CLERMONT

&

BEYOND

Julius Paul Montgomery

ii

Contents

Foreword

At the tender age of eleven years, I knew that I was not compatible with my community or family. The careers that dangled before this impressionable black boy back then were those of a construction worker, attending college and becoming a school teacher, or maybe working in the orange grove. My qualms with becoming a construction worker revolved around working for my older brother. If I became a grove worker, I would have had to work for a white man with an education probably inferior to my own. I had misgivings about going to college (my mother's wish) discussed in later chapters. If I could have selected a career for myself at that age, I would have probably opted to become an airplane pilot. However, when I was eleven, little black boys were not allowed to become airplane pilots.

I knew only a few people who could be called successful in my community, considering one's definition of success meant living a life per one's own desires. That is, at least, how I determine success. However, with the black mentality, which is usually subordinate to the white man's wishes, sometimes blacks were confused about their "success." If they were in their so-called station in life, perhaps kept there by a subtle or not-so-subtle force, they mistakenly thought they were successful. Using my definition of success, those men in my community who were actually successful have left an indelible mark on my life. One such man was my father. Not wanting to work for my older brother and unable to accept any of the other careers available to me, I enlisted in the U.S. Army. Everyone started on the same foot in the army, and everybody was governed by the same authority.

In other words, I felt that with everybody marching to the same music, I could become a success, and if for some reason I failed, I had no one to blame but myself. I knew there were some prejudices in the army, but I also knew that if I were given half a chance to succeed, I would. Within this country, one should never have to say, "For lack of a chance, I was not successful." However, the fact of the matter is that we all know there are still communities within this country with little or no chance. I am sure some communities have even lesser opportunities than what my community offered me some thirty-two years ago. This book is about experiences and the people who framed my life, including the lives of those black people who lived in similar circumstances as me over the years. It is about those actions we had to undertake to make our lives better. This book will talk about life before my army career and those who were not as lucky as myself. I feel that after you have read this book, you will agree that if our experiences have not made life better for ourselves, our communities, or for our race, then our efforts are rendered useless when compared to a more progressive and productive culture, community or society if progressiveness is defined as not to be bound by authoritarianism or orthodoxy or traditional forms. This book will let you be the judge, allowing you to draw from events as they take place in our lives over the years. From there, the book will grant you the opportunity to judge those events in contrast with the purpose the greater society says we have served, whatever that purpose may be. Regardless of whatever conclusion you might reach, I can say one thing for sure. There are certain moments in our past, and I am sure in our future, that society will not be able to judge, for they can only be experienced. They encompass fear, devastation, anger, rage, paralysis, and slaughter.

What Will I Be When I Grow Up?

It was an afternoon in early June 1952. The school was turning out for the summer break, and our community was about to experience an exciting first. My older sister Deloris and several other students from our community were graduating from high school. That afternoon, my mother, five brothers, baby sister, and I waited eagerly on the front porch to congratulate my sister. As we waited, we started a conversation about careers. My mother spoke of one of the boys, who had several opportunities now that he had his diploma, "Tom can be a foreman in the groves now that he has his diploma."

I very much objected to my mother's expectations for Tom and said, "Once I am out of high school, I am going to become an airplane pilot." My mother countered me with, "Boy, you know you are colored, right?". Before I could respond to her comment, she began explaining that the U.S. of America had not yet made room to train black boys to become airplane pilots. That was not acceptable to me and made me feel that I was being physically raped. My mother continued, "You will have to work in the orange groves just like every other colored person, or not eat!" Deep down within me, I knew I would not work in the groves for an extended period. Sure, if I needed some money to spend on the weekend or to buy presents during the Christmas break, I might have opted to work in the Groves, but that, too, would have been a temporary arrangement. For the time, I had enough talk about careers and left my mother's presence to play a mind game with myself. Mind games were my greatest pastime. Even at eleven years old, I seldom played with either of my five brothers or anyone else for that matter because questions always came up, and most of the answers that my peers gave were unacceptable to me. My older brother (13) and I were totally incompatible. His greatest concern was being accepted, and I could not give less of a damn about being accepted.

I wanted to be respected. In my mind, I was able to overcome any barrier with all the right answers. I could even become an airplane pilot. However, on this day, the day that gave our community its first graduating class, I needed a real answer to why little black boys could not grow up to be airplane pilots. And the only method I could think of to answer this question was through the mind games that I played with myself. My first question to myself was, "Who had airplanes?" My answer was the U.S. Army had airplanes. "Who did I know that was in the U.S. Army?" I knew Arthur. Arthur was one of my classmates. Some people said that he was the smartest in the class. However, I knew better and would one day prove different. In any case, he was my only hope of an answer to my question.

Arthur's father, Mr. Henry Dean, was a sergeant in the army, and I had to get an answer from him or through him on whether or not blacks could be airplane pilots in the U.S. Army? Now that school was out, Arthur would be playing in the big field across from his house or playing basketball tomorrow. The only problem I had at this point was mustering enough nerve to talk to Arthur. After all, he was the smart kid, and I was someone who kept to himself all the time. We had nothing in common. However, I felt I was just as smart, but Arthur was an exceptional athlete, and I had two left feet. To accomplish my objective, I decided to use a third person who was also an athlete. Aaron was a super athletic kid but was kind of slow academically. I had often helped Aaron with his homework, and he was one of the few kids in my community I played with. My strategy would be to start an argument with Aaron about Mr. Dean and ask Arthur to verify my point. I decided my argument would be that Mr. Dean was an airplane pilot. Naturally, Aaron would have to disagree, and we would have to call Arthur to verify. It would make little difference as to whether or not he verified my point. What mattered would be the following question: whether or not he knew any other blacks who were airplane pilots.

The following day I put my game to the test, and I was successful. Mr. Dean was not an airplane pilot but rather a radio repairman; however, Arthur knew of Colonel Davis, an airplane pilot who commanded a squadron with all colored pilots assigned under his authority. All of these pilots had received their training from an all-black school in Alabama. That was good enough for me. If blacks could fly airplanes, and the army was the place where my dream could become a reality, nothing could stop me from joining the U.S. Army. By this time in our national history, the air force was being established. However, I used to believe that there were no other branches of the armed forces except the army. In my mind, I thought that it was the army that gave black men the opportunity to fly airplanes. I would enlist for sure as soon as I became of age. After enlisting, it would take another six years before I would be old enough. Only then would life change for me.

I realized what I wanted to do in life, and for that reason, I felt that someday I, too, would be somebody respected. Because I decided to become an airplane pilot, my family discouraged my ambitions, including my parents, older brothers, and sisters. Maybe, it was because I talked about my goals all the time. Or, perhaps, it was because my father had already started a family business that comprised home building, and he wanted me to be part of it. Anyway, my family would make statements such as, "how is it possible for you to become a soldier when you can't take orders?" or "you said you could not work in the groves, or how would you be able to make it in the army where everybody ordered you around?" I think my family failed to understand my objective in life. And at the age of eleven, I was not prepared to explain it to them, nor could I accept that my father's business could one day be successful enough to employ my five other brothers and me. Besides, I don't think I could have ever worked under my older brother, which I am sure I would have had to do if I had agreed not to enlist myself in the army.

During that period, my father's business barely kept him at work. My mother worked in the orange groves daily, and my older brother worked in a kitchen at the local white folks' hotel. During the summer months, we all worked in the groves with my mother. Honestly, my summer experiences are experiences I will never forget. The days would start at about 5:00 am, and we would gather firewood for the old wood-burning stove so my mother or older sister could cook biscuits for breakfast and lunch in the orange grove. After breakfast, we would all catch the crew truck for the grove. Normally our ride on the crew truck would be about an hour, and after arriving, we would wait for the dew to dry off the trees. It was somewhat hazardous to pick oranges while the trees were still wet. One could catch a cold, or the poisons used to spray the trees to keep the fruit flies down would stick to your skin and cause irritation or even death.

My cousin Edroy was poisoned, and to this day, he is unable to walk, nor can he support his family on his workman compensation insurance. I hated the groves and the white bosses that were in charge. It was hard for me to understand why my mother could not accept my feelings. I was willing to take orders, but I could not accept a dead-end career. I was also willing to work, but not under these bad and hazardous conditions. I could even get used to working for a white man, but only if a white man would agree to work for a black man. To me, wanting to be respected was an easy enough thing to understand. However, for the blacks within my community, respect was a one-way street that belonged to whites only! After several summers of working in the groves, for whatever reason, possibly because my father's business was growing, or possibly because my mother knew I did not respect white men, my father asked me to work for him after closed for the summer break.

My father had several maintenance contracts, and one such contract required the upkeep of an all-white apartment complex. My job was spot painting. In doing my job, I had very close contact with the white tenants and one family, in particular, Mr. And Mrs. Mims. The Mims family was from South Georgia. Interestingly, my father, too, was of South Georgian descent. Mr. Mims and my father seemed to have a lot in common, and, in any case, both Mr. And Mrs. Mims quizzed me almost daily whenever they got the chance. Most of the questions they asked concerned the bible. However, we did discuss other subject matters as well.

One day Mrs. Mims asked me, "Paul, how did you get to be so smart being a colored boy? You are too smart to be colored, not that I don't think colored folks could not be smart." I came to resent those statements after I learned her meaning. However, her words sounded like a compliment to me. Mr. And Mrs. Mims became a good part of my life while

I was growing up in the little town of Clermont, Florida, and even after I was in the U.S. Army. After a while, however, I think I outgrew them and stopped visiting their place. The other whites that I remember affecting my childhood life were the county nurse, the icemen, the grove foremen, the building supply delivery men, and salesmen from the building supply.

Looking back at it, Mr. And Mrs. Mims were an exception, as I could never leave the presence of white persons soon enough. In their presence, there was little I could do to protect myself if one of them suddenly decided to hurt me. It was almost as if I was the prey, and they were the predators, even the ones I felt were good people. I did not trust them. My school nurse only came to our school during the immunization period. However, she always gave me a complete physical, after which she handed me a note to take home to my mother. Once I was examined by Mr. O'Brian, I was given a note for my mother, which included instructions on caring for the ground itch. My mother refused to respond to the note, which led to my principal, Mr. Whitehurse, visiting our home.

On this particular visit by my principal, we were enjoying beans and rice for supper. For whatever reason, he dared to comment about the food we were eating, saying that an unbalanced diet was the reason for my foot's condition. My mother asked the principal to leave. To this day, she blames me for his visit to our home. My foot healed from this very common Florida fungus with little or no outside help except the coming of winter. The following year the process would repeat itself, and life would go on in the small colored community of central Florida. From dealing with white folks, the most lasting experience in my memory was with the icemen, Troy, and one called Red. It was Red who frightened me the most. Red was about six feet four inches tall, with freckles and red hair. I always thought of him as a Klansman, and to this day, I do not count out such a possibility. In any case, whenever I saw him, I ran for the nearest hiding place, but I think he always saw me. He would have his ice tool in his hand and would shake it in front of my eyes. The ice tool had sharp hooks at each end and was bent to hook into a block of ice, which could be carried for short distances. I just knew for sure that one day he would catch me and hook me like he would a fifty-pound block of ice and carry me away. Whenever I was in the house and saw any white man, I would hide under the bed, for it had only been a few years that the local Sheriff had killed two of our neighbors. I was only seven years old back then, but that event left a lasting impression on my memory.

The KKK had also burned several crosses in our community. The Sheriff and Klansman had framed four colored men for raping a young white woman from the Bay Lake community, twelve miles west of Clermont. When that happened, the national guard was called in. I was told they were there to protect the colored community, but it was a terrifying experience for me. They had real guns, and they were all white. For sure, I did not feel protected. This incident was called the Greenlee case, named after the youngest of the four colored men accused of raping the white woman from Bay Lake. The Greenlee case became a statement to the young black men of Central Florida.

My question was, why did the National Guard not have black men? After all, was not this the same army that allowed black men to become airplane pilots? It was explained that even though it was the same army, black men were not permitted to serve with white men. This caused me some problems. However, I still wanted to become a pilot. My mother had always protected my five brothers and me in her own way. I was instructed to stay away from white women, always say sir to white men, and not look any white folk in the eye when they talked to me, and those were the rules we lived by as a colored family. Otherwise, my siblings and I would be whipped by our mother for disrespecting white folks. Troy, the second iceman, had several daughters who helped him from time to time. The girls were very beautiful and flirtatious, and, sometimes, I would see one of Troy's girls in the woods, near our house, with various white men of the white community. They were not picking berries.

Due to my mother's persistent counseling, I would hide and admire the girls from afar, fearful of how my mother would react if she found out what I was doing. Troy himself seemed to be an ok man trying to make a living for his family. For as long as I could remember, my mother was up at 5:00 am, making biscuits, grits with bacon, and sausage from the smokehouse. By the time I was ready to go to school, my mother would have already caught the crew truck for the orange grove. The crew truck was a rolling death trap, and several of our neighbors had already been killed while riding a crew truck to the picking field, including my mother's younger sister. But it was the only way for black folk to maintain an adequate lifestyle, especially when there were twelve mouths to feed.

However, that kind of lifestyle was not for me, and I was sure that I would beat the system. But in one way, the system was not all bad. During the late forties and early fifties, few if any banks made loans to the black community, even though we needed extra money to buy clothes at the beginning of the school year and to buy big-ticket items such as stoves, ice boxes, and other furnishings for the household during Christmas. When these needs arose, my mother would take the entire family to the grove, except for my father, who had started his own home repair business but was not making money to take care of our family. We could double our income and buy whatever we needed, including a family car, through these means.

In most cases, the car would be bought from a private owner, possibly the boss man or someone the boss man knew. Sometimes we would even triple our income. My older sisters and brothers were hard workers and accepted this way of life, and I was just along for the ride, because of which I got extra whippings for not doing my part and not doing all the little things that little black children were supposed to do to gain the respect of the white boss.

Times were hard, but we could not have been considered poor. My father made fair money from his business, and with my mother's income, we had almost everything the white folk had, if not more. We owned a large home that was several acres wide, a 1949 Chevrolet car, a pick-up truck for my dad's business, a television, and even a record player. We had inside plumbing and electric lights and always had hot food on our table. I guess one could say we were doing good. For the most part, this life was accepted by my brothers and sisters, and for my mother and father, they felt we were doing great as a family. They saw no reason why my sisters, brothers, and I could not go to an all-black college and become a school teacher or something that a black educated person was allowed to do in the fifties. It was not great, and I saw no reason blacks could not compete with the whites in all facets of American society. Why was there a water fountain for whites, a water fountain for blacks, a school for whites, and a school for blacks, and most importantly, why were whites less educated than blacks permitted to direct the lives and the communities of black people? The most memorable memory of my young life had to do with the white foreman who was poorly educated. Yet, he controlled and manipulated black men who were physically more powerful and also more intellectually sound.

This indelible period of my life caused a profound separation between my older brother and me, and even to this day, we rarely talk to each other. I was fourteen at the time, and my older brother was seventeen. For several years my older brother had told me about his boss Willie and how he would take half of his crew's money every payday for whatever reason. This, according to my brother, made Willie clever, and he felt it necessary to give me a fair warning not to bet with Willie now that I had started working in the groves on my own. It was June 1955 when I started working there. Even though it was an experience that I would rather not remember, since I must, here it goes: The hot Florida sun shone down on our bare backs with a temperature index of about 110 degrees. At midday, the sand under our feet felt like a fully fired furnace, and the only protection I had to my feet were cloth sneakers, which offered little to no help.

For the most part, the sneakers would get filled with hot sand that the hoe kicked up when it was pulled down to cut the weeds from around the newly planted orange trees. Our foreman, Mr. Willie, as we were required to call him, sat in his Jeep pick-up, some distance away, with his eyes glued to me. On occasions, he would holler, "Catch it up, Paul. If you don't, you will have to work through the lunch hour." The lunch hour was the hour most embedded in my mind. In actuality, it was really only thirty minutes long. However, within those thirty minutes, I would be able to empty the hot sand from my shoes, eat and get a cool drink.

Most importantly, though, I would ask my older brother to slow things down. There were eight black men in Mr. Willie's crew. Most of the crew comprised older men, my older brother, Sleepy, Lester, and me. As I looked up at the row of small orange trees, there were seven of us far ahead of me, with my older brother, James, in the lead.

James was some twenty trees out front when lunchtime came, with the others scattered in between. The rule was all rows must be caught up before lunch and quitting time. When the boss blew his jeep horn for lunch, the others would double back and help me finish my row. The older men would always make remarks: "Boy, if you are too lazy to keep up, you need to stay home with your Mommy," or something to that effect. My older brother James would also counsel me on the subject during lunch hour, telling me to keep up. My personal thoughts were how dumb it was to work in 100 degrees while one man sat in the shade making all the rules.

Moreover, why did we need to compete with each other in hoeing an orange tree? It was all so crazy to me because chances were we would never be rewarded for our extra efforts anyway. After being on the job for two weeks, I had my first and last confrontation with the foreman at the orange groves. On this day, at about three in the afternoon, the other field workers and I were working in the tree nursery under the close supervision of our boss, Mr. Willie. I asked him for permission to go take a crap and was given permission to do so. Upon my return, Mr. Willie began setting me up for my first bet. The other field workers were busy pruning trees with their pruning knives. As I kneeled within my own assigned row and opened my pruning knife to catch up with the others who were far ahead of me, Mr. Willie said, "Paul, I bet you five dollars that you pissed before you took a shit when you took your crap. I accepted the bet."

"Ok, all of you know everybody pisses before they shit, right?" He asked the other field workers, who nodded their heads in agreement, including my older brother, James. I became irate, mostly because all the blacks supported the white foreman, and especially when my brother refused to stand by my side. I stood up in my row, with my knife to my side, "Mr. Willie," I said, "you can not prove I pissed before I took a shit unless you go and find the pile of my shit, and I will not give you five dollars until the bet is proven." Mr. Willie checked the reaction of the other workers, who were staring at the ground by this point. I am sure it was the negative reaction of the workers that inspired Mr. Willie to make his next move. He charged me, saying, "Nigger, I am going to kill you. I will kill every nigger in Clermont-". I stood my ground, ready for him, and he stopped mid-sentence just before he could say "Clermont." All the other workers continued to work without looking up. I was very scared because I knew the penalty for standing up to a white man could have very well been death, the same as being accused of making advances toward a white woman like our neighbors had been. But still, I felt proud of my actions as we stood there, looking one another in the eye for several seconds. Finally, Mr. Willie gave in. His demeanor shifted to something I had not expected. It seemed that he became almost human and recognized me for the first time as to what I was: a fourteen-year-old boy. For this, I gained a little respect from Mr. Willie, but I lost all respect for my fellow black workers, including my older brother, whom I had once looked up to. I was naïve enough to think that all of this would be soon in my past, and I would become a pilot, flying airplanes in the U.S. Army.

Mama's Black Child

My older sisters and brothers were what colored folk called yellow niggers. Being of a darker complexion. I was called a darkie and was not accepted by my mother's eleven sisters or my extended family. The color of my siblings' skin ranged from yellow to a very fair shade. Blacks born during the 1940s to a family of fair-skinned blacks faced a serious dilemma. The color of skin within the black community established a very defined stratification. During my early childhood, a darkie needed to develop enormous skills, with a quick savvy to establish himself or herself. An argument could be made that the skills developed by self-conscious blacks could and did account for our success in athletics and entertainment. Some who achieved monumental success, such as Jackie Robinson, Nat King Cole, Jessie Ownes, and James Brown, just to name a few, might have faced the same dilemmas as I did during the forties and early fifties.

My older brother was everything I wanted to be. He was muscular, tall, fair-skinned, and had lots of friends. He was also loved by our nuclear and extended family. In my eyes, I could never measure up to him; however, after the incident in the orange grove with our boss man. Mr. Willie,

I felt better about myself. I had a power inside myself that I felt exceeded his personality. I know that now. But what I did not know was where this inner strength and power would lead me. Was it a power that could be properly honest? Or would it lead me to destruction within this uncertain world that I needed to face?

My Grandmother was a strong-willed and self-educated woman. She was a winner at any cost. She lost her husband early on in life, but not before he had fathered 14 children for her to raise. I would say her origin was American Indian, Scott Irish, and African American, all inferior as far as the greater American society was concerned. But within our community, she was a winner because of her complexion and beauty. Now the question was, where did this leave me? During those years, the only true thing we had was our family, with the extended family being just as important as the nuclear one. Big mama, as we all called her, was very much in charge. There was no doubt about that. Big mama derived her income from farms and some timber properties that were passed on to her after my grandfather's death. Some 300 acres of land gave her a manageable income to take care of her family.

But can you imagine what it must have been like being a member of a family of about 50 when you were the only black face? Well, for me, it was almost as bad as being a member of the KKK. The only difference was that everyone had a sheet but me. Maybe, that is an exaggeration, but not to a large degree. Life was not easy under those conditions, and it seemed like I had nothing to look forward to in life. Big mama's house sat beside Highway 50, which ran East and West through the black quarters of Clermont, Florida. It was a big two-story house with lots of flowers and fruit trees. About one mile west of our house, two blocks off the Highway, Highway 50 crossed Highway 27. These were the only two highways I knew of in the whole world. From conversations between my uncles and aunts, I knew that Highway 27 ran north toward Georgia, where big mama's land was, and south to Miami, where her sister, aunt Mitt, lived.

Highway 50 ran east to Orlando, about 25 miles away, and west to Tampa, about 70 miles away. I had never been to either of the places. However, I knew where big mama's house was. It was the place where everyone went for guidance and new dresses made for the girls and the women in our family. It was the place where everyone was considered family, except for me, it seemed. I am sure my mother and father loved me, but with the other pressures from the extended family, that love was lost somewhere.

We visited big mama's house for fun, which mostly meant playing with my fair-skinned cousins. Corn liquor at big mama's house was reason enough for the entire family to visit her place. It was sent from Georgia, and every adult in the family enjoyed drinking the liquor, except for my parents. Of all the fuss that went on in big mama's house, the only source of satisfaction for me was that I, too, was a part of this big, happy family. I also felt happy playing with my fair-skinned cousins, but that sentiment soon withered away once I realized that I was not accepted as an equal. After making that discovery, I learned to play by myself. I also learned some important lessons from my family, such as that black nigger kids only got what other fair-skinned niggers did not want. Whenever candy was passed around in big mama's house, I only got what was left after everyone had gotten what they wanted. Similarly, when dinner time came around at mama's house, I was never allowed to sit on a chair at the dining table. Instead, I had to sit on the floor with a tin plate and no spoon.

During my childhood, there came a time when the only person I identified with was my father. It was not because he, too, was a blackie like me, not at all. Instead, I appreciated his company because he actually made an effort to talk to me. He always gave me the candy I wanted, unlike my extended family, who only passed me leftovers that had already been picked apart by my cousins. I was always allowed to select a piece of my choice, and I appreciated that. I was allowed a seat at the dining table in his presence, and sometimes, I sat on his lap and ate from his plate, which, perhaps, is my fondest memory from my childhood.

But even in the case of my father, my brother always stole the spotlight, and I came in second. I would like to think that it was not because my brother was fair-skinned but because he was older. I think I am correct in making this assumption, or, at least, I hope so. But many problems did stem from the fact that my complexion was darker than my siblings and cousins. My mom, too, treated me the same way I was treated at big momma's house. However, there was one exception. Whenever I said something about how she treated me differently from the rest of her kids, I always got a killing of a whipping. I was whipped from the top of my body to its bottom, and I mean it.

However, my mother failed to realize that whippings did not stop me from feeling how I felt. They only made me want to leave home, and I knew I would do so as soon as I got the right opportunity. I was about 10 years old when I heard my mother talking to my father in the wee hours of the morning. The conversation went along the following lines. "James (my older brother) can work at the hotel after school. Paul... I don't think he can, and I feel you will have to take him to work with you when you need help," my mother told my father, who did not say anything in response. I will always resent that my dad took me to work while my older brother went to school. Even today, I resent that my parents made me go to work without worrying about my education. During my sixth grade, of 270 school days, I missed more than 90 to help my father at work. As such, I had to repeat sixth grade.

I felt like I should have been the one at school instead of my older brother because I was just as smart as anyone else. I am also sure my parents were aware of this fact. However, I also know that my parents thought that a smart black kid had little or nothing to do with success. In their minds, it was one's complexion that determined the degree of success they would achieve in their lives. After all, were not white men always in charge of black men regardless of their intelligence? But to me, success was not just putting food on the table or having your own place. To me, success was standing up for what you believed in and standing on one's own two feet. There were only a few people in our neighborhood who dared to break the barriers set by their skin tone, of which one was my father. Another was Uncle Joe. Of course, he was not my real uncle. We just called him Uncle Joe out of respect and affection.

Uncle Jow was a black man. I would even go to the extent of saying that he was a proud black man. As a child, Uncle Joe embodied my idea about what black men should be like. He was also Arther's grandfather. I am sure you remember Auther, my classmate whose father was in the army. He was the one who told me about black airplane pilots. To me, Uncle Joe was a successful individual. When one fails to stand on their own two feet, it makes little difference how much money they make. Life will always find a way to take it all away. I think my older brother fell into this category. He, for the most part, never stood on his own two feet, figuratively speaking. He always followed others' ideas, like thumbing my head, which originally was Abraham Jones' idea, and my older brother and Pop Hodges would always follow his suit. If I told my mother about the thumbing, I almost always ended up getting a whipping.

Let us talk about Uncle Joe. Uncle Joe was about 5'7" in stature. He wore bib overalls, a long sleeve shirt, and an old felt hat even during the hottest days of summer. In his right hand, he would have a long stick, which reminded me of the shepherds in Jesus's time who watched their flock through the night. You know the story of the three wise men. In my mind, Uncle Joe could very well have been one of the wise men in every sense of the word. At times, I would watch him for hours from a distance because he would not let anyone get close to his livestock. He had hundreds of turkeys, cows, and one hell of a bull. Uncle Joe's homestead was a two-story house made of old fieldstone. It still stands today and is one of the most beautiful pieces of architecture I have ever come across. Within his drive would be a new Lincoln car, and his yard was decked with several types of flowers that were always in tip-top condition. An assortment of fruit trees, including peaches, oranges, pears, grapefruit, and other citrus fruits common to the Florida environment, also surrounded his homestead.

He never had to catch the crew truck to the orange groves. All he did was watch his own place and stand his ground as a black man. To me, he was what a man should be, a protector of his rights. The only person I could think of to give you a real account of the impression he made upon my childhood would be William Beckworth, the black cowboy.

The latter led wagon trains west to California along the Beckwourth Trail during the days of the early west. Uncle Joe's stick only needed to be replaced for a Colt 45 and his sitting place for a saddled mustang, but other than that, he had all of the qualifications needed to be a Beckworth's doppelganger. His face always seemed sad and cold, with several wrinkles that showed he had endured 70 years or even more of life.

Once a year, there would be a community Barbecue, of which Uncle Joe was one of the men in charge of cooking the meat. A deep hole would be dug, and old bed springs would be hung over the fire burning within the hole. With several other older men from the community, Uncle Joe would place entire hogs on the springs, preparing a delicious meal for the 20th of May to celebrate the day that slaves were freed within Florida in 1865. These were great times for me. They allowed me to sit by the fire and listen to Uncle Joes' tales. He talked about times when he would drive white men away from stealing his life stock with a shotgun and how he had owned three homesteads in his lifetime.

As a child, I had never heard of a black man chasing away a white man, and that too with a shotgun. This, within itself, made Uncle Joe one of the most outstanding black men in our community. Standing up to a white man, boy! Maybe it was Uncle Joe I was thinking of when I stood up to Mr. Willie in the orange grove later in life. I would watch the hog sizzling over the fire, hoping to get a piece of the cooked meat and listening to Uncle Joe's tales. I would stay there until I would suddenly realize that I would get a whipping for missing supper. I would run home prepared to get whipped by my mother. At the same time, however, I felt that my time with Uncle Joe would more than account for it.

If I may borrow an excerpt from "Clermont, Gem of the Hills" to describe to you of a successful black woman who lived in my community when I was just a young little kid.

"Within the population of Clermont, there lived a modest, unassuming soul who for thirty years and more has been one of the most important characters in this community. She was called from her bed at all hours of the night away from her family more than she was with them frequently for many hours without sleep always a comfort and solace and genuine ministering angel wherever she is, mothers of this community and men and women grown, with families of their own calls Sally Townsand blessed. For three decades Sally has been the nurse attendant upon practically every mother and newborn baby in this entire community both black and white. No matter how strenuous her duties or how tedious they were she appeared to be happy in her work, never a crossword accepted her lips, and gentleness were in her every act. If angel Gabriel marked down the record of mortals for a reward in heaven, her book must be a great one, and when she is measured for flowing robes, wings of white and harps of gold, surly Sally Townsand will be fitted with the greatest in the heavenly wardrobe."

Sally Townsand was the midwife who delivered me from my mother's womb. She was indeed a success, for she was pleased with her place in life. I am sure she received many rewards. I, myself, am one of the babies she delivered, one who has grown into a healthy adult, all because of her kindness and will to help others

No Angels

The house that my father built sat off a dirt road, one and a half miles north of Florida's highway 50, on an acre and a half of land. To our southeast was Uncle Joe's homestead and to our west was big mama's house. We had a patch of sugarcane for making homemade syrup, which would be accomplished seven miles north of our place at the Isom's, who had a cane press pulled by a mule. I knew little or nothing about making syrup. However, we would cut the cane and deliver it to the Isom's, and several days later, we would pick up gallons of syrup that would serve as a condiment during breakfast time. We also had hogs that needed to be fed in the morning before we left for school and once in the evening after returning.

We would gather wood from the woodyard, and our only cow, Ida, would have to be staked out. We raised an assortment of greens, including corn, peanuts, Irish and sweet potatoes, and other foods our family needed. We grew almost everything from scratch, except for dried beans, peas, and flowers, which we bought from the white folks' grocery store. Occasionally, we would also purchase candy and other goodies to satisfy our sweet tooth. Our house had three bedrooms, a living and dining room, bathroom, kitchen, and a front porch, which had a swing that hung from the ceiling. In 1955, daddy added a garage for our brand new 1955 Chevrolet. My dad, James Wallace Montgomery, stands 5'7" tall. However, to me, he was almost ten feet tall. I thought there was nothing he could not do.

When I look back on those early days of my life, I realize that my father did do almost everything necessary or required to keep our large family fed and reasonably comfortable. If he had any fault, it would have been giving into my mother. The one thing that stands out most in my mind about him is seeing him pushing a homemade wheelbarrow that I am sure he used until he bought his first car to transport any and everything that had to be moved within our homestead, which included the grocery that had to be transported from the white folks' grocery store, some two miles away. The wheelbarrow was also used early in my father's business to transport his tools. He single-handedly built almost every black person's home within our community. The little help that he got was from me after I came of age.

From as early as I can remember, I have never seen my father smoke, drink, use a profane word, or miss church unless he were sick. I can only recall two times that my father was ill. Both times, it was from the poison ivy that he came in contact with while on a fishing trip. Hunting was his only form of entertainment. My father was not much of a disciplinarian. This department was, for the most part, left to my mother, which I think should not have been the case.

If working hard could kill, my father would have died at quite an early age. However, I can recall a few times he worked under the supervision of another man, black or white, and this was after he had entertained every other option. However, he never seemed to mind the rest of the family working in the orange grove. Maybe, he did but found it necessary, so he permitted it. It was many years later that I lost some respect for my dad. It was a trying time for all of us. My mother was in the hospital at the point of death, and I had flown down from my job in Greenville, South Carolina, to be with the family. We had taken my father's Lincoln from Clermont to Orlando, where my mother was hospitalized. In the lobby, I saw a very poor black girl who was pregnant and did not have a way back to her camp, where migrant workers were housed outside the city. I had asked my father to let me use his car to take her home, and he refused.

I could not for the life of me determine why he chose to say no at that moment. I remembered my father as a kind, compassionate, and giving man who was always willing and ready to help others. Was it possible that success had hardened him to the degree that he had forgotten what it was like to be poor or in need? Or did he feel like it was not his responsibility and that he should stay out of other people's business? Or maybe he felt others should have to perform the hard work he did, which included planning for the future. It was not until several years later that I got somewhat of an understanding of how my father felt. I had given up my job as a Recruiter Counselor with the U.S. Government. I thought

I could do freelance counseling and thought I could get help from him and my old community in Clermont. Together we would help one of the poorest areas in the U.S. of America to begin standing on its own two feet and begin the journey toward welfare.

My objective was to build a learning center for elementary and middle school kids and do job counseling for parents of poor families in the Clermont community. The center would be named after one of my role models, Mrs. Sally Townsand. Surprisingly, my father was not willing to help me in my endeavors. The primary reason for this was his inability to communicate with his peers, especially those who had struggled with him and made a life for themselves. In fact, most older blacks who had made good during an early era, almost in all cases, refused to join hands with another black who, too, was successful, even for the betterment of their own community. However, I found my younger brothers, who were of a different era, were able to help with the project.

Is it possible that my father, along with his peers, was looked over after reaching a degree of prominence within the black communities? Did this happen because of the new day of integration? And is it not possible that they thought that since most of us had looked to the white man all of this time for any sort of help, why should they help us when we disregarded them? Can I say and be correct that my father, along with his successful peers, were rendered useless by even their own sons and daughters for some time? Now I wonder if an apology could be made; should we, as sons and daughters, offer one? I would like that very much, for even at 92, my dad and other seniors still have a lot to offer. We still need their help in making America a better place for those who cannot help themselves.

My mother, Julia Mal Montgomery, was hard as nails. She stood about 60", and in her youth, she could use an ax, hoe, ladder, fruit sack, as well as a whipping switch better than the average man. In the kitchen, her cooking was outstanding. For as long as I can remember, my mother was up at five in the morning. If my mother had any weaknesses, it would be fear or too much respect for the white race. I think this fear goes back to her childhood and the power whites were given over blacks. I was never willing to show respect to whites that my mother demanded from me. In fact, I would rather not be bothered by them at all and always try to stay out of their way at any cost. Because of this, my mother and I were not very close, and I think she thought I was lazy and disrespectful. Because of my feelings towards whites, I knew I had to leave home as soon as I came of age. I am sure my brothers and sisters accepted my mother's reasoning that for a black man to keep employment in Clermont, he or she had to show respect to their white bosses unless they were self-employed.

I think my father was a fortunate man to find a woman like my mother. Without a doubt, I have yet to find another person like her. She worked day and night to help my father achieve his goals and ambitions. She also knew where to put a dollar to make a better life for the family. In fact, I am sure she made the best decision on behalf of the family when she encouraged my father to allow my older brother to attend school and work in the white folk kitchen and for me to be kept out of school to work in my father's business. The fact that my mother was partial to fair-skinned blacks was simply because there were no blacks in her nuclear family. To prepare me to live and survive in a world that did not allow black men to make accurate, meaningful decisions, she must have thought that being strict was the right course of action. The whippings I got almost daily were justified. However, for me, leaving home to escape the pressures of my family was also the right decision.

All needs considered, my mother is a perfect mother and wife to my father. My mother wanted better things in life, which also inspired my father to make a better life for all of us. If there was one thing in life that I hold against my mother, it would be her refusal to give me the assistance I needed when I called her from Vietnam after I had been involved in destroying a village with several women and children. I had been relieved of my duty and was under flagging action with instructions to be court-martialed.

The Vietnam war was unpopular, so none of us who fought it got much help and assistance from home when we needed it. I am still looking for the strength to forgive my mother and others who chose not to support us when we needed it the most. In any case, the charges against me were dropped some six months after I was assigned to my new unit in the states. I was allowed to finish my military career and retire. My nightmares, however, have not gone away. I still see the mangled bodies cut to pieces from the ninety millimeter main gun of our M48A3 Tanks. The only thing I can do now is pray for forgiveness so that I, too, might forgive. My older sister Gloria was a passionate and compassionate young lady. At one time or another, she fell in and out of love with every teenage boy in our community, or so it seemed.

She finally married an eighteen-year-old migrant worker who lived over at Juke Joint. She was seventeen at the time she got pregnant. From as early as I can remember, she had been like a mother to me. With my mother working in the orange grove, it was Gloria who I looked to for most of my needs. She was seven years my senior and had looked after me from as early as my birth, doing everything from changing my diapers to fighting my fights for me. My second sister, Deloris, had a completely different personality, and I wanted nothing to do with her. The only reason I can come up with for that is that Gloria had somewhat of a lighter complexion than Deloris. I had been taught that fair was beautiful, and dark was ugly. In any case, my older sister helped me through some pretty rough times, and I almost resented it when she got married.

But as it turned out, Gloria's marriage was like getting an older brother. For me, that was good. My older brother James and I had nothing in common, and with Speedy, as we all called him, I would get some positive responses from a more senior brother figure. Speedy was not all whom I thought he would be because if my older brother James was a hard worker, Speedy was a super hard worker. The two of them had everything in common, and in a way, this too was good because now James gave most of his attention to speedy as opposed to his other crazy friends who used to thumb me on my head. Now I was allowed to tag along once in a while, and I think Gloria might have had something to do with that. But, even now, I was an outsider. It was not long before my father's business grew to the point that both Speedy and James started to work with my dad and me.

At first, this was good because I knew more about the work that we were doing, and for a short time, we were all equals. But soon as we took on more work, both James and Speedy had already pulled ahead, and it was not long before both moved out on their own as block masons. About this time, my dad had pulled me out of school. He said it would be only for one year, but now it had been two, and I was getting closer and closer to enlistment age. At this point in my life, I faced a dilemma. If I joined the army, it would seem that I had deserted my father when he needed me the most. However, if I stayed to help him, I am sure I would live to regret it. My older brother James now had a family to look out for on his own, and my sister, Deloris, was still in college. It looked to me that I pretty much was the only person left to assist my father and my family.

I had four other brothers at home. Alexander had always been the infantile type. Willie was only ten, whereas Wilbert and Lawrence were six and four, respectively. My other two sisters, Marshanell and Maryon, were eight and two. I knew that my dad needed all the help from me that I could give. But I was now eighteen and had been out of school since my sixteenth birthday, trying to help my father make it to the point that he could do his work by himself. Deep down inside, I knew that would be several years coming. Finally, I made a decision. If my dad bought me a car, I would stay and help. If not, I would join the army. I did not feel right about this decision, but then again, my dad was not paying me a salary,' and at this age, I felt I needed to do something for myself.

An Escape

We were all sitting on the front breezeway of our new house that we were all so proud of. My dad built it in 1957. For some, it was the only grandiose house within an otherwise poor black community, even exceeding Uncle Joe's house in terms of its architecture, or for that matter, most houses in the white community. I had discussed with my father the possibility of buying a 1951 Ford parked on Highway 50. It was at the station down from big mama's house. My dad had told me it would have to be discussed with my mother. This setting, I thought, would be a good time to bring the subject up, if there ever would be a good time. I had a hard time convincing my family to buy me a car.

I knew the problems my family already had. The loan we had taken from the bank to build our new house needed to be paid back. My sister, Deloris, was still in college, and five of my younger sisters and brothers were still in elementary or high school. I had thought I should not buy that car from that cracker anyway. He would not even let black folk get a drink from his water cooler or use the bathroom. But I wanted the car! I thought it was only fair to have something of my own. After all, I had worked for two years without pay. Did that not deserve something? I brought up the subject carefully, "I am now eighteen, and I think I should be paid for working."

My mother replied, "Your daddy can't afford to pay you, boy. We have a loan to pay back, and your sister is still in college".

"Well, daddy, how about that car that I showed you at the service station? Eddie Bass has a car, and he only works in the orange groves on weekends," I asked, turning my attention towards my father, who did not respond.

Instead, it was my mother who spoke, "You are not Eddie Bass, and we can't afford to buy you a car, let alone insurance, and that is the end of the matter."

I think what I said next hit my dad pretty hard. "Well," I said, "I will be enlisting in the army on Monday."

The following day, which was a Sunday, I missed church to say my goodbyes. Eddie picked me up early afternoon, and we made our way north about eight miles to High-Way-In-The-Hills, an all-white resort area where we could buy beer after 1:00 pm. Blacks were allowed to drive through the drive-through package store for carry-outs. We hit the drive-through, bought a six-pack, and headed back to Clermont. For the next few hours, we drove through the colored quarters making several runs back to the package store for beer. After all, we were saying our goodbyes.

Eddie had lots of girls to see, but I was mostly along for the ride. I had dropped out of school at sixteen and had lost almost total contact with people of my age group. I was beginning to get pretty drunk, and I am sure Eddie was too.

We were speeding through the colored quarters when we finally stopped at the local Juke Joint. The music was good and loud, and for a few dollars or a pint of liquor, we could have had any of the women that hung around the joint. For that matter, being young and handsome, we could have then nothing at all if we played our cards right. However, our objective was to let everyone know that this was our last day in Clermont. So, we just danced and acted like fools. We told everyone that come Tuesday afternoon, we both would be soldiers in a man's army. We both hung around until past midnight and agreed that if we were going to make it to Jacksonville on Monday, it was best to call it a day. Eddie dropped me off at my parents' house, and with some effort, I made it to the back door leading downstairs. I managed to get the door opened. My four younger brothers were sound asleep. I fell on the couch in the living area downstairs and was only awakened by the noises of my brothers getting ready for school the following morning.

By the time I made it upstairs, my mother and dad had already left for work. That was just fine with me after the night I had had. It was about ten O'clock when Eddie pulled up outside in his 1951 Mercury. I put a few things in a paper bag. We were ready for our trip to the main recruiting station in Jacksonville after a quick stop at the local recruiting station in Leesburg, where we were supposed to receive our instructions and meal and lodging tickets. The Mercury had loud pipes, and Eddie made it a point to make sure everyone knew we were leaving. We took off from my parents' house like a bat out of hell. We left a cloud of dust on the dirt road leading to the black community, letting everyone know we headed north towards Highway 27. In about 20 miles, we would be in Leesburg.

After getting lodging, food tickets, and instructions from the local recruiter, we were northbound again. As we headed north, I could not help but think of my dad. For sure, he was a good man, and I began to have second thoughts about leaving him with the heavy load that he and my mother would have to carry. I remembered the first time that I had come this far north. My father's sister had died, and my mother and father had agreed that I would be the one to accompany my father to Georgia to attend the funeral. But first, I had to have a suit, so that was when I got the opportunity to visit Orlando for the first time. We had shopped on Church Street at a department store run by Jews. I remember the price of the suit that my dad had bought. The shopkeeper stated the price to be $30.00, and my dad's final offer to the Jewish gentleman was $19. 00.

The offer was accepted, and I received my first lesson in dealing with Jewish merchants. We had now been on the road about an hour and passed through Ocala, Florida, a town known for breeding racehorses. There was also the Florida National Forest. Both the horses and forest were a sight to see. Long white rail fences were stretching as far as the eye could see, and occasionally, we would spot a group of horses so pretty that it should have been a sin to ride one.

The National Forest was abundant in deer and wild boar. Hunting was allowed by permit only, which could only be obtained by rich white folk. The forest and the pastures were so green it felt like we were in a movie. Eddie had been talking about one thing since the time we had left Clermont, which was the most effective approach of getting into a girl's panties, of which I believed he was an expert. One reason Eddie wanted to join the army was to get away from several girls who said he was their baby's father. One of the girls he had impregnated was my first cousin. I wanted to change the subject, and I had made several attempts by talking about basic training and asking what careers would be offered to blacks in the army.

I also wondered how soon it would be before I could attend flight school after basic training. No matter how the subject started, it always ended up on some little sweet thing in Clermont, Leesburg, or Groveland, all of which were areas of the Lake County community who attended a single high school in Leesburg. I had attended Leesburg, Carver Heights High School for two years, finishing only the tenth grade. Eddie had his diploma. I was somewhat worried about my chances in the army without a diploma. As far as the girls' talk went, I had never been serious about one and was constantly reminded by my mother and Sunday school teachers of the responsibilities that came along with getting a girl pregnant. Eddied also attended the same Sunday school class, but even then, he only talked about girls to the point of trying to set me up with his sister. The next city after Ocala would be Gainesville, Florida, home to the University of Florida. The most exciting thing happening in Gainesville back then was the story of Mr. Hawkings, the first black law student to be enrolled at the university with the help of the Florida National Guard, the NAACP, News Media, and whatever other force that kept the KKK, or the local law enforcement, from bringing Mr. Hawkings educational inspirations to an abrupt end. Mrs. Hawkings, Mr. Hawking's wife, had been my algebra teacher in tenth grade.

His younger brother was the star running back on the Carver Heights champion football team. In fact, Lake County had a whole group of people from the Hawkins family, and they all had reasons to be concerned about their health. It was now getting close to the lunch hour. We would soon need to make a decision about what and where we would eat. Public restaurants were not open to blacks, and it was somewhat difficult to find a black community in an unfamiliar city. The normal thing for traveling blacks was to hit the closest grocery store and buy whatever grocery was needed to put together a simple lunch, consisting of pressed ham, bologna, a loaf of white bread, soda water, and a spread of some type. We decided to do the usual and had lunch outside of a small convenience store.

We later realized that it was not smart for two young blacks to have lunch along the public highway unless they were working for the highway department. Even then, they needed to be near their white boss. Our next stop would be the big city of Jacksonville, Florida. Highway 27 had turned into Highway 301, just outside Ocala, and now we were past Gainsville. I thought how close I was to my father's birthplace, a small Southern Georgia, turpentine community, of the town of Moultrie. He was 52 years old at the time, and I wondered what life must have been like for him or if there had been any improvement during the past 52 years in the area. The answer had to be yes because, for sure, there were no black airplane pilots 52 years ago.

Highway 301 would take us past the Florida State Penitentiary. I was told it was the point between the State Penitentiary, and the Lake County Prison, where the Sheriff's department had killed several people from my community involved in the Greenlee case. My hopes grew higher that I would meet all the requirements to be accepted into the army. If enlisted, I would be able to leave my childhood memories buried somewhere, along with the past that had brought me this far. However, I could never forget my father and his workload. I thought how strong he had to have been to have obtained the success he had achieved in life. I thought about how he had made his truck and his lawnmower available to me on Saturdays so I could have some way of earning money. Wasn't that enough?

However, I knew I was making the right decision to leave Clermont and Lake County, Florida. I could never be like my older brother or sisters, and the next time I stood up to a white man, he might not be as understanding as Mr.

Willie. We made it into Jacksonville at about 3:30 pm on the 13th of October 1959. Our first objective was to find the motel that we were instructed to check into on the black side of town. It was against the law for blacks to be housed in the Holiday Inn or any other major motel exchange in the south. After hitting the black side of town, it was easy to find the right motel. There was only one this side of town, or in the city for that matter, where young black men were housed by the U.S. Government to be enlisted into the armed services.

Now that we had found the motel, Eddie's suggestion was to blow the dull joint and find some women and get some pussy. The closest thing we found to women, who were willing to give up some pussy as Eddie had put it, were hookers. The going price was twelve dollars, ten dollars for the girl, and two dollars for the room. For this sum, one would probably get a dose of crabs that the army would have to treat, provided we were lucky enough to get in. After talking with several girls and not getting to first base without money upfront, we decided to buy a fifth of liquor and watch an X-rated movie. The place was very dark. We had to feel our way to our seats, bumping into old men or some pervert playing with himself. After several minutes we managed to find a seat and focused on the action on the screen. This was a first for me. I was not so sure if I was enjoying myself. However, I found it somewhat erotic but was unsure whether or not I would enjoy some woman sucking me off and kissing me with that stuff still running from the side of her mouth.

We sat and passed the bottle with our eyes glued to the action on the screen. The movie was getting pretty intense, to say the least. I had to ask Eddie where was the guy putting his dick in her butthole or her pussy? The answer was both. It was truly amazing to see a woman being pumped from behind by one guy while she sucked off another. However, I continued to watch in amazement. I asked Eddie about the things I did not understand, trying to elicit an answer from the more experienced eighteen-year-old. We sat through two showings of this erotic free, during which we finished the fifth of alcohol we had purchased. By the time the second showing was over, we were very drunk. Eddie assured me he would get us back to our motel. It was after midnight when we knocked on the motel door, and we were told the motel was closed for the night. We had no choice but to sleep in the car and hope for the best.

We were awakened at about 6:30 am by the constant rumbling of the cars driving by us. It was around breakfast time, and if we were going to survive the morning, it was best if we ate something. We made it to the closest washroom within the motel, washed some of the terrible taste of alcohol from our mouths, and joined the crowd for breakfast. Breakfast was at an all-black cafe that sat next to the motel. The place was so small that we had to wait in line to be served. The menu was grits, bacon or sausage, eggs, and biscuits. It was possibly the best food I had ever tasted, possibly because I was famished. I asked for seconds, and a very sweet old lady loaded my plate up with a good-sized serving, and I had almost recovered from the events of the previous night by then. A few minutes after I had finished breakfast, a very impressive black army sergeant entered the cafe and announced that the bus for the Recruiting Main Station was being loaded out front. As I stepped up on the bus, to my surprise, I realized that it was half full of white boys. The black Sergeant that I had been so impressed by was very clear in his instructions when he said, "On this bus, the state of Florida laws do not apply; you colored boys can sit anywhere you find an empty seat."

For me, that was somewhat uncomfortable, and I made my way to the back of the bus. Eddie and I found a seat together. I already felt that I was in a different world. In fact, I think all of us, regardless of whether we were black or white, were totally uncomfortable. One could hear a pin drop from when the bus departed the cafe until we reached the main recruiting station. Upon arriving at the station, we were ordered to form a single file queue and enter the double doors leading to the main building. Once inside, we were told to follow a yellow line that directed us to an open bay. I was very much unprepared for the next words that came out of the Sergeant's mouth. He ordered to us disrobe. I could not help but look around the room, mostly to see who was looking at me. I saw phalluses of all sizes, both black and white. I quickly confirmed that all men were not created equally, with the latter being more unacceptable than the former ones. We were ordered to bend over, reach back, and spread our buttcheeks. After that, men in white-colored coats armed with flashlights examined our assholes, using the light of the torches in their hands.

They rammed their middle fingers as far as they could straight in our buttholes. Afterward, they came around in front and gave each of us a short inspection. We were then told that we could put back on our underwear. From that point onwards, the physical part of the exam was not so bad. Chest x-rays, a look at our ears and eyes, a deep breath here and there, a few pricks in the finger, and that was just about it. After getting dressed, we were seated in a classroom and given number two lead pencils and a booklet. The proctor instructed us not to open the booklets until we were told to do so. The first test was concerning reading, word definition, and arithmetic. At this point, I wished I had gotten a good night's sleep. I looked around the room for Eddie to see if he was having any problems, who was just sitting there staring blankly into space.

After several tests, Eddie was still sitting idly, basically doing nothing. I did the best I could with the test and hoped I passed. After the testing phase, we were all sent to a waiting room to learn if we would soon be soldiers. The roll call occurred several hours later. The Sergeant informed us that if he told us to fall towards the left, we would get a one-way ticket home. If he asked us to join the group on the right, we would be given a one-way ticket to Fort Jackson, South Carolina. I was told to join the group on the right. I felt good about myself. I was going to be a soldier, possibly an airplane pilot. Eddie was told to join the queue on the left. He would have to drive the Mercury back to Clermont all alone, back to the orange groves with dead-end jobs, to the signs that read White Only, to a world where black men always had to bow down in front of their white bosses. Back to where there was little to no justice for black men, where dark-skinned individuals were slaughtered in the name of justice, and where education was more of a dream than a reality for most of them. Eddie would have to return to a world full of disparity, but even in such a world, some men had made a life for themselves despite the odds stacked against them. My father was one such man; however, even then, I knew Eddie did not fit the category of those men, but I genuinely hoped that he would.

After roll call was over, my group was briefed for our swearing-in ceremony and the subsequent train ride to Fort Jackson, South Carolina. It was somewhat of a funny experience. I was not afraid anymore. I knew I would be a good soldier, and I was sure I would not leave the army until retirement because I was already familiar with the hardships of living in a black household, having grown up in an environment where whites were always right, and blacks had little to say about their career, education, and other such things. The train ride from Jacksonville to Fort Jackson felt as if I was stuck in a vacuum at a juncture between two worlds. The world that I was leaving behind contained many things that were dear to me. However, it was a world where I could never have control over those very things that were dear and precious to me. The world ahead was something that I had dreamed of for more than seven years. It was a world that allowed black men to fly airplanes and made them in charge of men regardless of their skin color. For sure, the world ahead would have been a better fit for me.

I was a person who needed to always be in control, even if the jurisdiction of that control was limited to a few men. I thought of Colonel Davis, who Auther had told me was in charge of a squadron of black pilots. At that moment, I could not help but think of how honorable it would be for me to meet this black Colonel. I would ask him how it felt to be in command of a group of intelligent black men. I had heard of men in the army working their way up the ranks. Maybe if I was a really good soldier, I too could become the commander of a fleet of black airplane pilots. That would really be something, wouldn't it? I also thought of Eddie. I wished that I had asked him whether black people did what we saw in the X-rated movies. I am sure he would have had an answer for me. I also wonder why he had not tried to pass the army test. Did he think he did not have a chance? Had the night of booze and X-rated films been too much for him?

Maybe, he had got cold feet and didn't want to leave the world he felt he knew so much about. I have often wondered how black men could be so comfortable in the world where Eddie had decided to return. I was so caught up in my thoughts that I almost missed dinner. A tall black service soldier was placed in charge, who reminded me it was time to eat and directed me to the dining car. It was only yesterday that I could not eat at the same cafe or sleep in the same motel with a white person. Now I was encouraged to sit and eat with them in the dining car and with a black man in charge. Why were things the way they were back at home? Could the things happening on the train be accepted outside of it? From where I was sitting, I could see black men, women, and children living in run-down unpainted shacks, waving as we passed by them. Would there ever be a time when they, too, could also enjoy a better life? When would they have a more productive way of life, or was that simply too much to ask?

Jackson: A New Beginning

It was past midnight when the train pulled into the station at Columbia, South Carolina, and the army was out in force to meet us. There were four Sergeants, of which one was an American Indian, one was a Puerto Rican, and the rest were Whites. The army bus that they loaded us on was driven by a civilian. Upon arriving on base, the Sergeants were the first off the bus, and they positioned themselves in front of the bus, standing at an equal distance from one another. The Indian identified himself as the first platoon Sergeant. The two white Sergeant were in the second and third platoon, and the Puerto Rican was in the fourth platoon. We were ordered by a fifth Sergeant with more stripes than I could count fall in front of the first platoon Sergeant if we were between five feet to five feet six inches tall in height. If we were five feet seven inches to five feet eight inches, we were supposed to form a queue in front of the second platoon Sergeant. If we were between five feet nine inches to five feet eleven inches, the third Platoon Sergeant awaited us. Finally, and if we were six feet or over, we were asked to fall in on the fourth platoon Sergeant.

I was exactly six feet tall, according to the physical that I had taken in Jacksonville. However, I knew I was six feet one inch. In any case, it looked like I was in the fourth platoon for the night. It took forever to get everyone in the right place. The temperature was about 36 degrees, and I was still dressed according to the weather in Florida, which meant that I was freezing. After everyone was in place, the Sergeant with the extra stripes on his uniform told the other Sergeants to take charge of their men and lead them into the mess hall for chow. It took some effort to get uncle sam's newest recruits to respond to army drill commands. However, after several attempts, all of us formed a single queue, facing what seemed to be another batch of new recruits standing behind the serving line, ready to serve us our very first army chow.

We were now armed with metal trays to receive our midnight meal. The menu was steak and potatoes and coffee if you wanted it. I found it very odd to be sitting in a big dining area past midnight, with some hundred or more men eating steak and potatoes. However, this was a new beginning, and I am sure I would come to know and do many other odd things before seeing home again. The steak was tough as shoe leather, and I had some trouble cutting it with my knife. If I was at home, I would have used my hands, but I gave up on the steak and ate the potatoes instead. No sooner than I had finished the potatoes, the Sergeant with all the stripes stood in the middle of the dining area and shouted at the top of his voice, "First platoon! Second platoon! Third platoon! Fourth platoon! Fall outside on your Platoon Sergeant."

His voice scared me almost to death. The new recruits were knocking over tables and chairs until the Sergeants in command screamed at them to pick up the chairs and straighten the tables. After we were outside, it was left to us to find the position that we had been in prior to going into the mess hall. At this point in my army career, I was about ready to throw in the towel, and I had been in the army for less than one hour. The recruit that I had been next to was Robert Lacorn Jr., a black boy out of north Florida. It was Lacorn who found me and helped me get into place because I was hopelessly lost in a sea of new faces that had meant nothing to me. However, through this experience, I learned my first military lesson, which was when standing in a military formation, you are always responsible for the man to your right. After everyone found their places, we were marched to our quarters, which was a wooden framed two-story building. The number 4 was scribbled in black on a white background next to the entrance to let the new recruits know that they were in the fourth platoon quarters.

The top floor of the same building was occupied by the second platoon. As we approached the building, our Puerto Rican platoon sergeant made his way to the front of the group, holding a very impressive instrument that looked like a foot-long bullet between the thumb and forefinger of both his hands. He marched backward, and when he was just a few feet away from the building, he made a fancy foot movement and ordered the group to halt. In broken English, he introduced himself as Sergeant First Class Quinnones and welcomed us to the U.S. Army and the fourth platoon. I was so cold I just knew that if I touched my ears, they would have fallen off. Finally, he instructed us on how we would file into the building. The first single line to the right, which included me, comprised recruits between six feet and six feet and one inch tall. It was the smallest of the squads that made up the fourth platoon.

The second squad was made up of recruits between six feet two inches to six feet three. Members of the third squad were about six feet three to six feet four in height. Lastly, the fourth squad consisted of soldiers that were six feet five or above. The first squad was instructed to file into the building, march to the end of the structure, do a column left at the bunk beds to the far side of the room, do a column left at the first bunk bed, and stop at the last bunk bed that was not occupied. There were ten men in each squad and ten sets of bunk beds on each side of the building. This put me at the very first or last set of bunks as you entered the building of the fourth platoon. The second squad was instructed to file in and occupy the bunks on the right side of the building. The third squad marched in and was instructed to take to a position behind each man of the first squad. The fourth squad was instructed to march in and take a position behind each man of the second squad. Now that we were all inside, Sergeant Quinnones walked to the center of the room facing the first and third squads and commanded them to do a left face, make an about-face, and commanded the second and fourth squads to do a right face.

After we were done following his instructions, all the squads in the room were left staring at each other, and that was when bunk assignments were made. The first squad was assigned the bottom bunks, with foot and wall lockers to the left. The third squad was assigned the top bunk with foot and wall lockers to the right. Sergeant Quinnones did another about-face and made bunk assignments to the second and fourth squads. I was really impressed. I had been on an army post for less than two hours and had had a meal with more than a hundred men, learned how to execute military movements, learned how to fall in and out of a military formation, and had been assigned sleeping quarters. The next order that Sergeant Quinnones gave was not an easy one, "Now that you have your assigned areas, each of you will get to know your bunk buddy."

My bunk buddy was a six feet four Mississippian and a bigot. Sergeant Quinnones's final instructions to the platoon for the night was for us to know who fell to our right. I was the last man in the first squad, so no one fell to my right. Robert Lacorn Jr. was to my left, and the bigot from Mississippi was somewhere in the fourth platoon, and even then, he was too close. That night while lying on the first bottom bunk, on the left side of the hall with a white bigot occupying the top bunk over me, I reflected on my eighteen years of life. I began by backtracking the events as they had occurred just hours prior. I was concerned about what part the Sergeant with all the strips would play in my life in the next few weeks. For sure, he was in complete control. Even

Sergeant Quinnones sounded angry whenever he spoke. I had never seen anyone that could instill the fear of God in so many people, simply by his presence. The events that had gone down in the mess hall were a first for me. Not even big mama could have gotten so many people to move so fast.

However, the biggest worry at the forefront of my mind was my bunkmate. He was about six feet four in height and must have weighed more than two hundred pounds. The top bunk swayed two and fro whenever the mammoth from Mississippi rolled from one side of his bed to the other. I don't think I would have been so afraid of the bigot if I believed that everyone would be treated equally in the army. However, I knew that things were far from being equal because of my past experiences.

To begin with, my bunkmate was white, and I was black. The most powerful man that I had seen within my short army career was also white. He was the Sergeant with all the stripes. Even if Sergeant Quinnones was on my side, how would a Puerto Rican and a black boy fair against a bigot from Mississippi and a harsh white sergeant? My experience in life had proven to me time and time again that blacks could not win against the whites. I was also sure this rule included Puerto Ricans.

As I lay there on my bunk with the sun beginning to rise, I wondered why I had not thought of these questions before. It had been more than seven years since I made up my mind to become a soldier. From the very beginning, I believed that once I was a soldier, I would have escaped bigotry for the most part. The morning arrived in no time, and I had failed to get any sleep. I was up before the big Mississippian and had already showered and was half-dressed when he began to complain about having to sleep with niggers. He dragged himself slowly out of bed and made no attempt to give me room to finish dressing as his long body stood in front of me. If I had been on familiar grounds and believed that all people were equal in the army, I would have kicked him in the nuts.

He positioned his body directly in front of me as I attempted to tie my shoes, and there was simply nothing I could do at that point. The morning reveille formation had improved quite a bit from the previous night, and everyone fell in their places without any difficulty, including me. A few minutes later, we were off to the mess hall for breakfast. Army breakfast was a new experience for me but one I could get used to with little or no trouble. The menu included bacon, eggs, grits, potatoes, toast, milk, fresh juices, and coffee. Considering all the talk I had heard about soldiers missing homecooked meals, I found it hard to accept that the army fed so well. After breakfast was over, we were ordered to get in formation all over again, and that was when I grew to despise my Sergeant. There was so much hollering and yelling going on that I could not even breathe peacefully.

The rest of the day was devoted to receiving our army-issued equipment, including an M-1 rifle. I had never seen so many articles of clothing in all my life, let alone two pairs of quality boots and lots of underwear. Life had improved for me. I was willing to acknowledge that. However, by mid-day, I wished I was back home helping my dad paint houses. The weight of the duffel bag full of my army issue was almost too much for me to bear. But I knew it was a small price to pay. I began to feel that I, too, could become a man. This was new to me. I had never experienced anything close to it back in Clermont. There, if you were black and under sixty-five years of age, you were still called a "boy." If you were older than sixty-five, you became an uncle, even if you did not have any nieces or nephews.

Suddenly, I felt as if I could be anyone in life. I felt empowered, thinking that I could be whatever I wanted to be. The black Sergeant who I had met on the bus to Jacksonville had demonstrated that he was a man through and through, and so had the Puerto Rican, Sergeant Quinnones. It was rewarding to know that I had made the right decision by enlisting in the army, even though I still needed to find a way to deal with my bunk buddy, the bigot from Mississippi.

A Transformation

I was still somewhat troubled by how Blacks, Puerto Ricans, and Indians could be in charge of white men. But more than that, I had doubts about confronting my hunk of a bunkmate and living to write home about it. I felt this way because it was simply unacceptable for blacks to even question white men where I came from. I still had vivid memories of losing my job in the groves when I confronted Mr. Willie. I was only fourteen back then, and I did not want to repeat the entire process.

Even when I ever did find the nerve to confront my bigoted bunkmate, I could never write home about it, for it would only have caused more pain, anguish, and anxiety to my parents. In my parents' world, whenever there was any disagreement between blacks and whites, the only suitable course of action was to "put the matter in the hands of the Lord." One would think that I, too, would have shared my parents' faith and told myself that the "Lord will take care of my needs." However, it did not take me much time to realize that all I needed to do was kick some butt. Even today, when I look back over my life, I was treated because my skin color caused me much physical pain. The hurt is almost unbearable.

I was stuck in between two different worlds. Either I could simply revere my parents' standards and wish things were as simple as they perceived them to be. However, such a world would have left me with loneliness, fear, anger, and even rage, because I knew the world was much more complex than that. My other world required me to kick some white man's butt. However, I was so often reminded of how defenseless I really was, being a black man reared under my parents' standards. The fact that the greater black community shares my parents' opinions further outraged me. So, my question was whether or not the transformation I would undergo in the army help me in the long run. That is the question that I will answer in the next few pages.

Could the leadership I would learn in the army help me and others like myself? Would it help me navigate through my parents' world, where the white rule was accepted as supreme, a world where I would have to return to someday to establish a life for myself, my sons, and my daughter? Would I be able to control myself to not misuse the power against the very system that trained me? Perhaps, the army's objective was a real effort to bring black men and other minorities to an equal footing with white men. However, I don't think one would ever get the greater part of the black community to accept this reasoning. I believe that blacks would say, "The army's effort was simply to use the American human resources as a defense line for the country." I, along with other black boys, just happened to be some of the individuals available for this purpose. In any case,

I had begun to accept that the efforts of the United States Army were for real and without recourse and that its training objective was for each man to be able to stand on his own two feet. How else could a soldier be effective, be he black or white? From this perspective, I knew it was just a matter of time before I would kick the bigot from Mississippi's ass and move closer to finding that self-respect that I felt to be missing from black communities.

But it was also clear that the only rights in our training environments were earned rights. If I wanted to kick my bunkmate's ass, that right could only be allotted to me by the approval of the rest of the platoon. I needed to gain that approval through demonstrated ability. In the army, an individual's demonstrated ability was something that could not be taken away from him, ever. However, over the chapters of this book, you will learn social acceptance, or the lack of it, has a way of destroying one's abilities and skills, even if they were once demonstrable. Basic training began after we were issued our full field equipment, including an MI Springfield semiautomatic rifle. The first week was called zero-week, or one might call it going through the motions.

In other words, it was simply an observation week so that the platoon sergeants could assess the strengths and weaknesses of the personnel assigned to each platoon. After zero-week ended, the platoon sergeants gave leadership positions to those of us who came on top, including an acting platoon sergeant, per each platoon, and four squad leaders.

The squad leaders were subordinate to the acting platoon sergeants and were in charge of four different squads. I was not awarded any leadership positions, but neither was the bigot. So, we were still starting out even, and I knew I would outdo him. It was my plan not to give him any reason to think that I was anything more than the southern nigger he had taken me to be. After all, he must have thought that all southern niggers were afraid of "white men"?

I did all this so, in the future, he would know that it was a scared southern nigger, who kicked his white Mississippi ass, and I wanted him to know I had done it with most of the fourth platoon looking on. However, to do that, I needed the platoon to be on my side, but that was harder than it seemed. From the moment I came up with the plan to humiliate the bigot, I knew that I would have to work very hard to get on my platoon's good side, not because I could not kick the Missisipian's butt, but rather because I needed their support when the time came.

It was a nearly impossible task for me to train carrying my full field gear. It was designed to secure some 45 pounds on one's back without any form of external support. It was scary just looking at my duffle bag heaped there on the floor in front of my footlocker. I soon realized that dealing with the field gear had put all new recruits in a puzzling dilemma. Possibly, there was just one person in the entire platoon who had the experience to deal with our predicament. Privet Knox, the assigned acting platoon sergeant, had one year of college Reserve Officer Training under his belt. I had found him to be a great asset to all of us. So, I called upon him for assistance and found myself waiting in line because almost everyone else needed his help as well. The hardest thing for me to accept in trying to secure my full field gear was that once it was secured correctly, I needed to be able to March 20 miles with it on my back, with an additional nine pounds that came in the form of an M-1 rifle. It was finally agreed that private Knox would help each of the four assigned squad leaders assemble their full field gear. Then it would be the leader's responsibility to help the people assigned to his squad. My squad leader was the only black person chosen for a leadership position among the five blacks assigned to the fourth platoon of forty new recruits. Private Whiteside was almost a typical southern nigger, with one exception. He had a college education.

Even though he had a quick savvy about himself, he had one trait I just could not stand. Every time Private Whiteside gave instructions to other blacks, he spoke so loudly that everyone in the squad bay could hear him. When he was helping one of the white recruits, no one knew he was around. However, I was sure Private Whiteside would soon become sergeant Whiteside after basic training. He just had all the right things going for him, including knowing his place. He often told me not to make trouble with the white boys if I wanted life to be easier, even in the army. I am sure that was good advice because, at the time, my life was far from being easy, especially with the "Big bigot from

Mississippi." My bunkmate continued to call me nigger and got in my way regardless of what I did. He had been assigned as my bunk buddy, and he started terrorizing me from day one. After Private Whiteside had helped me assemble my backpack, I tested it and was even more convinced that neither I nor my duffel bag could walk for twenty miles.

I was told we would have to walk for twenty miles every day, and it was supposed to start soon. I was still having difficulty handling my entire field pack when we were issued a new set of instructions under the supervision of Sergeant Quinnones. We were marched to the arms room to be given our weapons, "the MI Rifle." For me, this was a special occasion. It marked the beginning of my transformation from an ordinary civilian to a resilient and determined soldier. But even with my understanding of the significance of this event, I did not really understand its far-reaching effects. I did not realize the kind of challenges this instrument would cause in my life from the first time I felt its weight. On our return to the fourth platoon barracks, now armed with the one item that truly made us different from the average Joe Blow, Sergeant Quinnones began introducing us to our weapons. He told us we would become more familiar with the M1 rifle than we were with the palms of our own hands and that it would be closer to us than our own mothers. He told us that our weapons would become an extension of our own bodies, and at times, we would feel more naked without our guns than we would if we were not wearing any trousers. Over the next 21 years of my life, I found all of what Sergeant Quinnones said to be accurate, much to my own chagrin. However, at the moment of its introduction, I found it exciting and eager to learn more about this almost intoxicating machine.

One week was devoted to training us about the MI rifle. During this time, we learned this weapon piece by piece. First, we learned the four major groups, which included the field scripting of the weapon, the trigger housing group, the bolt group, and the barrel group. We were required to break the rifle down into the four major groups and reassemble the weapon while being blindfolded. The idea was to take the gun apart during darkness for quick cleaning. The time to accomplish this task was one minute. Our next block of instruction was detailing the weapon, which required us to break the gun down into the four major groups, which were then scattered about on a table. We were supposed to identify each part and its role in any one of the major groups. After learning the physical structure of the M1 rifle, the next step was to know the weapon's characteristics, i.e., range, velocity, rate of fire per minute, effective killing range, and weight. It was not until this killing machine had intruded the most intimate part of my mind that we were allowed to pick up our weapons before or after physical training. Some mornings we were required to take physical training with weapons, and other mornings we took physical training without them.

However, before it was drill time, we were required to secure our weapons from the arms room. Drilling with the rifle is, in most cases, the most colorful and memorable part of basic combat training, but I also think it was the final step of ramming these machines right up our asses until they became parts of our inner guts. At one time in life, I thought the different marching positions, such as the right shoulder armed, left shoulder armed, present arms, armed salute, etc., were simply taught to us to understand how to handle a rifle. Now, I know there was more to it. It really was a form of indoctrination. The final act with this killing machine was to fire it. During the last few weeks of basic combat training, all of the above was deleted. We were up at 5:00 am, had a quick breakfast, rushed back to the barracks, where we put on on the forty-five-pound field pack, hustled to the arms room, took up the nine and a half pound rifle, and at 6:00 am, we were in formation sixty pounds heavier than what we were before we were kicked out of the bunk. Over and above all of this, I was still putting up with the bigot from Mississippi. I found it hard to accept marching twenty miles with fifty-nine pounds strapped to my back from the very beginning. I found that I was not too far off base.

The twenty-mile march to the rifle range was a bit too much for most new recruits, even after the past four weeks of physical training and drill. The hills of Fort Jackson, South Carolina, were of sandy loose soil and made marching for a short distance tiresome. Those who had problems with the earlier physical training found themselves dropping out after five miles of hard marching and occasional double-timing. However, my friend, the bigot, seemed to take it in stride.

The two weeks of going to the range and firing the MI rifle, for the most part, was a rewarding experience. It was the first phase of our training where our results could be recorded. I fired no better than my bunk buddy. In fact, at this stage of our training, I found myself hustling just to keep up with this guy. However, I made sure my boots and lockers were the best. I was sure I had won more friends than he had, simply because I had tried harder to win friends. We were more than halfway through training, and I was still putting up with the abuse from the big guy from Mississippi. I knew I would soon have to take care of this business, or it would be too late. I figured I had to do it before graduation, and as such, I needed to come up with the right time and place to execute my mission.

Saturday was a training day, and most of us went to Church on Sunday. So, the most optimum time for the job would be thanksgiving morning, which was the next holiday before graduation. I began to think the whole thing out. It would have to be early in the morning before anyone was out of bed. Because otherwise, I felt there would be too many distractions. At this stage of the game, I thought I needed all the help I could get. Already I knew this guy was not going to be a pushover. My final plan was to attack from the bottom bunk. Early on Thanksgiving morning, I would lay on the bottom bunk and kick upwards, knocking him out of the top bunk. I would be ready for him when he hit the floor. Then a kick in the nuts, and I felt that about that time, most of the rest of the platoon would be out of their bunks to see me finish him off. It was only a week before I would have to make good of this plan. If it did not work well, I could kiss my future goodbye. The week before Thanksgiving, 1959, was the longest week of my young life. I had had only one previous encounter with a white man, and from that experience, I had lost credibility with my mother because I lost my job. If this plan didn't work, I could lose it all, including a chance at a career I had dreamed of since my eleventh birthday. My dream of becoming a pilot and the opportunity to win the respect I always wanted from my family and community could simply disappear.

My plan needed to work. I don't know what others thought of my behavior from the time I made up my mind to take care of this bigot on thanksgiving morning, but I am sure they must have thought I was acting weird because I was scared as hell just thinking about what was ahead of me. This guy had me by a good twenty pounds. What if I did not kick hard enough to throw him out of the top bunk? What if I was not ready for him when he fell out of bunk? If that happened, I would have no choice but to get hammered by his fists. All these were questions I had no answers to.

Well, what could I do? I had made up my mind, and I had a good plan. On Thanksgiving morning, at about 6:00 am, it was still dark in the fourth platoon building. I laid on my back, looking up at the bulge in the top bunk over me. That bulge represented about 210 pounds of tuff bigot, who soon was about to receive the shock of his life. It was possibly something he would never forget, but I was sure I would never forget it either. I knew I had to do it. But that did not help the knots that had developed in my stomach. I took one last deep breath and kicked upwards as hard as I could. The big bigot from Mississippi hit the floor with a shout, "you nigger!" By that time, I had kicked him right in the balls and pushed him to the floor, landing on top of him.

I started punching him out. With every blow, I reminded him that it was a nigger kicking his ass. To my surprise, the whole barracks was cheering me on, including the acting platoon sergeant, Pvt. Knox. I threw some final blows and reassured myself that I had done the right thing. I felt I had a future with the U.S. Army. Several days later and very much later, my bunk buddy spoke to me kindlier and gently. Believe it or not, we became friends before graduation and the Christmas leave. It was at that moment that I felt I had become a man.

Doing Manly Things

This was my second trip to Columbia, South Carolina. My first had been with a white friend Private King, who had been the leader of my cheering squad when I kicked the bigot's ass from Mississippi. For the most part, my first visit to the Capital City of South Carolina had been one with mixed emotions and questions. Why had King and I not been allowed to go into the picture show together? Why did King climb the rails of the picture show and come to the area where blacks were designated to sit after agreeing to go into the section for whites? And why did two white guys come up and escort King and me to the door? Moreover, after leaving the show, why did King decide to become a captain as soon as can? Why could the Military police not accept that King was an Army Captain taking a stroll on the black side of town with a black Army Private?

I learned several lessons on my first visit to Columbia. The first one was that black policemen arrest white men as long as the two of them belong to the military. The second lesson was more of a fact than a lesson. It was that some white boys are really dumb. The third and final lesson I learned was that life could be amazing if white folk would not interfere. For the greater part, I did not have anything against good white folk; however, until this point in my life, they had caused me more pain than I cared to remember, especially when I was present in the state of South Carolina.

At this age, I was unfamiliar with the art of perusal and seducing lovely young things. Plus, I had little time to learn that art with everything on my mind. I wondered if the United States Government had planned the setting I was presently experiencing, and if so, where were the technical manual to explain how to operate the system. The answer to my question was just a block away, in the form of the USO. I quickly learned that the purpose of the USO was to serve the serviceman. If you could not get what you wanted from the front desk, just wait for your turn. It would come to you. My answer was in the form of a young co-ed from the two institutions of higher learning that set just across the street, one facing the other. Both institutions came highly recommended by the black community, and who was I to say the product was not quality. The young lady who came to me was a very presentable package. She had big brown eyes, a light tan complexion, black hair, and I guess her dimensions were around 34-24-36. The only thing she said to me was "ten and two," and I knew just what she was talking about, recalling a similar experience when Eddie and I first visited Jacksonville, Florida. Jacksonville seemed to be another lifetime away, and maybe it was. But that life was less than two months in the past.

As I recall from my first trip to Columbia, Alien University was set at the corner of Harden and Taylor, and Benedict College was in the next block on Harden and Blanding. The USO was just down the street on Harden. The young lady had taken me just around the corner to a rooming house. The room only had a single bed and a nightstand. The bed had no covering, just a single clean white sheet that was perfectly pressed. The room was not much to look at, but it was well maintained and immaculate. Again, I thought the U.S. Government must supervise this whole thing. Possibly, the U.S. Government was looking at the operation from the corner of its eye. In any case, once the co-ed and I were in the room, she disrobed with the light on, and to this day, I have not seen a more beautiful picture, including the playboy magazines that I have viewed over the years. I am sure the lovely young thing was putting on a show for me, and I enjoyed every minute of it. She could not have been a day over 20. However, I am sure she knew I had never been with a real woman from the very beginning.

I guess she wanted to make things easy for me. After disrobing, she took my hand and guided me to the bed, and together we sat on the edge and made small talk until I regained my composure. She taught me the art of lovemaking, and afterward, made a show of putting on her clothing the same as she had when she disrobed. Together, we walked the short distance back to the USO. On the second trip to this exotic city of the deep south, I was again seeking the company of the only real woman that I had ever known in such an intimate manner. But much to my displeasure, I was unable to find her. On the campus of Benedict College, there was a battle of the bands' concert taking place. Among them was the Rattler's band of Florida, A&M University. Several of my classmates were a part of the Rattler's band, of which one was a boy by the name of Harry Roundtree. We had started the eleventh grade together, and it was good to see him. However, I felt he had one step up on me, just from being a part of all the excitement on the college campus.

Poor me, I never even made it through the eleventh grade. After about an hour with Harry and the excitement of the band competition, I decided to look for female companionship outside of the college environment and headed for Taylor Street. Taylor street was lined with nightclubs with live band performances in each prominent club. My strategy was to find the club with the loudest music and the biggest crowd. There was a two-dollar fee at the entrance and more GI, all-black than you could shake a stick at. It was a BYOB, Joint. The setup was similar to the idea of an army training center-type operation. Persons 21 or older could bring their booze and get a set up at a table for an additional five-dollar charge. All of us less than 21 were left to stand around the wall. Frankly, it felt like we were ducks in a shooting gallery.

The working girls could almost take their pick, and they did. The routine was the same as if these girls had their own union. They will select their target from a distance, using their eye contact. After an approving nod from the prospective client, the working girl would walk to the spot where the client stood and whisper, 10 and 2, meaning ten dollars for her services and two dollars for a room. Typically, the rooms would be in a dull house, but often they were located in the back room of a family residence. I am sure the army accepted this arrangement as long as the GI was not taken advantage of. However, on this night, on my second go on the merry-go-round of pleasure, I learned that all working girls were not honest, even in what seemed to be the best working relationship between the army and this thriving black community.

While doing my thing in the back room of a dwelling house, my trousers were hung on a chair. Once the action was over, and I went to put on my pants, my wallet was nowhere to be found. I made some fuss and refused to leave. On my return to the club, the wallet was returned, along with an apology, but for what? You be the judge. After all, I was just eighteen! But in any case, I learned my second lesson about women of the evening, which was not to trust them. Once, I saw a peculiar incident involving one of the working girls. This girl, who had an admirer or lover, apparently wanted her to give him some attention. But it was evident from her behavior she did not want to be bothered. However, he continued to follow her as she tried to do her business. Then, suddenly, she pulled out a razor from her bag and cut off his nose with a sweep of the instrument with little to no effort. Blood was everywhere, and within minutes, so were policemen and military policemen. The city policemen took the man and the woman away, and business went on as nothing ever happened.

I had one week to go before graduation, and then I could be home for Christmas, which meant one more weekend in Columbia before I could go into my advanced military training. But I had already learned some valuable lessons, which went as follows: make sure you know who you fooling with, do not bother a working girl when she is trying to take care of business, do not lay your wallet around when dating around, and that it is a lot safer for black men to fool around at the USO and college campuses than on the streets of Columbia.

Christmas of 1959

Eight weeks prior, I could have never bet that I would accomplish all the things I would soon be able to boast about when I took my Christmas leave, which was just a week or so away. I had mastered the M1 rifle in this time, and now, I could march twenty miles with more than sixty pounds strapped to my back without any difficulty. Not only that, but I had also taken on and kicked the butt of a Mississippi bigot. I also had my first orgasm with a lovely little thing from an institution of higher learning. I really felt like a man. However, there were several things that I still wished had happened. I wished that I had received more mail from home. For weeks, I made mail-call every day and received only two letters. There were four other people of color in my platoon, except one. It seemed as though all of them received parcels from their families every day, including homemade cookies and whatnot. I also wished my family could be present for my graduation. But even with my strongest prayer, I knew there was no chance that was possible.

Our training lasted for only eight weeks, but it seemed like it had been a lifetime. We had only one final test, record firing of the MI. All other tests, including the physical fitness examination, were history. I had scored

450 of a possible 600 and also had qualified for airborne training, where you had to score 1000 of a possible 1200, which included a six-mile run. After record firing, the rest of the week was devoted to taking pictures and parade practice, getting ready for graduation day, etc.

The morning of record fire, we woke up as usual at 5:00 A.M. or 0500 hours, had breakfast at 0530, and were in morning formation at the sound of reveille, which was always sounded at 0600 sharp. On this morning, Sergeant Quinnones gave a right face command instead of his usual left face command that was in the direction of the rifle range some twenty miles away. We marched about the length of a football field and did a column left. In the dawn, we saw the outlines of three tractors and trailers there, which were referred to as cattle cars. Starting with the first platoon, we were herded like cattle onto the trucks. The seating arrangement includes a bench on either side of the trailer and one bench down the middle of the trailer, forcing each platoon sergeant to seat about sixty recruits on each of the three tractors and trailers. I think I would rather have walked. It was a tight fit, twenty per row, with full-field gear and an MI rifle. By the time we reached the rifle range, my backside was numb from the hard wooden seats. But I found consolation in knowing that if we qualified, this would be our very last trip to a field with a full field pack and rifle unless you were unlucky enough to be assigned to the combat unit as a permanent duty member.

Of the five coloreds, Private Green, from West Virginia, was the only one assigned to an Infantry unit after receiving advanced Infantry training, meaning he had to endure eight more weeks of the same training. I, with Private LaCorne, was assigned as a communication specialist. Private Whiteside had been assigned to the transportation unit. Private Gains, who was prior service, did not need advance training and was assigned to an overseas organization. I learned later that the cattle cars had been called in to speed up training, which needed to be completed prior to Christmas break. Our cycle had started on October 22, 1959, and Christmas break was set to start on December 23. The cattle car ride to the rifle range was scheduled on a Monday, and if I recall correctly, graduation was supposed to be on Friday, the 17 of December 1959. Saturday, December 23, 1959, 1 could revisit Columbia and have my first Greyhound bus ride along the highways of the great south. After we were herded off the cattle cars and assembled by platoons, we were each assigned a partner from one of the other platoons.

My partner and I were ordered to hold our rifles in the port-arm position. Afterward, we were marched to the ready line of the qualifying range. This range was not anything like the practice ranges we had been to so far. In fact, it took on the form of a jungle or forest. In my mind, I thought no way one would be able to see a target from where we stood. My partner was a short black kid from the first platoon who was as puzzled as me. The range Non-Commission Officer in charge was a six feet plus black guy with stripes that covered the greater part of his arms and the yellow helmet he wore. He introduced himself as Master Sergeant Jackson. He explained in no uncertain terms that he was in charge. His safety lecture was as brief as it could be. He told us to keep our weapons up and downrange! There was no running allowed, but we were ordered to walk at a quick step-pace, that too only when we were told to do so.

Score cards with a number two pencil were passed to my partner, who was now standing behind me. I stood with my rifle barrel up at sixty degrees on the spot-marked ready line. I pointed my weapon downrange as I had been instructed to do by the tall black master sergeant. His next command was, "This is a walk-through drill. You will walk to your first firing position, take a prone position, and engage your target when you are told. Scores, you will help the fire locate their targets. Move to the first firing position on the firing line". The first firing position was ten yards straight ahead of the ready line. It was marked by a path and a clearing in the bush where many other recruits had gone before us. I, with my scorer, walked to the first position and took up a prone position in the following order:

1) My knees made contact with the ground

2) After my knees were against the earth, I brought my rifle butt down to the ground

3) I slid my rifle alongside my body as I took the prone position

The drill was similar to what we had been taught to do at the training fire range over the past few weeks. As we looked downrange, our target popped up only ten feet or so in front of us. "That was your ten-meter target. I hope you all saw it. The next time you see it, it will be for record. Move to your next firing position," said the tall black man. Just another ten meters, we could see the fox hole and moved to take our position, with me in the hole and my scorer taking the prone position to the side of the hole. I engaged the target with the help of my scorer. "That was your 150-meter target. Move to your next firing position," were the next words to come out of the officer's mouth.

The next position was behind a post and was listed as the kneeling position. We moved to the kneeling position spot and were getting pretty good at finding our targets that popped up in various places throughout our line of fire, in the density of the vast forest that now engulfed us. The last position was the squatting one and was some 50 meters into the thickets of the forest, which was mostly made of pines with undergrowth in the sandy hills of South Carolina. We were ordered to move to the last position and engage our target, which was another 10-meter target. After the last target, the next command was to get in an about-face position. As we walked through the forest back to the ready line, we were reminded of safety and asked to keep the weapon up and downrange. Our next run was supposed to be conducted with live rounds and was for the record. We were reminded that failing to qualify meant that we would not graduate.

By the time I reached the ready line, the palm of my hand was wet since the temperature was more than 36 degrees. We were again reminded to keep the weapon up and downrange upon returning to the ready line. We were given a bandoleer of 96 rounds, eight per clip, and were told to go for it. Each target would stay up for ten seconds, with ten seconds allowed between each position. Standing on the ready line with my rifle up and pointed downrange and a bandoleer slanged across my chest with twelve eight-round clips, I waited for the next command.

I wondered if the targets had faces, what would they look like? The last war had consisted of the faces of the Koreans. What would the next face be? I very well could have fixed the face of our old iceman, Red, maybe the Sheriff who had killed my neighbors, McCall. But my upbringing would not have allowed that. My parents had taught me to love those who spitefully use you and abuse you. Like every other case, the faces on the target would be Japs. Why Japs? I think because the Japanese were the easiest for the Americans to hate. And was not I an American?

The Command that came next said: "Ready on the right." The assistants to the tall master sergeant signaled that the right side of the range was ready. "Ready on the left." The signal from the left was ready. "Ready on the firing line, fire, watch your lane, lock, and load one eight-round clip. Move to the first firing position, keep those weapons up and downrange, and fire when ready". I fired three rounds to kill the target from the first firing position and moved to the next firing position. From the foxhole, I got the target with the first shot. Next was the kneeling position, and with two shots, I knocked off the envisioned Jap. The command to move to the next target was given by an assistant who walked between firing lanes and maintained safety on the range. After firing 96 rounds, I had 68 kills, just two shorts to be declared a qualified expert.

Basic training for all practical purposes was over on the afternoon of Monday, December 17, 1959. The rest of the week consisted of preparing for the graduation, passing out awards, and finally, training for the parade that was supposed to be the grand finale. As I had guessed, my parents were not present on the day of my graduation. In fact, of all the black, only Private Green's parents had decided to attend the ceremony. The theater where our graduation was held was nearly full. The four platoons were seated in the middle of the theater in reverse order. At the front of the theatre was the 4th platoon, followed by the 3rd platoon and so on. This gave an effect that everyone was of the same height when seated because of the slanted theater floor. We were all dressed in our Army Greens and our overseas caps, better known within the ranks of GIs as the "cunt cap," because it was said to take on the form of the female coitus when it was opened to be placed on one's head.

After the last official act of basic combat training, my first planned stop was to visit and view a real-life cunt.

However, I had no plans of putting my head into it. Seated to our right were visitors, parents, and friends of the graduating class of Company A, 19th Battalion, 5th Training Regiment of the United States Army. The left of the theater was reserved for visiting commanders and flag-ranked officers. Seated on stage were the graduating batch's company commanders and platoon sergeants. I have never been more impressed with anything in my eighteen years. The formal ceremony was very extensive and informative. The Regiment Commander was the first to speak. He had entered the building like a king. When his name was announced, everyone in the theater came to their feet, including the visitors.

His speech was centered around the history of the 5th Regiment, who had seen action in Normandy, Korea, France, Germany, and many other places whose names I can't pronounce. When he was done speaking, the Company Commander took the podium and called his command to attention as the regiment commander and his aid departed the theater. By this time, I was so proud that I was almost in tears that nobody from my little hometown of Clermont, Florida, was there to see me becoming a part of something that already had given me a sense of pride that I had never thought was possible. Why? Why was I so proud? Would I always be so proud, or would these conditions change? With my new uniform and having passed the test into manhood, would I now be permitted to sit on the main floor of the picture show in Columbia?

I did not have an answer to any of these questions. However, I knew I never wanted to lose what I felt. The Company Commander told us all why we should feel proud, and especially those who had performed exemplary. There were three awards that were supposed to be given for exemplary performance:

1) Physical fitness,
2) Weapon qualification,
3) Best all-around trainee.

There was one black man who was supposed to receive an award: Private Lee from the third platoon.

The next event was supposed to be the last event of the day, and probably the last most of us would see of one another. Straight from the podium, the Commander announced, "repair for passing review, platoon sergeant, take charge of your platoon". Sergeant Quinnones, our Puerto Rican Platoon Sergeant, came down from the stage, and I am sure I saw a tear on his cheek. He gave the command: "left face, and right file column right march!"

As we filed out of the theater, all the other companies around us were filing out of company theaters, and we could hear the 5th Regiment band from the parade field playing military marching music. The event that took place that day will forever be frozen in my mind. Damn! That was something.

I knew the home would not be any more than a family affair. I had no girl, and I did not even want a girl. However, at this point, I was thinking as soon as we march past that reviewing stand, I would be Columbia-bound and would meet one of the working girls from the institution of higher learning for lesions in sex education, again. My duffer bag was packed lying on my bunk. I already had my round-trip bus ticket to home and back to Fort Jackson. I would also be receiving my advanced training as a communication specialist here. LaCorne, Beardin, and Jackson of the Third platoon and I had already pooled our money for the cab to Columbia. We also paid an extra ten dollars to pay the cabbie to pick up the girls off Taylors Street close to Allen and Benedict College. It was part of our routine to witness the cab driver ask trainees if they required any extra services. It was as if one could almost always depend on the delivery. The business of prostitution in Columbia, in the black community, was business that made money. Nobody wanted anyone to know that the GI was getting a bad deal.

The coming together of one platoon after another, just through perfect commands from the platoon sergeants given in a timely manner, was something for the eye to see. One would have said that this was not possible had they seen us just eight weeks prior as the companies continued to file out of the theaters of the 5th Regiment until it was a full regiment marching in perfect timing to Army band marching music. As we took our position, one company after another, the Commanders, Parents, and friends of the graduating 5th

Training Regiment were mounting the reviewing stand. I felt as if ice was flowing through my veins, so effortlessly it felt as if it were a natural process. *Surely it couldn't get any better than this.* Soon the Regiment parade ground was full of left to right with perfect aligned columns of young men, black and white, standing tall side by side and feeling good about it. It was only a few days before Christmas, and for sure, one could not have a greater Christmas present than this. The next command was given by the Regiment Commander, who was now standing tall in the center of the reviewing stand. "Take charge of your companies".

Using the most direct route that led to taking charge of their respective company, all company commanders moved at their own pace. What was interesting was that they did so without any music. This part of the parade too was special, because it showed a sense of ownership. Upon the company commander reaching his company, he was greeted with a hand salute by the platoon sergeant:

"Sir, the company is formed."

"Sergeant, take your post."

Now a loud single bugle sounded from the band, and the Regiment Commander gave another command: "Adjutant Post."

This sent a quick-stepping Captain from the reviewing stand until he reached the very center of the parade field twenty yards or so directly in front of the viewing stand.

Once there, he was paid attention to with a snappy move and made an about-face. Now as he was facing the Regiment commander, he looked back over his right shoulder, and at the top of his voice, commanded: "GGGGuids Post."

He looked back to the Regiment Commander, "Sir, the Regiment is formed." An award was given at the Regiment formation to the winning recruit for Trainee of the Regiment. He, with his commander, marched to the center of the field and faced the commander. This time, the Regiment commander came down from the stand and marched to the center of the field, as his aide carried the award. "An army Commendation Medal".

The commander and his aide stood directly in front of the company commander and the winning trainee, and a citation was read loudly. It read:

"The trainee (who was from another Battalion) had brought great credit upon himself, his unit, and the United States Army."

Afterward, the regiment commander marched back to the reviewing stand, took his position, and made some comments to the effect that only the best of the best was awarded Commendation Medals so early in army careers, and some would have a twenty-year career without such an award. He then uttered the command: (the last command of an event that will be forever etched in my memory), "Passing Review"!

The band began to play, my company was positioned almost in the middle of the regiment, or for the sake of nonmilitary persons, to our right was about eight other companies, and to our left was another eight, or so companies. The next commands were given by individual company commanders who took the effect of a chain reaction: "Company, right face," as their voices echoed from one company to the another until the entire regiment faced one specific arena with perfect alignment. This was followed by another command:

"Left turn March,"

The command was passed as the guide arm (a flag carried by a select soldier, Called the guide arm barrier, which identifies the unit, and signal when the preparatory command is given by the commander) went upward, and came down passing review was on its way.

During the time that every company reached the left turn spot that was marked on the parade field, any and every individual could view the guide arm lifted high, and as the command was vocalized, the left turn would be made with the troops staying in perfect alignment, and the guide arm was brought down again. And as each soldier aligned their body perfectly to the beat of the drum, one thirty-inch military step after the other. Some ten yards or so from the reviewing stand occurs the command. It would be: "eyes right".

The guide arm will be dropped and held straight out in front of the barrier so the unit designation can be read from the reviewing stand and all persons with the exception. Of the right file will look to the right. The commander surrenders a hand salute. These moments are the points of pride time of any soldier life, for the command is saying to him, you have met my approval. It would be equal to the walk across the stage at a high school or college graduation.

At this stage, I had nothing else to do. However, I was not so sure if I wanted to visit Columbia; I was still somewhat high after passing the reviewing stand, with eyeball to eye ball contact with the regiment command who I perceived would directly say to me, "Well-done, son".

Nonetheless, I guess I had to go along with LaCome and the others; now, the plans were made. As we marched into our company area, the cabs were already lined up to receive their fair for our exit. Wherever we wanted to go, it took about five minutes for the four of us to go in, grab our bags and select a cab with a driver that we thought could fulfill our request. The cab was from the yellow cab company. The driver was a brawny black gentleman and he seemed to have a pleasant personality. There were no words spoken between us; he simply popped his trunk and began to try and fit our bags into it. The trunk accepted all of our bags except one. It was placed into the back seat with Jackson and Bearden. Still, there were no words spoken by any of the four. The cab driver's enthusiasm and vibrant energy cut through the silence that transcended our physical presence and existence in that cab.

"I'm aware you boys want some action?"

"Yes, but we want some of them college girls."

It was Bearden who placed our order. Now it was the cabby's turn.

"You know that will cost you an extra ten, and you'll have to pay in advance".

Bearden passed him the ten-dollar bill that we had given him. The cabby instructed us how to register at the hotel, where he would drop us to wait for the girls.

"You guys will have to give me your names on a piece of paper, and when you get to the hotel, you can get a room for two dollars each for one hour. The person at the front desk will direct the girls to your room when I drop them off."

The hotel was an old red brick construction with double wooden doors with peeled paint. The lighting inside the hotel was dim, and a young woman signed us in at the front desk.

Her only question was: "Will you be expecting company?"

We told her we would, and she replied:

"Make sure you print your name plain."

It was very clear that business was good, for there was not a minute that passed without the door being open and slammed. I viewed the register for a minor second and felt lucky that we ended up getting four rooms. We never received any keys until we learned all of these doors had sliding latches from the inside; we were instructed to only open the door if the girl that knocked knew our name. My room number was 16, Lacorn's was 14, Jackson's was 8, and Bearden ended up getting Room 2.

I went to my room, latched the door behind me and waited for the knock that came about twenty minutes after I had laid down on the iron frame bed, with only a fitted sheet. She called me by my last name, "Montgomery." I got up and opened the door. I felt as if I had been cheated on; the girl at the door must have been 25 years old and I can say with confidence that she was not a college girl.

I asked her, "Are you going to college?"

Her answer was, "Why? Ain't I good enough for you?"

I wanted to tell her she was not what I had asked for, though I still let her in. She was out of her cloth before I could pull off my shoes, and laying naked on the bed:

"Come on baby, I don't get any all day."

I wanted to walk out of the room, but she didn't. She was laying down on bed with absolutely no covers. She was slim, almost needlelike, but long hair and a tanned complexion. With her, I took my time. I looked at her which she seemed to enjoy very much. So, I thought maybe she isn't so bad after all.

I say, money first, honey. I gave her ten dollars. She got off the bed, walked across to the chair where her purse was and put the ten inside her purse. By this time, I was undressed. "You ain't half bad", she said.

My thoughts were half bad my ass, I am downright physical, and I was after the many mornings of physical training and marches to the rifle range the past eight weeks. I was 6"1 tall, 192 pounds, with a 28" waist and a 46" chest; *I was bad.*

The action on the bed was all business; after I had physically invested her. It was as if she was counting every stroke, and she knew which stroke would make me orgasm. "That's it, honey, you only paid for a one-time opportunity," I protested, but she made it very clear by slapping my back side that the action was over. Almost as soon as she left the room, there was another knock on the door, "Montgomery".

This girl was short, and had a dark complexion, who said my girl was in Lacorne's room. We still had time for another quickie at half the price. I passed and went to look for Jackson and Bearden; to find they had left for Fayetteville, N.C.; and said they would see me in January 1960, in Communication school. I waited for Lacorne at the front desk and in the short time it took for him to come down, I observed and counted ten couples that signed in and signed out of the hottest hotel in Columbia, S.C., two days before Christmas 1959.

The fair to the Greyhound bus station was $1.50 each; it was my first visit to a bus station of any type. There was one waiting room for the colored and one for the whites. The station was full of GI's just out of basic, some of whom I knew; there were more blacks than whites; however, the black waiting room was much smaller, with no eating area. There was a sliding window where you could order food from the white's side of the station. For the most part, the black civilians carried brown paper bags with food from home; (mostly fried chicken or lunching meat between white bread). The waiting area seemed to be one big picnic. For a newcomer like myself who was exposed to these environments, one would think that everyone knew the other, although I was glad, I had my ticket. I was already thinking this would be my last time buying a ticket to ride a greyhound bus.

The activity in the area was almost the same as Taylors Street. Prostitution, greasy pig, the money in the envelope trick. For the most part, it was the white boys that were being taken because the blacks had already been had at least once.

To be very honest, it was almost unsafe outside of the station once you had made it in because, by one means or another, someone was going to get your money. I checked with the person at the ticket counter for the departing time for my bus. I learned that the departing time for the bus to Charleston was 6:30 p.m. or 1830 hours military time. It was then 4:10, two hours and twenty minutes to wait in a place that was becoming more and more unpleasant by the minute. Lacorne were much more at ease; he had already made a trip to the little sliding window for food and drink. I wasn't hungry. I began to assess who was who and tried to figure out where they were all going. For the most part, they were Carolinians going short distances within the state of South Carolina, and some was going to northern states like New York, Chicago, and Washington, D.C. for the Christmas holidays. Some were complete families, with only a few days off from work, and would soon repeat this process after visiting families and friends, so they could be back on their jobs. All the college kids had departed several days earlier, so almost none of the travelers were from Benedict College or Alien University.

I was almost totally preoccupied as I tried to figure out why I felt so totally out of place with these people when Lacorne was right at home. Was it because it seemed as if they accepted everything as normal, and I felt it was not normal to be disallowed asset to clean and descent facilities?

The Charleston bus departure was announced. I stood to my feet to learn that that announcement was for whites only, and we would have to wait until they were loaded before we were allowed out of the waiting room. The second announcement was all colors for Charleston; your bus is now loading. I told myself again I would return by bus, but never again would I buy a ticket. While the bus was loaded, I saw trainees who graduated with me who now felt superior to me. I thought of King, who had to climb the rail of the theater in Columbia because we were not permitted to sit together. King had been kicked out of the Army because he had been ruled not trainable.

I wondered if he was still standing up for blacks; and how much trouble he was having in his hometown back in Virginia. As the bus pulled out of the station, LaCorne and I, fortunately or unfortunately, were one seat away from the last seat on the bus. Ideally, we wouldn't want to sit there, although it's not a bad seat. I had the window seat, and I saw the hustle and bustle of the streets of Columbia easily.

The bus departed the city. The city that would always be a part of my memory. Charleston, a city of great beauty, the capital city of the south, the city with rich history, and where the first shot of the civil war was fired. The city where my grandfather Wallace was born. The bus made many stops between Columbia and Charleston; I saw all the personalities at each stop, both white and black.

However, my mind mostly compared what I had seen to what my grandfather must have looked like as a young man in these environments. I had seen almost nobody from the Negro family or ancestry, someone who stood tall. It didn't make sense because I stood tall on the parade field during a passing review. For the most part, the older

Negros walked slowly with their head to the ground, and the younger ones moved about with no particular sense of direction. Charleston was founded in 1667; how long would it be before colored would display a sense of pride in these parts, and how could it be that within this same region, with only a fence as a divider, black men stood tall.

Walked with their head high; why couldn't black men have the same authority outside the Army as they had within the army? We arrived at the North Charleston bus station just short of 4 hours after departing Columbia; the only other rest stop had been Orangeburg; at Orangeburg, I saw only a few white folks and seemly hundreds of coloreds with none being in positions of authority.

Now, in Charleston, the condition repeated itself. But here, I felt closer to the people because out here, there were some places I had several great uncles, aunts, and cousins whom I would never see, unless someone did a search of the "Montgomery" family tree. A genes study, but who would ever have time to do anything like that? Maybe me? But when? I had no answers and shook Lacorne to wake him, for he had been asleep almost since departing Columbia. As LaCorne and I departed the bus for the colored side of the bus station, I was getting goosebumps; there were so many people who seemed as if they were well-educated men and women; there was even a dining room for color's; a colors to eat.

LaCorne and I ordered hamburger platters from the drill, and helped ourselves to a Coke from the Coke Machine and took a table to wait for the next bus to Jacksonville. I could not help looking at all these color's, thinking that I could possibly see a resemblance of my father, uncle, or one of my aunts, of which I was sure blood kin was with in throwing distance from my table. I can't remember my grandfather; however, I was told he often came to our house when I was just a baby and would take me for long walks until my mother would not allow him to visit anymore. She often had to hunt him down just to retrieve me. Afterward, I was told he would wait until no one was looking and would steal me away from the family. Before I was old enough to remember, the family had him put away somewhere in north Florida (Chattahoochee), just south of the Georgia line, only about 100 miles from my father's birthplace (Moultrie, Ga).

As we waited for our next bus, my mind was completely engulfed with the thoughts of my grandfather. I developed a habit of tracing his migration south to the birthplace of my father, some two hundred and twenty miles south of Charleston. I would also pass within a few miles of where my grandfather died while still confined to the Asylum in Chattahoochee, Florida. As I recall, this occurred in the fall of 1947. I don't recall a funeral being held, or some type of family observance, but it must have been a very hush-hush affair. I was feeling a great deal of pain when I called for the white folk to load the bus for Jacksonville. The City of Charleston, South Carolina, within itself represented a great deal of pain. For it could be called the birthplace of slavery, or the point of debarkation for the North American Slave trade, and also the place that started the war to defend the slave practices. My grandfather felt the need to flee this place as well, given the circumstances, fast forward to me waiting to load the bus subsequently to those whose ancestors had inflected this pain upon me and upon my predecessors. When it was our time to load the bus, I thought about how I could generate those feelings that I had experienced this very morning during my graduation.

I looked at the bright side and if I'm being honest, I could only assume that someplace somehow, I would feel proud to be an American, once again. In spite of the reality hitting us, for the next ten hours or so, I would be covering territory that could only generate more pain. Lacorne and I took our seats again, one from the last, at the back of the bus. He was generous and let me have the window. After we left Columbia and travelled back, I enjoyed the view and the energy of the window seat. He noticed it and let me take it again. He was asleep, again. I could not even spit out ten words from my mouth for him to hear. I wanted him to hear my grandfather's plight. The bus was headed south on highway seventeen to Savannah, and I remained awake with a million thoughts. My mind was racing at 100km/h with thoughts jeopardizing every other thought. For whatever reason, I thought of Al Joseph (the white man who painted his face to imitate blacks) and the Swanee River. I then thought about how there was so much litter, and I could not see any future for this country for colors because we really had so little to build on.

I then thought of Joseph again; why should I dislike him? Is it mandatory? Was he not painting a true picture during his minstrel shows when he imitated colors? We had our music, our love for the land, and our hope that one day God would end our suffering; It was possible that he told our story better through his ministerial shows than what we could ever put together. This was simply because he had a better presume. He was a white man. From my viewpoint, a young black man, who was a subordinate first to older black men of my community, who are subordinates to white men. It is unlikely our voice would ever be heard, and the only way my father's voice would be heard is through the favor of a white man, one would demand all of my father's loyalty.

There it was, as I looked from the window, the greyhound bus headed south on highway seventeen to Savannah. I knew I would be a soldier for many years to come because it would be as close as I could come to being my own man and having my voice heard in this country. It was past 3 A.M. when the bus pulled into the Savannah station. The bus driver and several other people got off, and other people got on; LaCorn only had a short distance to travel before he would be home. I thought about how much I would miss his presence and aura. LaCorne was a man of very few words; but when the man spoke, he spoke words of wisdom. His foresight was highly regarded and one that made many listen to him.

Comprising the basics altogether, he had saved me many times, and I know he will see much success in his life because he is composed of many genuine characteristics. However, I do wish he stood up for himself more than he normally did. The driver returned to the bus and walked to where we were supposed to check tickets. He possessed one characteristic that caught our eyes: he punched new passengers and simply nodded toward LeCorne and I to acknowledge that he recognized us as thorough passengers from Charleston. When he reached the front of the bus after checking his last ticket, he acknowledged and that was when we were on our way again.

LaCom was wide awake now and he spoke a bit about this part of the country. He told me he had worked as far north as Savannah, as he picked and loaded Cotton for almost nothing. He preferred loading instead of picking because while picking cotton, the bulbs would cut your hands, causing them to bleed if your hands were not toughened for the task. He also expressed a desire not to return to these parts because it held little to no future for man. But he had not yet committed to being a career soldier, and he thought he might seek young black employment in the city after the army. I told him city or no city, colored was colored, which spelled little or no hope for a long and productive life. I told him I knew schoolteachers marred to men who worked in the orange groves, and other teachers marred to teachers, and they too were tied down to the same old Saturday night routines as everyone else. Teaching school is about the highest position you can have in the colored community, except being a doctor, and it wasn't worth it. Most had so little money they couldn't. If you could be a funeral director or own a big nightclub, it was possible for you could have a future, but that would need a lot of money, so my only option was to stay in the Army as long as I could.

It was early morning when La Corn pulled the line to signal the driver to stop. Somewhere between Waycross and Valdosta, Georgia, in the middle of nowhere, is how I would describe it. But the driver pulled to the side of the road and stopped at a little country store; LaCorn found his handbag. And the driver got out and let him get his duffel bag from the bottom side of the bus. As we pulled away, I saw LaCorn step up on the front porch to a telephone that hung from the front of the little building. I turned and wondered who it was at the other end of the line. It was probably someone who was very upset, so upset that it disturbed me so early in the morning, especially since it was Christmas Eve, and one of the very few days I would have an off from work during these holidays. LaCorn had been the only person in my platoon who received fewer letters than myself from home. From this perspective, I wondered how my family would respond when I'd make a phone call from the Greyhound bus stop, just off the highway fifty less than a mile from Big Mama's house. Thoughts occurred to me, such as:

Who would come to pick me up? and

How long would I have to wait; in the poorer section, of the white community, of this very segregated southern town that I called home?

It was Christmas Eve; no doubt Mama would be busy cooking; or out doing last-minute shopping for my younger sisters and brothers, of which of the six, none had driver's licenses; with only one (Alexander), being older enough to drive. I felt that coming home might have been a mistake. A disruption to a very busy family who tried to make a living under the most adverse conditions. It was at this point that I decided not to volunteer for basic training or any of the experiences I had had in the past two months that I had been away from home. I had left home under very trying times; my father had just recovered from a serious accident due to which he had lost three middle fingers in his right hand; my older brother, James, was marred with a new baby; my sister Deloris was in her Junior year of College at Florida A&M University – she had also just delivered a baby, that mama would have to take care of the newborn until she graduated. I also had a younger brother, Alexander, who was somewhat of a slow learner. Alexander had spent the past year recovering from correctional surgery on his feet, which led him to drop out of school. My older sister, Gloria, had just built and moved into a new house, almost as big and beautiful as a mom and dad's new house. This was of course with her new family. It was pushing six in the morning, and the bus was coming into the city limits of Thomasville, Georgia, less than fifty miles north of Tallahassee as it slowed down, and I was able to see the shacks that colors lived in.

I thought of my father and mother's house, one that boasted five bedrooms and three baths; I felt more secure about who I was; and where I was going in life then. As it turns out, I was not so secure since I thought life was good just in my hometown. For whatever reason, my older brothers and sisters would say that life was just great. They were as equal and proud as who they were and thought they had a good future. I disagreed, though. I think life is not only about gaining wealth. For it was for sure, my family seemed to be on the right track to accomplish that. But rather, life was about establishing strong continuity between family members. In other words, it meant building a family that could enjoy an uninterrupted success base. I did not see that in my family; instead, what I saw right after my birth was stiff competition, and it was that way from the very beginning. I was at a disadvantage. I thought it was a rare fact that my father was a General Building Contractor, in 1959, in the most southern part of the United States. But what I considered even more rare was that a black family formed an equal partnership between family members, such as incorporation; that the success could be passed to each family sibling.

In a small southern town of Clermont, Florida, there lived several very successful black men, but I know of no successful black family as one unit that had developed into a co-operation. Was it something carried over from slavery that colors were ordained to be in continuous competition with one another? Or is it that black heads of families are so insecure that they feel threatened by other members of the family? In the short time that I had been in the U.S. Army, I had learned to trust myself, but I had also learned I was strongest when I enlisted both moral and physical help from others. Through the use of this support, there was nothing I could not accomplish. The bus pulled to a stop in front of a weather-bent structure that was marked with a metal sign - "*Greyhound Bus Station.*"

Several elderly-colored women with cardboard boxes waited for its arrival. They were dressed as if they were going to a Sunday meeting. Their attire included hats, which called for something. As the bus stopped, each woman held two boxes and struggled to the right side of the bus, where the driver waited to secure their luggage and take their tickets. There were several seats opened just in front of me, and I hoped (which was almost a prayer), that they would not take the seats that lay open in front of me.

I watched them struggle three steps up and down the aisle until they were just in front of me. They had been talking all the time; I found out that they were on their way to Jacksonville for Christmas, and one of their biggest worries was that there might not be anyone at the station upon their arrival to meet them. "Look a Soldier Boy," one remarked. While not saying anything directly to me, someone commented, "I know your mother is proud, you can send her a little money each month."

My thought was, "Why is it like this, though? Black adults looked upon their siblings as a commodity of some sort?" or "Why would she take for granted that I still lived with my mother?" It was a silly question, and I could not have looked over eighteen, which I was not quite evidently. Most mothers felt boys my age was not old enough to be on their own, and this old sister was no exception. However, when I thought of my old schoolmates, they were all married, except one or two, but most were no older than myself.

"God!" I thought.

How will they ever make it? But surprisingly, most of them were doing very well, even with cars and well-furnished apartments. In fact, many thought I was crazy for enlisting for a mere eighty-seven dollars a month. For me, money wasn't what it was all about. Firstly, I needed acceptance and respect. I wanted a career, and thus far, I had not seen any opportunity for any of the above in the community of Clermont.

The first direct question coming from the woman who got on the bus in Thomasville was, "Son, how far are you going?"

I answered simply, "Jacksonville."

"Do you live there?"

"No Maam, I live in Clermont."

"Ant never heard of that," she replied.

For the rest of the question that were directed to me, I did my best to answer with a "yes Ma'am, or no Ma'am." It was almost hard for me to admit; however, in my experiences in my short life of eighteen years, I had almost lost all respect for the wisdom of the black community. I was living in the hope that some black leader would come along to restore that respect, and the old women were not just 'somebody' or 'bodies.' At this stage of my life, I wanted absolutely nothing from the black community but maybe a roll in the hay with the woman of my choice, and I was willing to pay for that. It was a quarter to eight when the driver called for a rest stop, pulling into the Tallahassee Greyhound Bus Station. It looked almost deserted, it was Christmas eve, and most people were already home with their families. I thought maybe it would be best if I spent my Christmas in some other place. But I thought I'd quickly conclude it, go home and be of as much help to mom and dad as I could during the two weeks I had off from training.

For sure, they had worked hard to make a reasonable life for me and my nine brothers and sisters. Even if we never agreed on anything. I was getting very tired and knew I had another six hours before I would be home. But for whatever reason, it was impossible for me to sleep while traveling. For the rest of the trip, I promised myself that I would try and get some rest. At a minimum, I could close my eyes and pretend to be asleep. I thought, maybe the old woman won't direct any questions toward me? I almost wished I had a girl at home or that I was more like everyone else, feeling good about all the little things of the community of Clermont. But then I did a simple evaluation. First a girlfriend; what was there to do? Go to the movies, go riding in a borrowed car. Park in the orange grove and become a father. I mean, that's what already happened to most people my age. I know this with conviction because my old friend Eddie had fathered several kids. No, I don't want to be looking for any girlfriend any time soon.

The next thing in the community would be Church Participation. My brother James was big on church participation, and the only thing I think that got to him to date is a sanctified wife, a baby, and someone to tell him how to live his life. Not to mention how they seem to take half of his money to support the pastor. The pastor, who, for the most part, spent too much time around his sanctified wife. He might have been doing more than counseling. No, I think I could do just fine for a short time. I would be home without female companionship. The other things that were special were fishing and hunting, and people came from all over the United States for these sports; there was the Ocala National Forest for Deer and Boar, The Wetlands along the Kissimmee Lake Okeechobee, Saint Jones River, and over one hundred other Lakes in my home town county along; all this did for me in my early years was make it more frightening because everywhere I saw, there were white men with guns whom I didn't know. There was almost always some rumor that some black had been killed and buried in a cement vault that was designed especially for the purpose of covering up the rumor of missing black people. The sight of the vault was said to be someplace in the town of Mountverde, which was just ten miles west of my hometown on the Highway within the same county.

I think up until one point in time, I was almost fond of fishing until I had an experience with a truckload of deranged young white men with guns that fired several shots in my direction while I was fishing on the side of the road at Lake Louise in the southwest, Lake County. I ran off so fast I left the Warmouth I caught. I was unable to fish it from the side of the road since. So, when I'd get home now, I would probably stay close to the house or help dad out in his construction business. I had learned a great deal about myself in the past eight weeks: for one, I was very objective in nature; two, I had a deep desire to succeed and find a way to circumvent most people or things that got in my way. My mom and dad also had the need and energy to succeed; I am sure this is where my drive came from, but I was not willing to take or seemly sell my most inner-being to achieve success. In my hometown, many were, to include mom and dad.

I always thought of a childhood rival, Lester Cole, as one willing to sell his own family if it would win him a favor with the white man. My older brother James was almost as bad. I felt both sold me out in my first and only attempt to work for a white man in our home environment. I inherited 'me' personally from my grandfather, for I was almost always compared to him.

"Which was not willing to do that which was necessary to make a living."

However, as for me, this is not true at all. What was, and is true, is that I have never been willing to sell myself and others short for a dollar. Or anything of a material value. The driver made his usual calls to load the bus, and soon we were on Highway twenty-seven heading South.

We had passed the campus of Florida State University and Florida A&M University, where one of my older sisters was still in school. We also passed the State Capitol. Resting my head on my seat, I had pleasant thoughts again about who I was. First, I had thought of the Hawkins Family and Vergil Hawkins, attending the University of Florida School of Law, which was a first for a black man. Then I had thoughts of my very own sister with a college education, which would be a first for the Montgomery Family. My own family and the Hawkins, those I felt very close to, were indeed achievers: (Mrs. Hawkins, Vergil's wife, had been my high school algebra teacher), and I also felt good to be in my home state, even with all of its short, racial comings. Closing my eyes, I made a promise to myself not to open them again before Jacksonville. It was about 11:30 A.M. when the bus reached its final destination, of Jacksonville, Florida: I could only remember in part the three-hour trip. I remember the chitchat exchange between the old ladies and looking up occasionally to see the beautiful Florida landscape along the highway, but nothing more, so my guess was I must have gotten some sleep.

Here I would depart company with the old ladies and would have to catch the through bus for Tampa. That would drop me off in the small town of Clermont, between Tampa and Orlando; on Highway fifty. I again thought, who would pick me up? The departing time for Tampa's bus was 12:20. The larger city prior to my stop in the road was Sant Augustine, Daytona Beach, and Orlando, and the time elapsed for about five hours. I would again try and get some sleep. It had been eighteen hours since I had left Columbia, and I was just a little tired, if I'm being honest.

There was somewhat of a Christmas atmosphere in the Jacksonville bus station. There was a skinny Santa Claus, going from the color's waiting area to the white's, asking young kids what they wanted for Christmas. Times were good, everyone I knew had a job, so there was no reason to think that the Christmas of fifty-nine, won't be a good one for everybody. The kids were really excited to the point that I thought just for a minute, it would not be so bad to be married with kids of my own, but it was only a very quick and foolish thought. When the announcement for coloreds to load the bus was made, I took my new, most favorite spot in the back of the bus and positioned my tired body to rest. Without trying to see who else was getting on. I hoped my bags had been properly exchanged for my final destination. As the bus weaved through the city of Jacksonville toward Highway One, I looked up several times to see the abhorred position of the black community. The moment of Christmas joy that was sparked by the atmosphere of the bus station was extinguished. My pessimistic view of the environment that I would visit for the next few days was reestablished.

Again, I was able to get a little sleep between stops and I tried not to be distracted by others who were getting on and off the bus as it made it a minor and major stop. It was quarter to six when the bus driver announced Clermont. I stood up to let him know I was getting off. I looked out to see the old Army Barracks that my father still maintained and where I had painted and done other repairs. But I did not want to be caught in this part of town after dark. Mr. and Mrs. Mims lived just across the streets from the small bus station, and they were almost like family, however, white. Just down the street was the Pools property, Winery and all; also possible was a Pee Willie Pool, who was known to be mean real mean! My brothers, friends, and I myself had been harassed, shot at, ran oft- the road, and other things short of being tarred and feathered, the meanest white boy in Lake County. It was my objective to get my bags, call home and get out of there as soon as possible.

The driver opened the luggage compartment, and I reached in and retrieved the only duffel bag in the compartment, checking to make sure it was the right one. Afterward, I dialed my parents' number and was lucky. Fread Pinkney, my sister's husband, was there. He and my sister were on Christmas break from Florida A&M University, and my mother told me she would have him come pick me up. In about five minutes, Fread was there getting out of a fifty-five

Chevrolet to open the trunk for just one bag. I liked Fread a lot; we had so much in common; he liked to have a beer once in a while - so did I. Plus, he also had a car and would let me drive whenever he was around. However, I would not make that request of him now that he was married; because I wouldn't want to get in trouble with my older sister any quicker than I would under normal circumstances.

This was for sure that if she and I were at the same place for over ten minutes, we would be in a fight. That was simply a fact of life. When we arrived at the house, there was no welcoming party: just my mother, whom I kissed on the side of the mouth. After I met my mother, I set my duffel bag down and looked for Dad. But Dad was out doing some last-minute shopping, along with my three younger brothers – that is what my mom told me. My two-year-old baby sister was asleep. My older sister, along with my twelve-year-old sister, was down at my oldest sister's house just two blocks down the hill from my parent's house. Things at our house looked very productive. Our very large house, as per our community standards, was indeed the envy of both the white and black communities. So were my older sisters and her family home, and even I felt good about being a part of it all. The greatest thing about being home was the food. O boy could my mother and sisters cook! Food was everywhere, cakes of all types, sweet Potato pies, Pecan pies, Hams, Collard Greens, Cornbread, Turkey, and dressing. I knew I would put on ten pounds, and that was not good.

When my brothers got home, I had to arm wrestle with them or something to recognize their development, even though it had been less than six months since they saw me. This was true for my older (married) brother as well. I would be asked to go fishing and hunting. I would have to prove how well I could shoot now that I was a soldier. I knew I would not outshoot my older brother, and he was almost born with a gun in his hand. I would not attempt to outfish him because this was an everyday part of his life ever since he was six years old. In such arenas, I was considered a misfit. Because in their eyes, doing these types of things were what made boys, men. My dad did not have much to say after asking how I got along with the Sergeants, and after I told him I would be going to work with him after his one day off for Christmas. If it was not for my ability to box and wrestle in these parts, I would possibly be looked upon as a sissy. But because I was good with my hands and could probably out-wrestle almost everyone in the community, I was just considered a misfit to which I very much agreed upon as well.

Expectations & Pain

It was the day after New Year's, 1960 - the things that were being talked about were:

a) Could John F. Kennedy be elected President over Vice President Richard M. Nixon?

b) What would the United States do about the U2 spy plane incident?

c) Integration of schools after the landmark, unanimous decision, Brown vs. Topeka Board of Education; Freedom Riders, and sit-ins, led by the Reverend Martin Luther King, who had been brought to national prominence, following the Rosa Parks incident.

d) She refused to give up her bus seat to a white man on December 1, 1955.

e) The slaughtering of Emmett Till, the fifteen-year-old black boy accused of flirting with a Mississippi white girl.

I was not concerned with integration or the right to ride on the front of the bus because I was, but I was more concerned about my family and myself: how would daddy make it with so little help? What would my brother Alexander do now that he had dropped out of school? Would his feet heal so he could be gainfully employed? What about my twelve-year-old sister, who had problems in school? How would my two-year-old sister be raised now that my mother works as a maid for the white folks? Not just that, mother also undertook the responsibility of taking care of my elder sister's baby, the one who studied at Florida A&M University. She still had another year to go.

It was Fread, my sister's husband, who had brought me to the bus station and had agreed to wait with me until the bus came. We were in Lake County and could almost smell the fear of the blacks who resided in this area: from the slaughters of times passed, people slaughtered by the very hands of those who were committed to protecting us, not to mention the likes of Pee Willie, who lived down the road in a little place just away from the bus station.

The bus was on schedule, and as it pulled off highway fifty, we could hear the roaring of its distinct engine and it's shifting down to brake speed to make a very brief stop at a little bus station in my hometown of Clermont, Florida. Fread opened his door and soon had my single bag; we walked toward the approaching bus and stood parallel to it as the driver applied the brakes, and the bus came to a halt as the sound of air escaped its valves. Without recognizing our presence, the driver descended the steps and opened the lower baggage compartment where Fread stored my duffel bag. The driver took several items off the bus and placed them in the bin outside the small station designed for securing packages when there was no station attendant. He turned toward me, and passed me a tag and a pen, "Here, boy, fill this out and put it on your bag." Fred removed the bag without speaking as I filled out the tag with my name and destination: I thought the driver could have just as well greeted us when he first pulled into the station area as I had seen white folk being greeted by the drivers and commented to Fread, "You see how he let you put the bag on the bus without saying anything?" Fread whispered, "He is just a common southern cracker, and you have to be careful with them."

I shook my brother-in-law's hand, and his last advice as I climbed the steps of the bus was to take care of myself.

Seated in my favorite spot at the back of the bus, I waved to Fread as the bus pulled out from the station, as he stood next to his nineteen fifty-six fords. I thought he would have a hard time making it in Lake County, even if he had already finished four years of college at Florida A&M University. Fread and I had a lot in common: in fact, he was the only person in my family I could hold a conversation with without getting into a fight of some sort. We both believed that black men could stand on their own two feet and make a living without the assistance of a white man. We both would run our barbecue stand and earn fifty dollars a week rather than lay concrete blocks under the supervision of a white man for one hundred dollars a week.

However, Fread was now an elementary school teacher. I knew he would not last long because, as early as the sixth grade, I could tell black teachers did not have a free hand to teach black children things they needed to know to stand on their own two feet. I had refused my mother's offer to be sent to college to become a schoolteacher simply because I would not have been able to follow the white folk who supervised our school's agenda, nor would my brother-in-law. And when he'd refuse and suffer the subsequent consequences, the black community would label him a failure.

As the bus headed east toward Orlando, I began to reminisce on highway fifty. There were other college graduates in our community.

One was my second Cousin Abraham Logan, who was now a Second Lieutenant and was already on active duty with the U.S. Army: and T. C. Adam, who had been going out West to work for some big company. Both of them had a much better chance than I had of making it, sort of like how I had a better chance of making it than my brother-in-law Fread. Lester Cole, whom I had fought with from the first day I set foot in class with him. After his family had moved from north Florida, I thought he would make it, even if he had to sell out every other black in Clermont: in fact, he might even become Mayor because he had that type of quality about him. It was the same as my basic training square leader Private Whiteside; most blacks called it "Unele Tomish."

The Fogle brothers, Albert, George, Gean, Mack. These guys were so close that if one made it, so would the other; they had been raised that way by a single parent: Mrs. Rose after Mr. Fogle had left when we were all just kids in grade school. I had always envied these guys, and I wished my brothers were more like them. Jimmie, and Donnie Freeman, did not live in the black community perse, but rather with a white family whom his father chauffeured and took care of on the grounds of the white folk estate. Their mother was the white folk maid and owned a beauty shop in the black community where she styled black women's hair. They also owned a cafe and had a house in the black community where other people lived from time to time.

For whatever reason, I almost thought of the Freemen boys as not being colored, although we went to school together. Both Donnie and Jimmy would for sure someday become businessmen in one form or another and would have very little to do with the black community. Buster and Charles Chandler also lost their father at an early age. However, I have always had a great deal of respect for these guys as well, and the reason was because of the strong leadership of their mother, Mrs. Thama. The Chandlers were a close-knit family, and as for the Fogies, if one made it, so would the other. Jonnie King, a good running back for the Carver Heights Trojans, could have earned a scholarship to college. However, he did the right thing after getting Eddie Bass's sister pregnant. Even then, without a high school education, I thought Jonnie would find a way. I wish I could say the same for Eddie. And there was Lester's older brother Ollie, who was just one hundred and eighty degrees from Lester's personality. Where Lester would sell you out, Ollie would throw you his very own life preserver to keep you afloat.

There could have been maybe only two in our community who may have worked harder than Ollie. One was my older brother James, and the other was my eldest sister's husband, Abraham, alias, "Speedy." He had been named so because there was almost no one who could keep up with him in the orange groves (maybe my brother James), but between the two, it would be a race worth watching, and because of this, the two had bonded well.

Junior Floyd, at whatever cost, would be a success and would probably reach out to help many of his family members that lived throughout Lake County, Florida. The successes of these - the best - men of my community would probably never be heard of outside of the small community of Clermont and Lake County, Florida, and the reason was simple. One lack of trust for the other. My older brother and brother-in-law were already pulling away from my father. They would probably never become general contractors or incorporate my father, who was already a general contractor. Probably only because he was not allowed to practice his skills as a carpenter within communities at large, but rather was restricted to doing handyman work for all white folks. And after the civil rights legislation of 1957, under President Eisenhower, he was almost forced to take a general contractors license. But even now, armed with this most powerful tool, it would not be used for the greater good of extracting the weaker of a family, race, or community to a level of self-sufficiency.

I was still thinking of the ills and pluses of the men of my community when we pulled into the Orlando bus station, and the announcement was made that the bus had reached its destination. Connections would be made here on forward, for points north and South. My thought as I exited the bus was something like this: Colored was hunted by some slavery syndrome and/or dilemma, and this impairment had restricted colors to look out for number one because if he tried to help other colors, he would only worsen his dilemma.

To some degree, those successful within the colored community were correct. However, if our community were to survive and become a major part of society, these practices would change. How could a father demand a son be as strong as himself? What about those who did not have a father to teach them to be strong? Could a man become a man just because he possessed physical ability? Or would his physical ability be used only to serve a higher intellect?

I submit to you the latter, or in some cases, especially in cases where the physical young man had no one to teach him, "a father," the responsibility of manhood, the physical ability could lead to an own individual demise. As I sat in the Orlando bus station, I thought of the young men in my community whom I admired and respected, most of who were just a few years older than myself, some with fathers and some without.

Mack Jones, who was the brother-in-law of one of the young men who was killed following the alleged rape of a white woman from the Bay Lake Community, was physically strong, good-hearted, and worked from can-to-can't; (his father, Mr. Ruffs, eighty years plus). However, he had almost no sense of direction without maximum supervision and thus became a slave to the environments of Lake County, Florida. Mack had looked out for me for as long as I could remember; if I did not get anything for Christmas, Mack would make me something with his own hands. That sometimes took him days or even weeks.

One of my funniest memories is the tractor and trailer truck Mack made me for Christmas, of Forty-Seven. I was six years old. It was also the year my grandfather Wallace died; the truck helped me through hard times, and if I had had the foresight to protect it, today it would be a treasure. It would have been just as grand if Mack was the exception. However, he was a sure reflection of other young men of this central Florida community. Alex Newson was raised by his grandmother and was just as protective of the younger boys of the community. However, he had on several occasions been accused of having sex with girls several years his junior, and I think there was some truth to these rumors; because almost everything I know about sex, I learned from Alex. Oh boy! But it's insane how all the girls liked him.

James Qurton was one hell of a basketball player, but that is all he was – all he would do. I think he had a father who did handyman work for the white folks, and James, other than playing basketball, served the ladies of the community, and he would pick a few oranges from time to time.

If there was anyone young man in my community during these years, who was said to have a sense of direction, it would have been J. B. Four hands: the only person other than the black millionaire (Mr. Dock Jones), sons, and high school education. Before my sister Deloris and her graduating Class of 1952, J.B. had been educated in Orlando, at an all-black high school. Jones High and I submitted that blacks had little to nothing to do with this feat. It was simply the wish of the white community that he was educated, and so it was in this central Florida community. J.B..'s mother, Mrs. Babe, was a good, hard-working, God-fearing woman who took in washing and could make a white shirt stand along, and almost every businessman in the Clermont community required her services. And so, it was the businessmen who made sure Mrs. Babe's son had an education and subsequently ensured that he had a job. J. B. Forehand, almost as long as I could remember, were the only black foreman who supervised grove work. He took a complete operation of-grove work, including maintaining good rapport with both payroll and vehicle, and he always remained within the community.

Abraham Logan, alias "June Bug," and T. C. Adam, also were people of color and because of maid loyalty to rich white families, and I would also include the future of Donnie. and Jimmy Freeman To the loyalty displayed by their mother and father, James Freeman, to the family they had kept all these years ensured their kids an education. The Irony of black men being supported and educated by their own would have a harder time succeeding; In the case of black men to black men the old slave syndrome will come into play, I watch you while you watch me to ensure you stay in your place. Men, including fathers and sons, always sell out black men. So, in effect, Tom Wootson graduated with the other black men in the class of "52." He was someone who my mother thought could become "a foreman in the groves," I say he is someone who would probably not be successful, even after he were given the opportunity, simply because he was going to be sold out by one or more of his subordinates. Where J.B., Jimmy, Donnie, T. C., and June Bug had the security of bonding between the servant and master family, thus the chance of being sold out over the years was much slimmer, and they probably would be successful.

The chances of a prominent black man's son becoming successful in the fifties were lesser than the chances of a well-thought black maid's son that served powerful white families. The more I thought of who I was and where I was from, the more I became sure of making the Army a career. At the age of eighteen, I felt as if I had solved the plight of black men, even if no one would ever listen to my logic. It was simply to stay in an even position of servitude or subordinate to the white community. For the most part, no one cared how much money a black man-made, along with what he did are not due to encroach upon white men's territory or his women would be problematic

Black men who understood this within our community would be successful men within their rights, and those of us who broke the rules would pay, by one means or another. The rules were different in the Army, and besides, just by definition, we were the "Armed Services." We were subordinate to all civil communities. I was able to live with this. The call was being made for white folks to load the Charleston-bound bus. My thoughts were still back in Clermont, more specifically on my elementary school principal, Mr. William N. McKinney: here was a man who had to go to college under the loyalty scenario. His mother had been a God-fearing woman and a maid for white folk. However, McKinney was an excellent athlete, and after being accepted into Edward Waters College at Saint Augustine, Florida, under the servitude scenario, McKinney is highly successful; in fact, from many.

Perspectives: The most successful within my hometown by a black folk standard. He had been a football stand-out at an all-black college, he had completed graduate work to become a school principal, and now he had two sons. Now the call was for all going North to Charleston, "Last Call." I boarded the bus and took the very last seat on the left side. I did not wish to become as concerned with the demographic of the southeast as I had on my first bus ride south from the other, from Buch, brother, Columbia to Clermont. I just wanted to rest and be left alone. However, my mind would not rest. Did it seem to have become a computer of some type, bound to give the formula for the most direct past to success for disadvantaged male youth? And that youth was me. I thought Buch Mckinney, the oldest son of Mr. Mckinney; he was only thirteen at most. *But the reality was, he was already one specimen of a man.*

I had often protected my younger-ing of about the same age as Buch, simply because he could not defend himself against Buch's superior strength. Buch was also a good student, and a damn good-looking black youth. But from my observations, his chances of succeeding were minimum. First of all, simply by being the son of the black community, the top educator placed him on some invisible pedestal, and there were always challengers trying to knock him off. And with him being the competitor that he was, he would vigorously take on some or all newcomers, and chances were, occasionally, he would lose. But even a greater threat was the changing times.

The victory in Topeka (Brown vs. Board Education) caused the United States Supreme Court to strike down the separate but equal doctrine under which blacks had for so long been legally segregated in schools, which was six years in the past. Still, it would begin a political ploy, with nineteen sixty being an election year. And the chances with ploys were, it will be enforced: and now Mr. McKinney would have to compete with white men, the school principal's job. He was doubted for his chances of winning, but if he did win, even greater pressures would have to be endured by the handsome young McKinney. I conned town community; I thought of personalities, The Lesters Coles, of the people I considered my home. My community will always be looking to improve its stations in life. I even thought of my own family as to who would affect the enforced Topeka victory and who it would affect in the Community of Clermont, and Lake County, Florida.

The one conclusion I came to was that it would be bad for educated leaders of the black community and good for the "Uncle Toms." Now "suck butts" could improve their station in life get elected to different community committees and boards simply by sucking butt and selling out good black people. Still, the business of the black community will also be affected negatively, and black colleges, as we know them, would almost become something of the past. My father had been the President of the Community PTA for as long as I could remember, and now black people's participation in the educational process of their kids would become very limited if there was any left at all. The victory of the Brown vs. The Board of Education of Topeka, Kansas, possibly was only a victory for Mr. Thurgood Marshall and his station in life. And for suck butts who wanted to become assistants to white school superintendents. As the Greyhound bus headed north on U.S one toward Jacksonville, I, in my brand-new army green uniform with basic training already behind me, knew I should have been rejoicing.

There must be hundreds of young black boys who would change places with me. Why was I worried about the future of the black community of Lake County, Florida? The reality was that even my immediate family members had refused to write. It started to rain, and I could smell the scents of the very earth enter through the vents of the bus on this unseasonably warm January evening. Florida was the only place in the world that could produce this intoxicating smell - to understand what I am talking about, one would have to walk through the wetlands of the Kissimmee, or Saint John, River, or fish from the banks of more than a hundred lakes, in Lake County, or ride along with U.S. one on a warm raining evening. I could very easily understand how one could get attached to these environments. However, for me, the price was too high! And it would be hard to enjoy all the beauty of this wonderful land, from inside the state prison that set just a few miles off U.S. one, over by US 301; in Sarke, Florida.

It had been less than six years when I had given anything to go to school with the white folks. I could still remember the days I set on the back steps of our house and watched 31 seconds. We would enjoy the athletic facilities that I wished we had at our school, but that was before the run that someday with Willie on my first attempt to hold down a day job and see how black men would sometimes kiss up to white men, for even the smallest of favors. There existed a lack of having them in charge of others in exclusive black men for even short periods. It was also hard for me to understand how my father, brother, and brother-in-law could not form a production company together, and some could benefit other family members later on in life. They were the best at what they did in the county, so I assumed it should have been easy.

I remembered the first contract my father received in a community in Orlando. It was the summer of 1958, and I was restricted to mixing mortar and finishing up behind James and Speedy (who were both exceptional at laying). Nevertheless, if I had a choice, I'd rather be in management and sales. However, the argument was that I did not know enough about the business, and white folks did not buy from blacks and bricks, block and door to doormen. I disagreed because I made flyers and tried to get my dad to let me go door to advertise his business. My guess was this: if I could show black men building a house valued over fifty thousand dollars and one that could be sold at a reduced rate, people would be glad to be in business with us. Us. My father and brother only saw it as another one of my shams to hard work. If I'm being honest, they were right. But had not the white men done the same to get out of his scheme? And not worked to keep black men doing all the hard work?

I never or would never like work that constituted all black boys and no brain. God had given me "a black boy" and a brain! *And I wanted to use it.*

Now, what was wrong with that? It had been five hours since I said goodbye to Fred at the small bus station in Clermont. We were now coming into the big city of Jacksonville, and I could guess what the environment would be like over there. I was sure that I'd have to wait for a half-hour or so for the next bus. Regardless of why I came there, I wanted as little interaction from the black community as possible. Did this mean I had turned into some sort of nature-freak and eventually converted into a black bigot of sorts? I wasn't too sure, and I had many, many questions.

Another one of those questions I asked myself was rather reflective. Was I afraid of a relationship with a black woman of the black community? On the contrary, it could also mean I was the one who rejected and that I was simply looking for a higher level of intellect? I didn't know the meaning of these feelings, although I knew I would keep searching. This way, I'd provide myself the benefit of the doubt until I could find the truth about who I am.

The city lights of Jacksonville were impressive, and the only way I could make any evaluation as to what form of intelligence existed there – within - was to compare it with other cities or towns. If I compared it to my hometown of Clermont, I would have to multiply it by some one hundred times, and if by the size of Orlando, only about three times, and if by Columbia, only by two times.

These were the only places I had ever visited, and for the most part, I had only visited them with the hope of finding a quick piece of ass that won't cost me over ten dollars. So, in effect, Jacksonville would have one hundred times the Whores of Clermont, three times the Whores of Orlando, and two times the Whores of Columbia, if that was ever possible. However, I doubted if any place could have more Whores than the amount in Columbia. As cliché as this saying may go, it is also very true:

"You have to close the whorehouse to have the church."

The bus went through the city streets at about twenty miles per hour. We then passed houses that looked as if they should be condemned; they had little to no paint on them, and almost all the houses had porches that were overcrowded with poorly dressed children and had looks of despair on their faces. According to the sign that advertised the First National Bank, dusk reigned over us, and the temperature was sixty-two degrees. Cafes seemed to be the leading business, with an occasional barbershop, red and white peppermint signs every several blocks, and old buildings that were several stories high with dim neon signs that said hotel.

Girls colorfully dressed seemed available to whoever stopped to examine the inviting merchandise. We were in the colored quarters of Jacksonville, Florida. As we passed through the residential area that approached what seemed to be buildings of a more permanent structure, the bus driver announced: "Jacksonville," "there will be a thirty-minute delay here, all persons continuing north may leave your belongings in your seat, and may reclaim your seat when called to do so," this is "Jacksonville." There were only a few people on the colored side of the bus station, mostly servicemen returning to camp.

I had once passed through here, but it had been early morning; now, the area made a different impression; there was action on the streets. I walked to the waiting room door to check out the action but was too scared to go further. There were several sailors all white; walking fast toward the bus station with a shiny new Caddie following; about one hundred yards or so from the station, the Caddie pulled upside the sailors and stopped; the door opened, and a gigantic colored man got out with a razor pointing at the sailors: "Two of you guys owe me twenty dollars."

As the sailors quickly sifted their hands through their pockets, they remarked:

"We don't want no trouble."

They handed the gigantic colored guy forty dollars, and he thanked them. Everybody seemed happy. However, as the sailors passed the colored waiting room, I heard one of them say, "I can't stand nigger pimps."

I was impressed; I saw a civilian-colored man demand something from white men, who met the demand. It was a first for me, and I looked around the colored waiting room for even one person I could identify with, someone I could engage within the small talk. I saw no such person or persons.

Yet again, I thought: "What am I? 12?"

And my answer was, "A country nigger kid who's trying to find himself."

Again, I thought of the black pimp who confronted the four white sailors, and my question was: Where did he get the authority to confront white men in a civilian environment? However, one kinder liked the idea; I had no concept of a pimp and a prostitute's relationship, so I felt it was wrong to take money from any man by threat or force, but the idea was somewhat twisted at the back of my mind. I thought maybe, what is sometimes wrong could be right? The call soon came for the north bond to Charleston passengers to reclaim their seats.

This was the only time I was permitted to board the bus in front of whites and getting on the bus alongside white folks felt quite good. However, the feeling changed once I was at the threshold of the seating arrangement, and by law, I had to make the long march to the back of the bus. After I had reclaimed my seat behind the driver to the rear of the bus and was comfortable, I watched the other passengers, both black and white, fill up the seats closer to the front of the bus. The four white sailors were just four seats in front of me. I was able to access from parts of their conversation that I overheard that they were en route to the Charleston Navy Training center for advanced navy training.

"It was the sailor's idea, the one who's familiar with Jacksonville, black quarters, to go to a black whore house and not pay, and the others had no reason to doubt his authority to pull it off. I, too, felt almost any white man could have pulled this plan off with the smallest amount of resistance from the working girls of the black community. I know Pee Willie Pool and his gang; if they wanted to, they could have pulled it off in my hometown community; I never saw a pimp in Columbia, and working girls were everywhere, including college campuses.

From listing to the four sailors, they were little to no different than me, looking for the same fulfillment in life. If fate had it, I could like them. But for a brief period in my life, however, I am sure it won't be the last. I witnessed a black man taking advantage of a white man, and I was certain this would leave an indelible mark within my brain. I thought of Pvt. King again, how he had tagged along with me on our first trip to Columbia and how he always spoke about how beautiful many black women were to him. I always received the impression that he wanted me to turn him on to some black woman, of whom I had not yet experienced myself but found ways of not revealing the truth to King. I felt as if it were possible, King and I would have burst our cherry together, with black working girls, if he had not gotten himself arrested, for the impersonation of an Army Captain. Although I was glad that I got rid of him, I still think of the guy more favorably than negatively. On occasions, I have seen white Soldiers going in and out of clubs, getting involved in quickies with black girls, and had heard of black men with white women. However, I had not experienced such a phenomenon, not that I would not have liked to; but every time I think about a white woman, I first think about my mother and how she told me I could lose my very life by just looking at one; and of course, Emmett Till, *who lost his.*

It was shortly after nine when the bus pulled into Tallahassee. For the past three hours, I had been getting bits and pieces of the four sailors' conversation, and their biggest complaint was how far greyhound came out of the way to get to Charleston. Their argument was if the bus had taken the highway seventeen route, straight North we could almost be there by now; but the bus had taken highway ninety instead, and it would be ten hours before we would arrive in Charleston; and I thought Charleston, to Columbia for me, would be even another four hours. I was hoping that my friend Robert LaCorne, would catch this bus at his little spot in the road, close to Valdosta; however, if I knew LaCorne, he would wait until the very last hour to leave because he had a girl. It was very hard for me to consider having a girl, first by my family standards, she would have to be a light complexion.

I had met only one girl I liked a lot and one who fits the description, and I liked her a lot. Her name was Vivian Lora Thompson, and I was sure she liked me; however, she lived in Leesburg, and I lived in Clermont, twenty-three miles south in the same county. We had several classes together at Carver Heights High School, one of several Black high schools within lake county, Florida. I rode the county bus from Clermont to Leesburg for the three years I was in high school; until dropping out to help my father. I was sixteen when I left school; I felt the greatest loss was not have the opportunity to develop into a starter on the varsity football team. Secondly, I did not have the opportunity to develop a lasting and meaningful relationship with Vivialoria She would have fitted into the family, the hierarchy of women just fine, which was the higher authority in our family. She had fair skin and long brownie hair that fell almost to her buttocks when she let it down, which she often did. Her lips were full, and she walked with quick short steps, which caused her rear end to motion sinuous under her skirt.

Our relationship was only at stage one; I'd carry her books, play with her hair, and pinch her butt. I think simply because I liked the way it moved under her cloth, she would furnish me with pencil, paper, and let me copy her work in Mrs. Hawkins's algebra class. (Mrs. Hawkins was the wife of Mr. Hawkins, the first black, to attend the University of Florida, School of Law). Without her, I would never have passed algebra; Vivialoria was a very smart girl, and I am sure she would have a productive future. The call came for north bond passengers to reclaim their seats; I was just finishing off a greasy hamburger that I had gotten through the rear window of the white folk snack bar, from a colored boy who looked like he would rather not be there but was ill-prepared to be anyplace else.

The disparity was tough for me to undergo; however, I had seen it in the eyes of a multitude of colors, almost three months ago, as I was departing Jacksonville up and down the railroad tracks and on the highways, when Eddie and I first traveled to Jackson. I was sure, I would do anything not to come back to this dead sea environment, where all hope had left the eyes of its peoples.

I left partly to relieve myself of the hopelessness, but there was nothing I could do to change these conditions. Sudenlly, I noticed I was the only person left standing there; the others had already loaded the bus while I was caught up in the disparity of black folks. We departed Tallahassee on highway three until we reached Thomasville, Georgia; just a few miles from my father's birthplace, Moultrie Georgia, and could not help but wonder what the birthplace of looked like; I also wondered why almost everyone I knew came from northern Florida or Georgia. However, I think I saw the answer in the eyes of the people. What I saw was total despair. I tried to think of the families in my hometown who were not from northern Florida or Georgia, and they seemed better off than those who were immigrants. Mr. Dock Jones was born and reared in Lake County, Florida, and he was the only black millionaire I knew. Mr. Joe Odum was a Floridian, and he owned three homesteads and drove a Lincoln Automobile. The Deans were Floridian, and I thought they were also well off, or maybe they were from Georgia, or the Carolinas, or northern Florida, just like many other black folks, except Mr.

Dock, who I frequently heard bragging about how he had to run the swamps of lake county all his life.

The Coopers, too, must be Floridians, they too had money, property, and new cars; almost every colored in Clermont lived in a Jones or Cooper boarding house and drank Whiskey on credit from the Cooper liquor store. I always thought both the Coopers and Mr. Jones to be above the law and who took advantage of all the poor colored folk. Any loan from Mr. Cooper or Mr. Jones would demand fifty percent interest, and not paying meant a trip to Jail, and again, the bail bondsman were a Coopers or Jones. The rule was, pay me one way or pay me the other. The head Deacons of the local Churches were also Coopers and Jones; the Coopers, and Jones, were the keepers of the immigrant nigger, from the North. However, there were some exceptions; my father was an exception to the rules and had made good. He owned two homesteads and several other properties in less than twenty years. Mr. Cole, and his family, from northern Florida, beat the odds

However, both families had paid quite a price for success and hard work on part of the Hold family, including great personal sacrifice. The bus was just outside of Valdosta, Georgia on highway eighty-four. I thought it was where LaCorne had gotten off, but I could not see him, and I knew he would stay with his girlfriend up until the last minute before he'd report back to camp, so that meant he'd catch the next day's bus. As the bus continued on highway eighty-four toward Savannah, I decided to never live in Clermont, Florida again. I decided to never live in a town where I was only known by family, especially a member of the black community, surname in the white community was highly Respected, Blacks familys was cattorized as good niggers or bad niggers.

All the local rules, as they had applied to colored folks; and possibly the only town in this country, where the avenue was paved for me to become a reasonable successful nigger, my mother and father had seen to this by knowing and keeping their places; however, my reasoning was simple; I could not live the subservient life that my mother and father had lived, and the Army was my only way out. I laid back in my seat, but I must have fallen asleep because I briefly woke up to hear sailors talking about going to sea somewhere between Savannah and Charleston. I slept right after and did not wake up until the driver announced 'Charleston,' my final destination. I was glad to be in Charleston. This place was the only stop where restrooms and an eating area for the colored existed.

I wished I could meet a friend, but almost every story I had heard about meeting strangers in bus stations ended with someone getting ripped off. I had about twenty dollars on me, which had to last until payday, which I hoped would be in a few days. But even then, I would only get forty dollars, and the rest was always to help mom and dad with the family.

The bus pulled to a halt, and I sat and watched as everyone departed the bus; white folks looked so happy as they talked and hugged. The blacks hurried to the black waiting area. Given their situation, they lined up and ordered food. It was easy to understand; whites could get food at any place. The blacks, however, did not have much of a choice. Charleston was their only hope other than the back door of the white folk cafe, and even then, chances were, you would have to eat standing up. As I departed the bus and looked at the clock at the bus station, I noticed the time was six-twenty, the morning of January 3, 1960. Times were good, everybody was making good money, and the craziest thing in the world was for me to be in the Army; this was how my family felt about the whole matter.

At six in the morning, I was not in a hurry; I got at the back of the line, and when it was my time to order, I ordered eggs, grits, bacon, and toast. I took a vacant table and waited for the call for the bus to Columbia that was less than four hours, and I hoped I would make lunch at the mess hall. At about seven-fifteen, the call for white folks to load was made, and five minutes later, I was seated at the very back of the bus that would take me to Columbia, South Carolina; and I hoped never to ride a greyhound bus again.

Some twenty minutes of winding through the city of Charleston put us on highway one seventy-six, North; the countryside that displayed farmland, and unpainted shacks, and in many cases, conditions that were not suitable for human inhibitions. I now understood why so many had come south to live in the Citrus belt of Florida; at least, they had a better chance of not freezing. I almost became obsessed with what I saw in the light of day as I rode through the heart of South Carolina and made a promise that one day I would return here to do whatever I could to change these despicable conditions.

I thought of my grandfather again and what life must have been for him, and I also thought that I would, one day, do a genealogy study of the Montgomery family to find out more about my humble beginnings. When the bus pulled into the Columbia bus station, it was eleven-thirty or thereabout. I departed the bus and stood to wait for my bag as several taxis waited to take a carload of G.I. to Fort Jackson. The Irony here was those white boys and black boys were loading into the same car. In the presence of God and the whole world, who did not allow the mixing of blacks and whites, the difference was that cabs could not operate on base unless they operated on a first come, first-serve basis.

My thought was people could change, but the price had to be right; in almost any other city of the South, this scene would have been impossible unless it was a military town. We loaded the cab, five white boys and I asked to be dropped off at the fifth training regimen consolidated mess. I made lunch and afterward found a bunk at the reception station and waited for LeCorne.

Limitations

As I lay on my bunk at the reception station, I attempted to put the last few days behind me or at least to try and find something positive in my experiences over the holidays. The only positive aspect was my family. More importantly, the fact that they were healthy and had jobs.

For the great majority of my hometown community, the prospect of the future was bleak indeed. However, the saddest report was that very few knew they lived in the dead sea. If any river flowed into this dead sea to replenish it, it could spring back to life again. The school system that I had been critical of would soon be replaced. A system that the colored would have even lesser control over their own community did they under the present dictatorial white regime system. Much like myself, black males with youth would soon be doomed to work for minimum wages for eternity, and our young women who had babies as fast as one could count would gain little to no sense of direction to sustain themselves or their new families.

In other words, my community will be a proud welfare state that would come under the direct supervision of some subservient Nigger, like Lester Cole, or some other kiss ass who draws his breath through the butt holes of the white dictatorial regime. It was Sunday, hours or 2:00 o'clock, January 3, 1960. LaCome was probably catching the bus to be in camp for the evening meal and Monday morning reveille. It was 1400 hours, and I was worried about him because he would fall in love oh-so-easily. 'Uncle Tom' and I would probably be caught up in a no-win situation of an uneducated black man trying to support a wife and family. I almost knew he would not reenlist; because, all he knew to talk about was his woman, back home. Why couldn't he be satisfied with a quick lay in town? That's cheaper than trying to support a family. He got less mail than I did, and his woman was probably doing his best friend when he was not around. After every shot, she had to eat, and for sure, the seventy-eight dollars a month the Army paid us was not going to support any woman.

I thought this would be a good opportunity to walk around Fort Jackson. After all, the next minatory formation wasn't until six on Monday morning, and it was three hours before supper. I was already dressed in my army greens. I grabbed my jacket, put on my cunt cap, and just outside the door. I stopped to survey the organizational layout of this World War Two Era training facility. The temperature was about forty degrees, which was just about right for a good walk since I was dressed in a heavy woolen army green uniform. As I looked on toward the Northward direction, I saw the big water tank set on a hill that trainees referred to as *tank hill*. To the South were pine groves and the area we had come to know as the confidence, or obstacle course. On this obstacle course, I learned I had a long way to go to measure up to the best. It had taken all I could do to make it through the course, and for whatever reason, I thought I was in pretty good shape. I thought of my older brother and his friends and knew this course would have been right down their alley; however, it probably would not have been safe to try and negotiate any of the obstacles with them. This decision was simply because they would have had little or no concern for personal safety, and I would have been the one to get hurt. It always seemed to work that way when I was around those guys.

To the West was the gym for the fifth training regimen. I was on the boxing team and used the gym daily in preparation for my first fight. But on fight night, I was sick, and unfortunately, I lost by forfeiture. Early on, I had learned I did not want to become a fighter, even though this was about one thing – I could beat all of the guys back home. I think I did not like boxing because I knew that somebody would kick my ass sooner or later. Fort Jackson Boulevard ran Westward toward Gate One and Eastward toward the East Gate at the base of the tank hill. I decided to go North to Fort Jackson Boulevard and discover my interest in Fort Jackson's main drag. It seemed almost unreal to be walking freely along a major roadway, with little to no fear of anyone. At this point in my life, I had found a few places where I, a young, six feet tall, one hundred and eighty pounds heavy, black teenager, could walk freely with no fear of physical harm.

I enjoyed this feeling of freedom, and I continued

to walk toward the East gate. I stopped along the way at a snack bar I discovered on the Boulevard and ordered a hot chocolate. I sat down to have my drink and listened to the chitchat of the crowd that was already inside the snack bar that was more familiar with Fort Jackson. I had spent eight weeks of training here, on the training range, and inside the fourth platoon training area. I learned from listening that in advanced individual training mode, one would have almost total freedom after class was out for the day to include passes on a limited basis. I never had complete freedom under any circumstances. In fact, the most freedom I had ever gotten to experience to date were the recent bus trips to and from home; and even then, I was afraid to leave the bus terminal and waiting rooms. I was very much scared to travel alone, if I'm being honest. This new freedom was not freedom of movement; my observation from adult men of my community made me think I would have to learn how to handle it. Like the freedom to sit in a public eating area with other ethnic groups and whites and have a lot of hot chocolate – I had never done this before, *alone.*

After I had finished my hot chocolate, I continued my discovery walk that I was sure I had learned. However, I wanted to reflect on things that happened on the Boulevard. As I walked to a place I did not know, my first feelings re-surfaced as infamously as on highway fifty. In my hometown, big mama was in the house established as early as preschool, there were *'fair-skinned people, who were superior to other people - the premise dark skin.'*

I had made several attempts to dispel these premises. However, it was clear that I had not done so. I felt guilty as I sat near it, thinking if they had whites in the snack bar, I had not earned the right to be in their presence. I had stood up for myself, from an age as early as fourteen, when I refused to give Mr. Willic my hard-earned money after a foolish bet. I lost my very first job and the respect of my family. I kicked the bigot's butt too, from Mississippi, who was my primary training bunk buddy, and I seemingly had been rewarded for it! Basic training also taught me that man was limited only by two natural phenomena: physical and mental ability or their lack thereof.

On the right side of the Boulevard, I discovered a golf driving range that I could tell from afar because I read the sign. I had never seen a golf driving range. Regardless, I was amazed at the accuracy and the distance at which the players hit the little white ball. I stood and watched for several minutes and promised myself I would play the game as soon as I got the opportunity. While I stood there, I thought to myself, 'If I was so confused about who I was and what authority I had as a man, what about other black boys who looked up to me? They looked up to me because I was in the Army and stood up to Mr. Willie in the orange grove, and I kicked the bigot's butt. In the sight of only three other blacks whom I knew would be in my advance individual training class, I was a hero. But they did not know the real black frightened country boy I was. What frightened me the most was the thought that I may not make it through Airborne training after advanced training. I established a new record – a 12-minute run. The pace was faster than double time. I made sure my exercise was in order and did not miss out on anything. In five minutes, I completed my sit-ups, pull-ups, squat thrusts, and forty push-ups. These exercises did have an adverse effect, but I decided to keep the secret to myself, which included a swollen knee.

There were several reasons I hadn't told anyone. I was afraid I would be kicked out of the Army if the knee was X-rayed and required major surgery. I liked being a hero and didn't want to appear weak to those who had elevated me. I could not afford to go back to the dead sea community of Lake County, Florida, especially not as a failure. I would have had to endure the pain and occasional giving away that could have been stopped with an ace bandage. After reaching the East Gate, I walked through the picnic area at the very end of the post and sat on a bench as I looked through the fence at the passing civilians and across the highway at the exclusive all-white community. I was not jealous of the community's houses across the highway from the post because my family had also lived in a big ranch-style house back home. However, I did not like something. I think it was because all this money and opportunity were concentrated in one area, and seemingly so, the rest of the world was their servant. That the white could complain and everybody came running!

We could complain for a lifetime in my community, but conditions would not change. That caused me to become angry when I looked or passed through these exclusive, privileged areas. I even paid a visit to the shacks of the heartlands of Carolina, where so much of my ancestry lived, and looked and saw several blacks cleaning yards and wondered if they lived in houses like I had seen when I was on the bus earlier today. It was now four o'clock, and I wanted to see what lay on the other end of Jackson Boulevard. Before heading West, I briefly stopped to watch the people on the golf driving range, and indulge in supper. I attracted the special attention of several blacks who hit the little white ball. I felt better just by being close to the blacks who took part in more than a fifth Sunday for meeting back home reasons unknown to me; to meet on festivities to May 20 celebrations of Freedom Day in Florida. However, I had been to several football, and basketball games played within the black school district in Central Florida, those were the good times, ones that the black community remembers positively.

The athletes of the Central Florida area were exceptional; many had received college scholarships to various black colleges in the South. However, I doubt if their education would advance their station in life.

For whatsoever reason, though, I have always watched progression in unity. It almost took us some inherent responsibility. I never had any system in my life, all of us had to depend on our livelihood, and if one left the invisibility umbrella to become independent, chances are one would drown. My dad's independence was a tight rope; *act, work cheaper and do better than white peers*. Build homes in the black community with an independent financier, a Jew gentleman who owned most of Clermont's downtown area. Everyone knew the setup, but one could afford to cross the wealthy Jew.

However, speculation was when the Jew died, and the Montgomery's would stop being productive. The Jew lived and was active until about ninety, and afterward, his son-in-law kept the same arrangement with my father. On the right side of the Boulevard, I discovered a theater, and the movie of the day was *A Summer Place*. It was supper time, and the mess hall was a mile away. I took off at a double-time and prayed my knee would not give away.

I reached the mess hall just in time to find LaCorn, Jackson, and Bearden. A black private introduced himself to me as private Wheaten from North Carolina. As they came out of the mess hall, I shook hands with the newcomer to our ranks and made a beeline to the serving line.

The menu was meatloaf, potatoes, broccoli with cheese sauce, bread, and milk. I was able to get a double serving because the line was closing down for the evening, and I was glad I was able to eat along without all the tells about the girls back home. However, as soon as I got to the reception station sleeping billets, I knew that everyone would be talking about the girl they had left behind. The earliest movie started at five, and I opted to take it in instead of hearing about it at the back at the barracks.

The movie, *A Summer Place,* was about first love and a young girl losing her virginity. It starred Connie Stevenson and some fidget, who was supposedly a superstar by the name of Troy Donahue. At about 7:30, I made it back to the barracks with Burden, Jackson, Wheaten, and LaCorn, who was hard at a game of bid whiz. Wheaton was the loud one, and from his outcry, one would have thought it was hog-killing season back home.

"Montgomery, find a partner because this one is all over, but the shout; I am running a Boston, on these mothers."

I had no idea what he was talking about. It was a sin against the church to play cards back home, and I had never considered it a game. It was just for fun. Wheaton had an engagement ring displayed beside him on the footlocker he used as a bench. He took time out of the game to pass on the ring to me.

"Montgomery, feast your eyes on that. It is for my woman, and you are already invited to the wedding. I am getting married as soon as this course is over, in my Airborne uniform."

Damn, I thought all these guys were crazy. Or was it just me? How could any of them support their wives? Or how could they be married and be so far from their new bride? I looked at the ring. And passed it back and told him I never played cards.

I looked through my duffel bag, took out my boots and shine kit, and brushed the boots to an acceptable shine. I heard Jackson tell Wheaton *'to put up his body to see this, the ring was gone,* someone took it. Wheaton pulled out a straight razor, "I want everybody to see this nigger cut the balls off a nigger, a cracker too, if anyone taken from me," the ring showed up back on the footlocker within minutes, and Wheaton let the ring remain displayed on the footlocker.

It was about nine-thirty when I returned from the shower. The game was over, and I noticed the jump boots Wheaton had displayed in front of his bunk. One could shave in them.

"Montgomery, how you like them boots?"

I went closer, "I'll show you how it is done. It takes about three hours. I learned this from real Airborne troops; get a better look. Back home, at Fort Bragg."

I felt pretty bad about my boots. However, I was not going to attempt to match this guy. It was drawing close to ten o'clock, and I knew lights would be out soon.

As I lay on my bunk with the lights out, my first thought was how Wheaton got away with carrying a straight razor and if he really would have cut someone. Secondly, I thought if I had not established a reputation as someone who stood up for himself, this group of guys would not even talk to me. From my perspective, these guys were far more advanced in life than me. With this group, sex was a full-time involvement. By their conversation, I could tell sex was almost like food, a three-time-a-day requirement, and the rest of the day would be confirming their prowess.

My only experience with sex was the visit to the whorehouses in Columbia. As far as I was concerned, there was no real urgency to become involved with one woman. But still, from the deepest pits of my insides, I wish I had some personal sexual conquests to boast about. From my position, the three other colors in my platoon had almost no limitations and had experienced a whole life, almost like my friend Eddie Bass. However, my life had been very controlled and sheltered, with many limitations. As our second training phase ended, I knew one could not win without the challenge.

I felt like a winner in life after taking on three severe challenges. These conquests could very well be my impetus to manhood. The time when I stood up to Mr. Willie back in 1954 will never be forgotten by me or those who were there as witnesses in the orange grove on that hot summer day. The tall Mississippian basic training was a test that won favor on my behalf. However, the platoon and the basic training circle made it possible for me to say that I was ready for the next test that life would send my way with a degree of confidence.

My Knee and Ankle

A dvance training was completely different from basic training. It was more like a lack of training at regular school with books (field manuals) assigned to everyone. There were problems to be solved and obstacles to overcome.

However, the field communication crewman course was not a high-tech course. Circuit boards and the installation of switchboards were the only areas that required one to think. Another circuit installation was simply to follow the illustration in the field manual.

The school was eight hours a day for eight weeks, and after that, the rest of the day, except for the evening meal, was free time. Bunks were not stacked, and this time, I did not have to put up with the big guy from Mississippi. There were still acting Platoon and squad leaders assigned to the platoons. Their jobs were to make sure that the assignment was posted on the bulletin board and weapons and gas masks were maintained.

All through the advanced training, Robert LaCorne was my only friend. One Sunday morning, he even convinced me to go to church with him. Then, after the mass, he also introduced me to Virginia, a young high school student I encountered several times while in advance training.

It was all so square to me. At eighteen, my early visits to Columbia had taught me girls meant automatic sex. But with Virginia, it was a totally different ordeal. I can't say that I had fun with Virginia because something was always missing. And to top it all off, our kisses only magnified the problem.

After ending things with Virginia, LaCorn still visited to Columbia to see his girl. I questioned him if he was still in love with his girl back in Georgia or not. He said she had stopped writing. Of course, she never wrote. Meanwhile, in Columbia, I continued to visit the USO, where one could connect with girls who were working their way through university and college.

For a guy like me, times were good. There was nothing physical in the advance training, except climbing telephone poles which were a week worth of instructions prior to graduation. One was required to mount a fort foot pole and play a game of catch with a basketball from that height. My knee and ankle could barely pass that climbing test. I just hoped that my knee and ankle would be one hundred percent when I graduated from advance training.

Airborne training was completely physical. Participating in the twelve-mile run was not an easy task, but I did it to qualify, and it was only a one-time thing. Also, I had to hold that physical image. I had established among the colored boys in basic training because they looked up to me.

My only fear was that if my knee and ankle did not cooperate, my career with the army would be over. What will become of my life then?

Reflecting on my feelings towards women, I didn't need them for sex only. I didn't need a girl like the rest of the guys. They would die and go to hell just to be seen with a girl in public. I knew that one day, I would follow in my parent's footsteps too. I would find a girl that I wanted to be. I would be so sure that I would marry her and start a beautiful family with her. But eighteen was a little too early for that.

Finally, on March 4th, 1960, I graduated advance training. It was nothing like graduating from basic training, and the ceremony was at 10 am.

Having packed my bags already, I was loaded on a two-engine prop aircraft with about thirty other airborne bounds after lunch. This was my first flying experience. I kept feeling like the aircraft was overloaded. And the turbulence was so bad that I kept imagining scenarios about how our plane would crash.

But finally, after what felt like an eternity, we landed at Fort Campbell, Kentucky, home of the "Screaming Eagles" Airborne Division. I also realized that my knee and ankle were not going to hold out much longer. I had no idea what the army would decide for me. Then, at Fort Campbell, I was assigned to an artillery unit, Battery D, 105 Millimeter Houser 319 Battalion. There, I was settled on the second floor. What I loved about the place, at first sight, was how everything on the floor was so clean that it sparkled.

I knew that Weaton, the kid from North Carolina, would be on this floor too. I wondered where he was. Probably with some Airborne unit, comparing his boots or in jail for cutting someone with his razor.

The bunk I was assigned had a foot and a wall locker. Surveying the vast, windowless room, I noticed perfect displays on top of each wall locker that separated one sleeping area from the other. Under each bunk were perfectly aligned boots polished to perfection. All enough to scare an ordinary fellow to death.

I was afraid to unpack because I was sure that this wasn't the place for me. A Mexican trooper was assigned to help me get settled in. I asked him how everyone was being uniformed and strike. He told me I too would fit in, it takes time, and I would be given the help and time to bring my area up to par.

With that, I unpacked my duffel bag and arranged my belonging into my assigned lockers. Alex, my assigned trooper, showed me around the battalion area and afterward gave me some pointers on how to put an Airborne shine on my boots, a process that would take three to four hours the first time. I listened to him carefully, and after three hours of water and kiwi shoe polish, my boots almost qualified for that 'Airborne shine.' Still, I was a little skeptical about displaying them under my bunk as they still needed some work to be done on them.

My next stop was the supply room. It was where I would be issued my field gear that would be displayed on top of my wall locker. I had already wrestled with field combat gear in basic training, and I used to think that I would never get it right. I AM not sure if I ever did because it never felt right on my back during those long marches to the t-firing range.

The next day was going to be my first day of Pre-Back training. This training was essential to pass before entering jump school, which was mainly running and calisthenics. If I passed this training phase, I would become an Airborne Trooper. But if I didn't, I was going to suffer the fate ruled for me by the U.S. Army.

After breakfast the following day, I reported to the physical training area. My trainer, Stocky Mexican, Sergeant First Class, was about 5'8" and 210 pounds. I stood at 6'2" and about 180 pounds. If one did not know, they would have thought I was the trainer and the Mexican trainee.

Others soon arrived, and we became a total of six people. The Mexican was a man of few words. He called the roll and announced that we would be going on a six-mile road run. In the Pre-Back training period, a few facing movements were off initially. The six-mile run turned out to be a twelve-mile run. It was six miles one way and then the other six miles back. The tiny, fat Mexican did not break a sweat and only allowed two quick breaks that lasted about two minutes each.

Upon our return, my ankle had swollen so bad that it became unbearable to even remove the boot. So, I was taken to the aid station, and they took me to an orthopedic doctor. The first question the Doctor asked me was if I wished to continue in the army or not. I told him that that was only of the things I was very sure of. To continue my services in the army. He said that he would recommend that I be assigned to a holding company to receive treatment for my ankle and knee.

In the army, when Pre-Backs washed out normally, their equipment was thrown out of the window, and they were labeled as quitters on the battalion intercommunication system. I was afraid that I would get the quitter's treatment, but I did not. In fact, I was assigned someone to help me with my bags, and a company jeep dropped me at the Holding company. This was March 7th, 1960.

The holding company was made up of several World War II kind of buildings, warmed by coal furnish. People assigned to the holding company had no assigned duty but KP on occasion and to keep appointments. There was an assigned vehicle to transport assigned personnel to and from appointments. One was to have special permission to go to the town.

I had committed to myself that my priority was to get better and look forward to my next duty assignment, wherever it was. I had plenty of time on my hand and was idle most of the time. I would shine my shoes and rearrange my stuff. It was almost like being confined. It was the first time I wished I had a girl to write to.

The prognoses on my ankle were a high ankle spring. An ace bandage was wrapped around it, and I was advised to stay off it. I was prescribed pain killers to help relieve the pain and crutches for mobility.

It was in early April 1960, when I finally got my assignment for Hawaii's 25th Inf. Division. All I ever heard about Hawaii was that it was a paradise on earth. The question was a paradise for whom? Was this paradise also for eighteen-year-old black boys?

I had a thirty-day leave, after which I was to sell from Brooklyn Army Depot on May 19th, 1960. After receiving my orders, the biggest question was what I would do for thirty days at home. I did not have a girl, and the ones I hung out with in Clermont were not attracted to me. I could work with my father; God knows he always needs help, but my ankle and knee created an obstacle as I was in no shape to do construction. The other question was how I was going to travel to Florida? I had resolved that I was never going to take a bus ever. So that left me with only one option: to fly to Florida.

My flying experience was from Fort Jackson to Fort Campbell. This was not a good train experience; however, when I took the train from Jacksonville, Florida, to Fort Jackson, South Kentucky, it was a pleasant experience.

Finally, I concluded that I would visit a travel agency to work out my options. After talking with the travel agency, I found on the army post, I decided to take the train. I had bought a one-way ticket from Hopkinsville, Orlando train station.

The problem I had now was who would pick me up from Kentucky to Orlando, Florida. It was April 14th, 1960, at 7:30 pm when I boarded the train to Orlando.

Seated in an all-white coach, I could whisper around me. "There's a nigger soldier over there!" but the train attendees did not care. I thought of Martin Luther King and the set-in marches and started feeling a bit scared. Then, to add insult to the injury, a white girl boarded the train and settled right beside me.

Immediately, an older white gentleman called her out.

"Young lady, we have room up here for you. You don't need to sit there with that nigger boy!" he bellowed, making the girl shift her seat.

Having had dinner at the mess hall before leaving, I was not hungry at all. But I wondered if I would be permitted to eat in the dining car because I knew I would be hungry before reaching Orlando.

Thinking it would be wise to ask the conductor for another seat, I decided to do so. However, it felt like the sixties, and I needed to fight for my rights. I have no idea what the conductor was thinking when he assigned me that seat.

The first stop after leaving Hopkinsville, Kentucky, was Tennessee. A passenger entered my coach. He eyed me and thought that he had boarded the wrong coach.

I knew that I would not sleep before reaching Orlando because of how uncomfortable I was, and everyone watched every move I was making. It felt like I was a caged animal and not a human.

But I couldn't dwell on all of this. Because I felt good about myself. After all, I was going to stay in the army. I had an assignment. Hawaii did not sound like a good place for a black person, but I knew I would make it. And who knows, I might even like the beach.

As it was announced that the next station would be Nashville, Tennessee, many passengers started gathering their belongings to depart the train.

I wondered if Nashville had any country singers; after all, it was home to the grand old opera and the world's musical capital. But it was not a town for a black boy looking for things quail. My first train ride from Jacksonville to Fort Jackson had been different altogether. I had freedom of movement. Also, I could use all the facilities on the train freely. The only thing that saddened me was witnessing the living conditions of Black Folk along the tracks.

I still think the living condition along the tracks from Hopkinsville, Kentucky, was deplorable; however, I felt like a trapped slave on this trip. I was scared to leave my set. I felt like I had always felt in the presence of white people. Like they had the power to do whatever they wanted. They could call me whatever they wished, even take my life, and no one would bat an eye.

It was a long way to Orlando; there were many towns the train would stop at. I felt less secure when the train was stationary. Because that is when most of the comments were passed around about me. It would have been so easy for them to have thrown me off the train or form a bee lynch mob and did whatever they wanted to do with me.

These were the terrifying thought that swirled around in my mind as I sat frozen in my seat, trying not to move at all so I wouldn't get noticed because I had no defense of my own. Before reaching Orlando, Florida, there were eight more major southern cities from Nashville, Tennessee.

Suddenly, I felt the need to use a bathroom. But the train was stationary, so I decided to wait until it was moving again. Thinking it through, I compiled a list of questions I needed to ask the conductor.

After the train started moving again, before the colored conductor could walk past me, I stopped him and inquired about the bathroom. And being so kind, he not only walked with me to the toilet but also settled me down in the rear of the dining car and gave me a great meal.

Finally, I started feeling and being treated like a human being again. With the conductor's assistance, I made it back to my seat. And even though I still felt very much out of place, I felt a lot more relaxed after going to the bathroom and getting something to eat.

Our next stop was Chattanooga, Tennessee. I was not as scared as before, but I did not feel like one of the boys either. I wished I felt confident enough to get on and off the train like some white passenger, but deep down, I knew that was never going to happen. I almost wished I had taken a bus. At least then, I would have been able to see the outside world.

When the train started south towards Atlanta, it was about midnight. It becAMe too dark for me to spot the black fAMilies, but I knew they were there in the dark. After all, I belonged with them.

Looking back, I realized I was never afraid of the white folks. It was the environment of the train that was making me nervous. First his pride, second his women, thirdly, his position associated with his woman and himself.

Down here in the south, if a black man was caught in between the white man triangle, perceived as doing wrong or otherwise, he could lose his life.

At fourteen, I stood down a white man in his element with a pruning knife and lived to tell the tale. In 1955, four years after the Greenlee case, one black man was shot to death, and another was whipped to death for allegedly raping a 17-year-old white girl in Groveland, Florida. Groveland was just six miles west of my hometown, Clermont. However, that day in orange grove with Mr. Willie, I had been lucky to have survived against that white man.

I had challenged two white men in the deep south and survived. However, nether occasions were like being in the Deep South. With the big Mississippi bigot, everybody in the barracks thought he had picked on me one too many times, and it was about time I challenged him. So, I guess I was pretty much in my element. With Mr. Willie in the orange grove, I think he decided to spare me because I was just fourteen years old, and he would gain nothing challenging me.

My uniform was a factor that I had not been challenged on the train yet. I'm sure soldiers were common on this train route to the deep south, but maybe not the black ones. The objective of the deep south was to instill the fear of God All-Mighty in the black folks. In the case in Groveland, the white folks did not shoot a black man and whipped the other to death; they also burned down four hundred houses and forced the entire black township into the woods and swAMps.

The sheriff got three confessions from Shepherd, Irvin, and ACP from the beating, killing, and burning. All three men were convicted. The NAACP, headed by Thurgood Mar Marshall, appealed the conviction, and another trial was in Ocala, Florida.

During the waiting period for a new trial, it was decided to transfer Shepherd and Irvin to another facility by Sheriff Willis B. McCall. They were handcuffed together when the men were shot by McCall. Shepherd was shot to death, and Irvin was shot three times in the shoulder, chest, and neck. He survived by lying face down in the mud and playing dead.

Sheriff McCall's brutal actions caused an uproar. Newspapers from around the world sent reporters to cover the incident. In the upcoming new trial, the Judge assigned was Judge Truman Futch.

In December 1951, Judge Futch ruled that Marshell, and Jack Greenberg could not represent the proceedings. According to the Judge, they were a group of agitators who had stirred up trouble in the community. Marshall did not back down and called on the black church community of Florida to give him the support he needed. Because of the threats he received, the Marshall had two bodyguards with him at all times and did not stay in the same place two days in a row. In fact, the black community took turns in providing shelter and food to Marshall and his staff. Harry T. Moore, head of the NAACP in Florida, was not so fortunate as his home got bombed, and he was killed in the explosion.

Under threats of further appeals, Marshall finally forced Judge Futch to allow him back into the case. Even though the trial was back on, Marshall still received death threats from Sheriff Wills McCall's deputy. The jury was all white men. While Marshall talked to the jury, he noticed that they all had Shriner's pin on. Once the case was given to the jury, it took them ninety minutes. One court observer later told Marshall they took that long because they wanted mint to smoke their cigars.

The verdict, of course, was guilty, and Irvin was sentenced to death. Marshall appealed the case at every level until the Supreme Court refused to review it. But the lengthy appeals delayed the execution and gave Marshall time to work on other options to keep Irvin alive. Using political and NAACP contacts, he put public pressure on the governor and generated loud headlines week after week about various details in the case.

With the pressure building from all sides, three years after Irvin was sentenced to death, Gov. Leroy Collins changed the sentence to life in prison. Several years later, Irvin was finally released.

In 1955, when Irvin was convicted and given the death penalty, all-black Americans felt violated, but there was no public outcry. Colored folks were born into racism. It was our parents, schoolteacher, and church pastor's responsibility to teach us our place and how to appease the white community. One example is when you talk to a white person over the age of fifteen, you would look towards the ground and use words like, "No sir, or no ma'am." You were not permitted to look them in the eye as it was considered disrespectful. And it could result in you losing your job or even worse. There was no place for smart niggers in this community. So, there was no public celebration when Irvin won the case and was released from jail.

The train arrived in Atlanta, Georgia, "The Capital of the South." This was a major stop, and people got on and off the train, but I did not have the nerve to move. I knew the rules and did not dare change them. The other cities that we would probably stop before Orlando were Macon, Tifton, Georgia. Both Macon and Tifton had a bad reputation regarding racism. My father told me how colored men were whipped if they caused the white man any trouble here.

Savannah, Valdosta, Georgia were cities where colored folks would run away like slaves to escape their white bosses. Many of these runaways ended up in Central Florida just to start the process all over again.

The next stop was Gainesville, Florida. The big thing over there was the first colored to be accepted in the

University of Florida. There had been some demonstrations at Law School, but nothing like the burning and killing that we had in Groveland in 1951.

The next stop was Ocala, Florida, where Thurgood Marshall became the first colored lawyer to win an appeal for a black man and retry him for raping a white woman. In the first trial in Lake County, Frank Williams defended the three colored men: Samuel Shepherd, Walter Lee Irvin, and Charles Greenlee with Marshall's assistance. Samuel Sheperd and Lee Irvin were sentenced to death in the electric chair. Charles Greenlee, sixteen, was given life because of his age. Between these trials, Sheriff McCall shot Irvin three times, in the shoulder, chest, and neck. Shepherd was also killed by McCall. During this second trial, only Lee Irvin was left, and this time, Irvin was again convicted and sentenced to death in the electric chair. It had been eight years since the last trial, but just passing through the area gave me a feeling of helplessness, and I started feeling unprotected.

The thought that comforted me was that I would be getting off the train in Orlando in a few minutes, and I could call someone to pick me up. If I had not been so afraid, I could have called from Atlanta, Georgia, and someone would have been waiting for me at the station already.

It was April 15th, [th] 1960, at 10:15 am, when I used the public phone to call someone to pick me up. The Orlando Station was clean with excellent seats and not a bad place to wait. I was surprised when my sister pulled up to the station at about 11:30 am in my mother's new Buick Wildcat. We made small talk and asked about each other's well-being.

On highway 50, the main highway from Orlando to Clermont was about twenty-four miles. In the little town of Ocoee, it was rumored that colored men were lynched and buried there in a standard concrete vault.

It was said that no one ever questioned the men who a part of the lynch party were, even though everyone knew them by name. I was going to be home for thirty days, plus I had another five days for travel.

That was a lot of time when I had nothing to do due to my bad knee and ankle. If this was my brother James, he would fish for the whole duration of thirty days. James could fish anywhere and everywhere but not me. I tried fishing, but I ran into white men almost every time, and sometimes they had guns.

My older brother was a master of the lakes and swamps of Central Florida. I was ten, and he was thirteen when lynch parties burned and killed our neighbors in Groveland. My ankle was almost healed, so I found a suitable attire for construction work and decided to help my dad.

I visited all ten of my aunts and uncles and confirmed my heritage from South Georgia to Central Florida. My mother's heritage was colored but mostly Seminole Indian.

My mother, sisters, and brothers lived within two miles of each other in Clermont and enjoyed telling us stories of our heritage. I was the first in the family to be born in Central Florida and had six other sisters and brothers younger than myself born in Clermont.

The difference between me and my siblings was that I could never learn that colored folks had to be respectful to white men. For some reason, I felt that we were equal.

I told my family that the army was good for me because even black men could be in control and held responsible.

Finally, my knee and ankle were almost healed. I helped my dad in those thirty days and went fishing with James once. It was a good trip.

Now, it was time to leave. In a few days, I would arrive at the Terminal in Brookland to catch the ship, Pvt. Joe E. Mann for a seven-day cruise to Hawaii. After having the experience of traveling on a civilian train and bus, I opted for the bus to travel to New York.

It was May 14th, 1960, at 11:00 o'clock, when the bus was to depart the Clermont bus station. Fred, my brother-in-law, brought me to the bus station and waited until the bus came because I was uncomfortable waiting alone.

Mr. And Mrs. Mims were my white friends, and I visited them whenever I visited home. They lived a block from the Clermont bus station. However, Clermont was no different. Below the Mason-Dixon line, where colored were second-class citizens, the first stop north of the Mason. Dixon, public restaurants, and public toilets were not just for whites. They also were open to coloreds.

This meant that I could sit in any seat on the bus and eat at public restaurants. At the same time, Martin Luther King. Jr and his followers, dowers south were fighting for these rights; it only steered things up.

Whites in the south were meaner. This bus trip north would be my first. In the cities, I could see the poor and downtrodden. And every once in a while, I would see a soldier with his bags trying to make it to his next duty station, the same as me. If we came in contact, we would exchange information about our travel, about ourselves, expective duty station and other pleasantries.

My bus reached Ocala; a town seared into my brain. This was the town that almost every colored person in Central Florida knew about. With the intensity of the Marshall Marion County fight for the right to defend Walter Lee Irvin from the rape case, I got cold chills even thinking about it. First, the fight for a black lawyer to define a black man in the Marion County Courthouse was unprecedented.

The fight for Thurgood Marshall to practice in the county courthouse was a victory. However, after losing the case, it was a fight for him to get a retrial. Irvin was fighting to stay out of the electric chair. That was eighty years ago. Now sitting in the rear of the bus, as we pulled into the station, I couldn't help but wonder how whites remembered the Irvin trial.

To them, they had lost, even though they won the verdict to send Irvin to the electric chair. The idea of a colored man practicing law in the south was enough, but there was about as much as they could take in their courthouse. Thurgood Marshall was the first colored man to practice law in the Marion County Courthouse. There was a profound effect within our community and within our families. The widespread brutality affected the way mothers and fathers raise their children in the colored community after the death of three black men being shot to death or whipped to death. We didn't even feel safe walking in the woods, fishing, hunting, or taking a swim in one of the hundred lakes in Lake County.

I had nine siblings and protective parents, who were always suspicious of every white person they did not know. My mother was born to Mr. And Mrs. George Walker on December 2nd, 1918, in South Georgia, FitzGerald. She had a muscular physique and was about six feet. She only studied till sixth grade, but with the amount of knowledge she had, most people assumed that she graduated from one of the nation's finest universities. She was also an enterprising woman, and together with her husband, she built a home construction business that supported our family for fifty years.

When we saw a strange white person, our first thought was that maybe that person was a member of the KKK. We would immediately recall how four hundred houses were burned, how we ran into the swamps, how several young men were lynched, and the National Guard had to be called out for our protection. Life suddenly changed for all of us. My older brother James and his friends were the exceptions. They still fished at the lakes of Lake County and caught tons of fish.

There were also eleven other siblings to the Walker family and some three-hundred fifty acres of farm and timberland to manage. Thus, they all received their diploma from the "Walker Family" of timber management and cotton management. Mama accepted Christ at an early age and became a member of Mt. Calvary Baptist Church in Ben Hill County, Georgia.

She married my father, James W. Montgomery, on November 23,1933. Thirteen months later, my oldest sister Gloria was born. Some six years and three children later, the Montgomery family relocated to central Florida and established a homestead in the small town of Clermont in Lake County, Florida.

I was the first Floridian of the Montgomery clan, with six others that followed every two tears after me. However, childbirth did little to slow my mother down. Within the Central Florida heartland, the citrus capital of the world, those who knew her would tell you how she held her title within the citrus groves, among the best man or woman, even including the eight months of pregnancy.

"The Church of God in Christ" came to Clermont in the early forties. mama was one of the organizers within the Clermont area and was assigned as Missionary of the "Young Women's Christian Council." She worked as a teacher and mentor for young Christian women for many years while working in the fields and raising a most productive family. Mama's skills rivaled that of an experienced ship captain, navigating the ship through rough and dangerous waters but always sure of the state of its cargo.

Finally, the bus pulled off highway 301 north into the city of Jacksonville, a bus station that I had been at several times in the past six months. It was the old Southern Station, one side for the coloreds and the other for the whites. This was a break station, meaning that you could get off the bus if you wanted.

I opted to keep my seat and watch the activity at the station while I continued to think of my highly productive family. My sister Gloria, the oldest of the Montgomery siblings, had always been like a second mother to me. She fed me when I was hungry, fought my battles when the odds were too great and were often an intermediary when things got rough between us siblings.

Gloria was a born leader of the highest order. Together, with her extraordinary husband, Speedy, and my brother, James, they broke away from my father to start their own business. My mother always expected Gloria to be successful because she always assigned Gloria the heaviest assignments on her. I wondered if she thought she would do as well as she did. Gloria was now an employer, whereas, in the past, only whites were employers in the small town of Clermont and Lake County, Florida.

The bus pulled off U.S. 301 into Brunswick, GA, bringing me out of my world. At the thought of my other oldest Sister, Deloris, I smiled to myself. She was a young School Teacher in Lake County and had graduated from Florida's A&M University in 1959.

For as long as I could remember, Mama wanted Deloris to be a schoolteacher, so she became one. Even when she was just in elementary school, she had that exceptional reserve about herself; that was expected of schoolteachers within the black community. Whenever any scholarly task needed to be performed, the family called upon Deloris. She would do letter writing whenever Mama had a need to communicate with relatives back home in Georgia. She wrote the rent receipts when Mama's tenants paid their weekly rent and helped Daddy keep books in his construction business.

To go to college, Deloris picked Oranges. She took other odd jobs, including babysitting at night for not so-respectful white men whom Deloris had to depend on for transportation home. On occasions, I noticed Deloris was not okay. The first year, she always had tears in her eyes when she came home, and Mama would talk to her in private. Since she could raise enough money when she graduated high school, she took a gap year and tried to do so in that year.

Many would have given up but giving up was never in Mama's vocabulary. Deloris, too, was willing to hang in there. She started college in 1956, and in 1959 she was in her last year of school, graduating in just three years with a B.S. degree. I looked out and realized that the bus had pulled out from Durham, NC., onto highway U.S. 291.

I wanted to be like my brother James for most of my young life. He had the work ethic of our mother, the physical ability of Hercules, endless friends, and everyone loved him. He used those assets to make Mama proud. He also had a tremendous earning ability at a very young age. Almost no one compared to him within the orange groves of Central Florida, except our sister Gloria's husband. James was consistently employed by someone doing something all the time. During school, he waited tables within the local hotels that catered to the snowbirds from up north who were hibernating in sunny Florida.

I had tried my hand several times at waiting tables, but I was too dark-skinned or unable to keep up with the fast pace which was usually set by James. He took his pleasures from the environment of central Florida, which boasted more than one hundred lakes. I could safely say James and his friend, Pop Hodges knew almost every lake's location, whereas I was scared of the woods after the lynching and burning in Groveland.

In the form of Abraham Jones, there was also a third party that made up the fearless threesome. This was the team that I most coveted during childhood. The saddest I had ever seen James was when one of the three sons was taken away. Abraham's life ended when he wrecked his new 1956 Crown Victory Ford north of Tallahassee, Florida.

James and Pop's fishing continued and came in handy during summer's lean months when their catches were our evening meal. During winter, coon hunting started at dusk and ended at daybreak. You could always find James and Pop in camp with their blue tick and redbone hounds. Coon meat was a delicacy within our community.

As the bus pulled out from Lynchburg, Virginia, heading for Washington, D.C., I thought of my brother Alexander. Alexander always felt like he had nothing to look forward to. However, the mother had plans for all of her children. She would always say, "he is going to be alright." Alexander had deformed feet and could only stand for a short period without crying out in pain.

Often, he would sit on the front porch and cry because he could not play with the rest of the children. He could not play basketball, baseball, or football like we could, and he was also not good at his studies. Several months before my enlisting in the U.S. Army, he got admitted to Orlando's cripple children's hospital.

He was still in the hospital when I finished basic training and received my assignment to Hawaii. I saw him only once, and both feet were in casts. I was sure he would be alright because Mama said so.

Our fat twelve years old and believed he could win at any level. He did not remember the burning of Groveland and the killing and lynching but was still too afraid to go into the woods to play.

My other sisters and brothers were too young for me to remember much about. Marshall was a sweet little nine-year-old who played with dolls, and Wilbert was seven. All I could remember about Wilbert was that he was dark-skinned like me. I wondered if he, too, had or would have a hard time.

Larance was five years old with light skin. Maryon was two years old and got all the attention of the family. She was a pretty little girl with short, nappy hair who loved being held and sung. We were not a poor family as daddy had his own business. We lived in a five-bedroom and three-bath, beautiful and enviable house.

Finally, at about 11 pm, the bus pulled into the Washington D. C. station. I was pleasantly surprised to see black folks dressed in respectable and fashionable clothes. There were also several soldiers, sailors, and navy and marine troopers at the station. I felt safe again and finally decided to leave the bus to get some refreshments. Everyone at the station was colored, and I felt like this was a world I could live in.

The bu stopped for only about twenty minutes. I reclaimed my seat, and after everyone boarded, the bus started its journey towards Baltimore. It approached north, where the colored folks did not have to sit in the back of the bus, stay outside standing up, or eat at restaurants in a designated area.

North Baltimore was the end of the south. When the bus left the Baltimore bus station on highway 15, colored folks were sitting all over the bus, making me feel a little comfortable but more suspicious of the white folks.

I was still in my back seat when the bus pulled into Port Authority, New York City. Port Authority was one big station where a connection could be made to all parts of New York City and the rest of the country. This was the end of my bus ride, and I had to connect here for the Brooklyn Army Terminal. There were lots of soldiers and lots of cabs lined up. The cab drivers announced their destination, and I got my bags from the bus and perked my ears for any driver to announce Brooklyn Army Terminal.

I opted for a cab with three other white boys. We were all army and assigned to the USS Mann, a troopship bound for Hawaii. Sitting beside them, I smiled at how excited they all were about their assignments to Hawaii and kept wondering how a colored boy from the south would survive Hawaii.

It was May 15th, 1960, and the ship was going to sail on May 19th, at 07:00. The cab ride was about an hour. It was 3:00 pm when we unloaded our bags and squired up with the taxi driver. Inside the building, there were signs directing soldiers to sign in for the USS Mann. Bound for Hawaii on May 19th, at 07:00, we signed in and were assigned a bunk and reminded to keep our bags locked at all times.

For the next three days, we had nothing to do. There was ping pong, pool tables, card games, illegal poker, and crap games. I was lucky at the craps games and won several hundred dollars during the next three days. I was told the crap games would be better on the ship and immediately started looking forward to being a part of them.

The routine at Brooklyn Army Terminal was, 1st call, 05:30 am, headcount at 06:00 am, breakfast at 06:30 am, and another headcount and physical training at 07:00 am.

The next headcount was going to be at 17:00. On shipping day, 1st call was at 05:00 am, headcount at 05:30 am, breakfast at 06:00 am. Then the other headcount and loading were at 06:30 am.

The USS Mann departed the port on May 19th, 1960, at 07:00 am. It was named for PVT. Joe E. Mann was a Congressional Medal of Honor winner during WWII, and I was not comfortable on this hunk of iron. It was about the size of a football field, which I thought was way too small compared to the size of the Pacific Ocean. The captain announced that the trip from New York, Hawaii, was going to take seven days. He also informed us that the 1st calls each morning would be at 05:30 am and muster at 06:00 am. The afternoon formation was going to be at 17:00 and would be on the deck.

There were about three hundred folks on the ship, including soldiers and crew. Our sleeping arrangements were high stacked hamlets, and our bags were secured to the center post that secured the hamlets. There were activities below the deck, and for seven days, I spent my time playing poker and dice games. Nobody seemed to care as long as there were no fights.

I won three hundred dollars, excluding the money I won at the Brooklyn Army Terminal, and got a good start in Hawaii. I took five hundred dollars, locked it in my bag, keeping the rest to gamble on the last day of the trip. The dice were good to me, and I won another four hundred dollars, finally making over a thousand dollars.

Considering that my monthly pay was only $89.01, I was rich. I locked all my money up except ten dollars and decided not to gamble until we reached Pearl Harbor.

Hawaii

The ship docked at Pearl Harbor on May 26th, 1960, at about 15:00 hrs. I was glad to leave the ship, but I knew it would be hard to find dice games to match the games on the ship. Once off the ship, the Sergeants in charge on the ground made us form a mass formation.

The instruction was to listen up for your name. When my name was called, I was assigned to the Headquarters, Battery, Second Battalion, Ninth Field Artillery. I was told to board truck number one with all my belongings.

Once all the five trucks were loaded, we departed for Schofield Barracks, about twenty-five miles up the mountain. The temperature was about eighty degrees. Going up the mountain, all the Infantry Division could see was beautiful flowers, green trees, grass, and pineapple fields. The view looked spectacular. This was a paradise on earth. But I felt like it was too good for a black kid who had known nothing but discrimination all his life.

On our next stop, we were welcome to the twenty-fifth, by the Division Commander, Maj. Gen. Richardson. He told us how lucky we were to be assigned to the twenty-fifth.

"Here, we work hard, and we also play hard." He said.

He talked about the Brigade Football teams that played every Friday night and other Brigade level games like basketball and baseball. If you are good enough to make it into the Brigade team, you could be exempt from regular duties and play sports full-time.

"Get these men to their units." He instructed the Seargent.

Again, we were ordered into formation, and names were called with the unit you were assigned to and were told to board the truck.

It was about 15:00 hrs. when the truck stopped in front of my new unit, Headquarters 2nd Houser Battalion, 9th Artillery, in section K of hers and the 25th Infantry Division.

The person in charge of the quarters signed the new recruits into the new unit. We were given a bunk with sheets and blankets and told we would be assigned a bunk with the locker tomorrow. This was home for the next three years.

I made a friend in a new recruit named Willie J. Harris. We both had the same assignment, Headquarters Communication Platoon. An Artillery organization was broken down by Batteries. In Coy, a Battery headquarters were Battery Headquarters Platoon, consisting of the Commander, usually having the rank of Captain.

The first Sergeant usually has the rank of E-8, which is the second-highest enlisted grade in the army. A battery Clerk normally had the rank of E-4, and the commander driver also carried the rank of E-4. The Mess Section consists of a Mess Sergeant having the rank of E-7 with two first cooks, both of whom carried the rank of E-6. There were also two shift leaders, both having the rank of E-5, and there were four cooks, each carrying the rank of E-4. The Medical Section consisted of the Medical Sergeant, carrying the rank of E-7, one Senior Aid man having the rank of E-6, and four aid men having the rank of E-4. When the Battalion is tactical, medics are signed out to line units. The Survey Platoon consisted of the Platoon Sergeant, having the rank of E-8, three team chiefs had the rank of E-7, three assistance team chiefs had the rank of E-6, three recorders had the rank of E-5, and six tape men had the rank E-4.

The survey Platoon was responsible for surveying the gun positions. The Communication Platoon consisted of the Platoon Sergeant, having the rank of E-8, wire section Sergeant had the rank E-7, radio section Sergeant had the rank E-7, three wire team Chiefs had the rank E-5, nine wiremen had the rank E-4, three radio team Chiefs had the rank E-5, one senior radio repairman had the rank E-5, one radio repairman had the rank E-4, three radio operators had the rank E-4.

The headquarters ammunition Platoon. Platoon Sergeant had the rank E-7, assistance Platoon Sergeant had the rank E-6, six truck drivers had the rank E-5, and six assistance truck drivers had the rank E-4.

Battalion Headquarters, the Commander LTC. Colonel, Executive Officer Major, Sergeant Major E-9. S-1 Section had the rank of Captain, S-1 Sergeant, had the rank E-7, and four S-1 Clerks, each had the rank of E-4. S-2 Section had the rank of Captain, S-2 Sergeant had the rank E-8, (Sgt. Pryor), S-2 Clerk had the rank E-4, S-3 Section had the rank of Major, S-3 Sergeant had the rank E-8, (Sgt Jones), Battalion Fire Direction Center, Fire Direction Officer, Major, S-3 Sergeant, E-8, Chief Computer, had the rank E-7, three Fire Direction Operators had the rank E-5, and two Fire Direction Operators had the rank E-4. The S-3 Section was the heart of the Artillery Battalion.

The key thing about this organization and all military organizations was that each function had a slot. In most cases, slots were assigned by the Platoon Sergeant, while in others, slots were assigned by the commission officer in charge. Each slot had a rank or grade as an E-5 assigned to it. One could not move up in rank unless he was in the proper slot. Noone could be promoted to E-6 unless he was in an E-6 slot and met all other qualifications, like education, time-in-grade, and a written proficient evaluation for the slot he would be promoted into.

The 2nd How Battalion, 9th Artillery, stationed at Schofield Barracks, Hawaii, was a reasonable and just organization. Master Sergeant, E-8, Pryor, was in charge of the S-2 section. The S-2 section was responsible for the security of the Battalion, including security clearances for need-to-know personnel. Sergeant Pryor made his rank in the old Negro Army that started integrating into the regular army in 1948 by order of President Truman.

Talking with Sergeant Pryor made me realize how he was an extremely intelligent individual. He had no coloreds in his section. However, his presence made it easier for coloreds in other departments. Master Sergeant Jones was the other colored E-8 in the Battalion. He was the S-3 operation sergeant responsible for running the Battalion. As the operation sergeant, Master Jones was responsible for the day-to-day training, firing of guns, and special training, such as jungle war fair. Both Master Sergeant Jones and Master Sergeant Pryor were set-in on enlisted promotion boards. This made us colored soldiers realize that the boards were fair and that there was no distinguishing in the army.

In the communication platoon, there was no colored senior sergeant. One stepping, fetching, uncle, torn sergeant E-5, known as McAllister. As a private, I had established good reports with the senior sergeants and the other enlisted men of the Platoon. I was selected for almost every wire-related communication work assignment. On this day, Sergeant McAllister had been assigned to install an overhead wireline from garrison to a field terminal. He selected me to help him install the cable, so we loaded the equipment on the truck and made it to our work site.

Sergeant McAllister explained what we were going to do and gave me the pole climbing equipment. I had always been a good climber, but to climb four miles of poles with my bad knee and ankle was asking too much, even from me. But I still took the equipment and fastened it on.

On the first pole, my knee buckled and hit the side of the pole, making me fall to the ground. Instead of helping me up, McAllister continued to work on the wireline until he concluded that he could not do the job by himself. Finally, he asked me could I get up and walk, to which I told him to come and inspect my knee.

He did, but I could see that he was scared of what the Doctor was going to say about not getting me medical attention sooner. Somehow, he got me on the back of the truck, took me to the division artillery aid station, and, with some help, drugged me inside and laid me on the floor. It was another hour before the Doctor inspected me.

Once he saw me, he called the ambulance and two medics. Then he told them to take me to Tripler Medical Center, located twenty miles from Schofield, near Pearl Harbor. It took almost an hour to cover the twenty-mile and to go through the red tape and into a doctor's care. I had nothing for the pain, and it almost became unbearable by the time we reached it. Finally, I was given something for the pain, and my trouser leg was cut from the knee. I witnessed hopelessness in the Doctor's eyes, and it made me wonder if I would be able to walk again.

They moved me onto a gurney and rolled me along the long corridor into an elevator. The elevator stopped at the fourth floor, and I was rolled down the long corridor and deposited in an empty bed along with about twenty other soldiers, sailors, marines, and others who had one type of injury or another. I was given more pain medication, and I tried to get some sleep.

However, the staff had other ideas. Together, along with one Doctor, staff personnel, they took me to the x-ray room and x-rayed my leg. Afterward, they took me to an operating room, drilling four holes through my bone and putting huge pins through my leg. The pain was unbearable, but I knew I had no other choice.

Finally, they put my leg in traction with about forty pounds once I was back in my bed. I could lay one way only, and that was flat on my back, with my left leg extended to the ceiling. This went on for about a month, with the Doctor coming by every two or three days to drain my knee of any fluid buildups.

I had been in Hawaii for less than a month, and what I had always been afraid of had happened, a severe injury to my knee. I wondered how long my ankle would hold up. My birthday was less than a month; I was going to be nineteen. I was told by the colored soldiers to forget about sex, or finding a girl in Honolulu, to them Blacks was invisible.

They say the only possible sex for a colored soldier was with Big Red and her girls at $20.00 a shot. Big Red was a six-feet, good-looking woman of color. She ran a shop out of clubs on Hotel Street, Downtown Honolulu. I think Big Red was a very wealthy woman. There were also some good-looking nurses at the hospital who I know got an eye full of all the G and were not too bad looking themselves. I think I thought of sex twenty-four hours a day, and a pretty nurse passing by every once in a while, intrigued me more. No matter how pretty the nurses were, it was not fun when they brought you a bedpan. Being confined to the bed meant being in pain constantly. Pain medication was only given about twice a day unless you made a lot of fuss, and then you might get an extra shot. One morning, I was surprised that the Battery Commander, First Sergeant, and my Platoon Sergeant visited the hospital, had a bedside ceremony, and promoted me to Private First Class, to pay grade E-3, this was a big thing, since. Sergeant McAlester told me a colored soldier could not compete with a white soldier in the same career field and of equal intelligence.

After the grade of E-5, Sergeant McAlester said that colored soldiers seldom get an evaluation equal to a white soldier unless the evaluator was colored. Without a superior evaluation, you cannot get promoted unless competing with all colored soldiers. I thought of Master Sergeant Prior and Master Sergeant Jones, who were in charge of the Fire Direction and Intelligence Section that had got their promotions mostly in the all-colored army and was now in charge of two sections with no men of color. It was very easy to see that these two sections got faster promotions than any section except maybe the Gun Section in A and B Battery with almost all colored soldiers and colored evaluators. The difference between these sections is that one is all-colored, and one is all-white except Master two-line duty. Sergeant Jones and Master Sergeant Pryor were the evaluators for the all-white sections.

Most white folks had college degrees or at least some college qualifications, unlike most of the colored sections. Most people had either high school degrees or were high school dropouts in these units. As long as they competed among themselves, they got promoted to E-6 and E-7. When colored folks competed with whites, all area whites almost always win, sometimes making the grade two to three years ahead of the colored soldier. In most cases, the colored soldier's job will be manual labor, lifting heavy materials, being exposed to extreme weather conditions, working with snow, rain, mud, etc. Within the communication section where I was assigned, the duty was heavy lifting snow, rain, and mud with about fifty percent white and fifty percent colored. Sergeant First Class Portwood was our platoon sergeant and evaluator, I think he was a fair white man, and in most cases, he evaluated E-5s, E-4s, and E-3s justly. But if he had to evaluate an E-6 or E-7 and one was white, and one was colored, I think he would give the edge to the white soldier. Basically, the way Sergeant McAlester explained it, he had been in the army for almost twenty years and was just an E-5. I was excited about my first promotion, and I would work very hard to compete with all soldiers, white or colored. I had to overcome my injuries for my next promotion, which could take two or three years to heal. Even though I was there for two or three years to be the next E-4 in the communication platoon, the hospital I would work hard to Platoon was half white.

I was told that I would be going back to surgery for a knee reconstruction to put my leg out of traction. This operation meant that I would be in the hospital for three more months. After surgery, the leg would be put in a cast, and I would be given crutches to get around the hospital area. There was a club on the Pearl Harbor side of the hospital that I was looking forward to sitting in my wheelchair at the club, sucking on a gin and tonic. Although I was only nineteen, and the drinking age in Hawaii was twenty-one, I was told they did not check ID cards at the club. The club was about one hundred yards downhill from the hospital, and I was sure the hill could be negotiated on crutches. I did not know how long it would take before the surgery. However, I was told the recovery period would be about three months in the hospital, given the severity and special treatment this type of injury required. If Doctor Tensely were the head surgeon, I would brief him before the surgery date.

Several days later, Doctor Tensely finally spoke to me about surgery. He said the kneecap would be removed, and a rasp would be used to file and reshape it because it was cracked. Some cartilage would also be removed from the bone that interacts with the kneecap. He said this procedure constituted a total reconstruction of the knee and a timely procedure that would require a great deal of effort on my part to help my knee normalize. I told the doctor I would do my part because I wanted to make the army my career, and my surgery was scheduled for June 21st, 1960. I can remember lying on the operation table, being told to count backward, starting at 100, getting to about 95. I woke up in recovery with fifty or more stitches in my left knee. A nurse in the room made sure I did not hurt myself until I was fully aware of where I was. The nurse asked me where I was and then my name. For the next two weeks, I was in bed with an ice pack on my knee, and the doctor would come to draw fluid off my knee every few days or so. This experience was an excruciating one. After about a month, my leg was put into a cast, and during this time, I also had a birthday, but there were no gifts.

I was able to walk with a crutch to explore the hospital ground for the first time since my hospitalization. On the hospital ground was a hobby shop to make leather crafts, basket weaving, woodwork, etc. There was also a concert hall where entertainers came to entertain the patients. I looked forward to these concerts, and I also made my way to the small club I had been planning. I had my first gin and tonic and did not visit the club again because of the legal limit to drink, and I wanted to be an example of what a soldier should be. For the next two months, my leg was in a cast, and I was in an ough to lift fixture in the hospital area. Visiting one place to another was boring, and my leg itched like crazy. When the cast was removed in early August, I had been in the hospital for almost four months, and physical therapy had not yet begun.

I was introduced to the physical therapist, and she explained the exercises I would be going through. 1) there will be warm-up exercises, 2) there will be flexing of the muscles, and 3) weightlifting. After each session, there would be a whirlpool, at 112% for thirty minutes. This routine was at 9 am, and 3 pm until the knee was 100% again. After a month or so, I was about eight pounds with my left leg and was directed to use the loom in the craft shop between 9 am and 3 pm to make a rug. The loom was powered by paddling with the feet and using the hand to put material in place to construct the rug pattern. It took me about a month of working about an hour a day to construct the first rug that I sent home, hoping that this would establish better communication between home and myself. I got a letter telling me how much they liked my handmade rug and hoped I would be out of the hospital soon. In October 1960, I was discharged from the hospital and reassigned to the communication platoon and was given temporary duty as division petroleum and gas clerk at Division Artillery.

This duty required me to supply the division with gas and oil and record the gas and oil used by division artillery. In September 1961, I was assigned back to the communication platoon as the senior switchboard operator. In October 1961, I was promoted from private first class to specialist fourth class, the first of my group to be promoted. This step-up caused a lot of fuss in the Platoon because I was in the hospital from May 1960 to October 1960, about six months, and from discharge until September 1961. I was assigned a division petroleum specialist for another eleven months for seventeen months and was the first to be promoted. The platoon sergeant, Sergeant First Class Portwood, explained how I have professionally carried myself and demonstrated extraordinary leadership traits. With all of my setbacks, I was on track to having a successful army career. Now I was back to regular duty, and I thought I would check with personnel to put in an application for a flight school to learn that I was not qualified because of the knee operation. Now, I would have to decide if I wanted to stay in the army.

The Big Island

Preparing to go to Big Island for training required all of the unit's vehicles to be high in readiness: fluid levels and maintenance upto par. The load-out was on the Pearl Harbor Naval Base, and the battalion-size team would be loaded on a Navy Ship (LSI) and Barge; this included about one hundred or more vehicles and counting. Headquarters Battery, two Gun Batteries A, and B. Headquarters Battery are responsible for ammunition for the guns, also for (S2) security and maps, (S1) personnel, and (S4) supply.Each battery are responsible for their vehicles and equipment. All batters were secured within the ship and Barge within a week's time..

The voyage would be from the Island of Oahu, the Big Island, passing Molokai, Lanai, and Maui. Along with the vehicle's equipment and about a hundred officers and men. It's about a day and night's voyage, culminating in the landing site some thousand feet below our training camp. The road from the landing site to our campsite was almost straight-up my three-quarter-ton truck with trailer were gear to make the climb; it was tricky to climb up the mountain to our training site). The area between Mount Kilauea an active Volcano, and Maunakea is the highest mountains within the

Hawaii chain. On the side of the snowcapt mountain, and at about forty degrees, the other one was a spewing volcano.

The mean temperature in the mountain terrain were about. forty degrees The lava beds were treacherous and,a paired of combat boots, lasted only about a week. Nearby was the Kings Ranch which became a tourist attraction to hunters; understand there were bighorn sheep and pheasant on the ranch. On occasions, we took a break to have fun on the beach and at a resort hotel. In Kona, it was all about Lobsters and Scrimps, untouchable dancing girls, and lots of beer and drinks; however, the drinking age was an issue. Our second break was at the beach with our sleeping bags, where the locals wrapped our food in a banana leaf and cooked it underground; this was called Luau or Hawaiian. There were also dancing girls doing the Hawaii hula but were, again, untouchable. Training on the Island was demanding; it lasted for weeks and reversed itself. Going up the mountain and then coming down was even more challenging; some experienced brake failure that required towing or assistance. Loading the ship barge was possible because we had a great workforce. Every section was responsible for loading the Barge under the supervision of the non-commission officers of the respective section.

There were poker and dice games at the training site on the Big Island almost every night we camped. We played games whenever we could, but the senior Switchboard Operator took most of my time at camp and field training.

I lost a few and won a few; I think I was about fifty dollars ahead. There was no gambling on the voyage of the LST between Islands; maybe because there was so little room, everyone was topside most of the time. At topside, you could see dolphins running alongside the ship. I was sure I had impressed my platoon sergeant First Class Portwood, Sergeant McAllister, and the section sergeant of the battery because I had made sure each section within the headquarters battery had communicated with the battery switchboard and could communicate with other sections as well as with the civilian switchboard so they could call home whenever possible. There was only one terminal in the camp that could reach an outside line, and that terminal was open to Headquarters A and B, so it was busy most of the time. Gambling was not legal, but everybody still did it; it was the only way you stood a chance of having enough money from one month to the next.

I was lucky I often won when I gambled. Back at Schofield, I had it pretty good. I had money even if there was little chance of finding a girl or a reasonable working girl. I went to the best spots once or twice a month, i.e., Waikiki Shell for Concerts, with my friend Willie J. Harris; I always call him Willie J. Willie J. was in the communication platoon and made Specialist 4th Class in November 1961, a month after myself. We did everything together; he always had money to spend and did alright with dice. Headquarters had several gays who were discharged for their conduct and were not allowed to become soldiers or conduct homosexual activity while on duty. One was Privet First Class Batcher, Specialist 4th Class DeLazasa, and a couple in the medical section, Specialist 4th Class Brown and another Specialist. Training on the Island of Oahu was just as demanding as training on the Big Island; the difference was red mud instate of lava. Mountains were almost too hard to negotiate, and there was Jungle Training where we negotiated mountains with Artillery Pences using block and tackle. We trained against an aggressor force that had capabilities equal to our own and real prison of war camps, with umpires to decide who was winning the war games by using guidelines determining the number of kills and loss of equipment.

This type of training was almost constant within division artillery units. In Oahu's jungle terrain, we rotate from the training site to the garrison and back to the training site every two weeks or so. It was almost always raining, and the mud was ankle-deep and hard to wash off. Once back at the garrison, wash pads, or racks as we called them, were always busy using high-pressure hoses to try and wash the everlasting mud from our combat vehicles. On return from the field training sites, after washing and cleaning vehicles and equipment, they were displayed on a Saturday morning for inspection by the Battery Commander, the Battalion Commander, or the Division Commander. There was always an inspection of some type on Saturday mornings. Section equipment in a headquarters Battery for the communication section would include all of the equipment used for combat training, such as radios, telephones, vehicles, reels of wire, equipment for laying wire lines et cetera, and along with the display will be a loading plan on how the equipment is loaded for field or combat deployment. (53) fire direction would lay out their equipment such as charts used to compute artillery fire slide rules, computer maps, et cetera.

Individual soldiers would lay out their individual field equipment between the section equipment, including mess gear, tent half called shelter half, tent poles, entrenching tool (a small shovel), and other equipment necessary to survive comfortably in a combat environment. All section would lay out their equipment for inspection every Saturday morning when in garrison, including the gun batteries. The 25th Infantry Division was a combat-ready jungle division, fully trained in jungle warfare.

Thailand

In February 1962, the Second Brigade of the 25th Infantry. Division including Second Battalion 9th Artillery was designated to Airlift to Thailand, fully combat-ready; this included live ammunition for each combat-ready trooper and basic loads for each Artillery Gun Section. (The threat was the North Vietnam Communists). The load-out was from Hickem Air force Base close to Schofield. The equipment load out was on C 130s Hercules Aircraft. One such aircraft could carry two-gun sections, with ammunition or about four two-and-one-half ton trucks fully loaded. The troops loaded out on C 147s, and the destination was Korat Thailand Royal Air Force base.

From there, we would travel south on Thailand friendship highway about ten miles south of Korat and set up base camp. The camp would be called Camp Friendship. It was the edge of the jungle and under every bush was a snake of some type, mostly cobras, and lots of spiders. Cobras were so common that I was soon picking them up by hand, before they could come to a striking position, and cutting them in half with a machete; machetes were a must for life in the jungle. For the spiders, though, you wore a long sleeve shirt and kept your pants' leg tucked into your boots, and made sure that anytime you went to bed your mosquito net was properly tucked in.

If Hawaii was almost devoid of female companionship. Thailand, known as the *Sin Capital* of the world, made girls available twenty-four-seven. Upon arrival to our base camp, *strips* or *sin cities* as they were called were already set up in make-shift huts across Friendship Highway from our base camp. The girls wore western attire and made every attempt to get the attention of the GI, which was not hard to do. By global standards, they were very attractive women. There were almost no restrictions on visiting *Sin City*. However, safe sex was preached by the medical section, which issued protection upon request. There were other services offered by the strip across the highway, such as haircuts cold drinks and laundry. One objective of the 9th Field Artillery was to test the mobility of a Field Artillery unit using both track and wheel vehicles in the jungle of Southeast Asia. The 9th would cross Thailand from bottom to top, starting from the most Southern tip to the most Northern tip of the country; this included following along the Macon River and along the Laos border.

There was also mountain area that would be negotiated. Every time we moved, the *Sin City* would follow by one means or another. I am sure they were not always the same girls, but girls from the closest village would make up what it took to service hundreds of American GIs. Upon arriving to Thailand, a GI could get a girl for about an American dollar. After about a month in the country, it was five dollars; I guess you had to pay for the price of doing business and travel together. The service in Thailand was considered combat duty; however, there was almost no contact with the enemy. Special Forces had gone across the Macon River and had reported contact, but they were with us only a few days, and I don't know what their mission was or if they had any KIA or WIA. Once we reached Macon, I was tide and ready to return to Schofield in Hawaii. Of all the girls, I had one encounter with a very young girl that I would always remember even though she was a working young lady.

I am sure if given the opportunity, she would have done well in America. I spent a lot of time with her; of course, this is possibly true with many of the girls who were forced into prostitution. I thought of the working girls back at Fort Jackson and how different they were or was there any difference? Some of the GIs fell in love with these girls and even wanted to marry them. However, I don't think I would ever go that far, or maybe I would do under the right circumstances. Some of them were downright knockouts; even the high-ranking officers were hung up over some of these girls. On one occasion, the girls were put on a show in a makeshift club; they were strippers. Two officers had a fight over who would spend the night with her. So, it was not just the enlisted men, it was also the officers, and West Point say they were gentlemen. It was now June of 1962, and we had been in Thailand for four months. In November of 1962, it would be my time to make a decision to reenlist in the Army. Since I could not be an airplane pilot, chances were I would not stay in the army either.

But I had almost nothing to look forward to back home. I would probably work for my brother, and I have never done well when working with him, but maybe it could work. I understand there was lots of work, and the pay was good. I could buy a car since I had enough money in the bank in Hawaii to pay for a late-model car, and maybe I would find a girl. The Communication Officer was an adventurous guy, so I got to see a great deal of the country; we visited various restaurants and sampled all types of Thai food, and we met girls who were willing but did not work in forced prostitution. Other cities that we visited were Phitsanuloke, Chiang Rai, Mae Hong Son, and towns along the Macon River. It was now June of 1962, and we had been in Thailand for four months. The first two months had been at camp friendship fighting cobras, and the remainder of the trip had been all about crossing the country and fighting – fewer – snakes. We saw lots of elephants doing logging work in the jungles; they were amazing workers.

Once we left Camp Friendship, there was no need for a switchboard operator, and for the past two months, I had been given the duty as the Communication Officer Driver. When the Battalion returned to Hawaii in late November 1962, a Mexican Specialist 4th Class by the name of Preseodio was promoted to Sergeant E5. This was a promotion that Sergeant First Class Portwood and I thought I should have received. That is when I made up my mind that I would not reenlist. On the fourth of February 1963, in Oakland, California, Willie J. Harris and I were honorably discharged from the U.S. Army.

My pockets were full of money – more than a thousand dollars – that I had withdrawn from the 1st National Bank in Hawaii as well as my last payment from the Army to include travel pay. Both Willie J. and I were invited to a Coming Home party upon our return by one of the soldiers being discharged with us, who lived in Oakland, and we accepted the invitation. We all pooled our money for a taxi for about a thirty-minute ride over to the colored side of town to our new friend's house, where there was music, a barbecue, and mostly family members of our new friend. We were introduced to his family and enjoyed the barbecue. We all had beer till it got dark.

This was not really what Willie J. and I were looking for. We wanted to hear some jazz music, interact with some women and go around the town. We wanted to hear Coltrane, Monk, Mild Davis, or a better-known jazz artist of the day. We thanked our friend and his family and called a taxi to leave. Upon entering the vehicle, we asked the taxi driver where the jazz artist was playing. Apparently, it was not in Oakland. The taxi driver informed us that it was perhaps across the bridge in Frasco and would be a fifty-dollar fare to check out Frasco; for that kind of action, he would have to call and find out what nightclub had live music.

We gave up on that idea and asked the driver to take us to a decent local hotel, and maybe round up a couple of decent girls for the night. He agreed to do that for twenty dollars, and in less than twenty minutes, we had two women in the car: both good-looking and well-dressed with no resemblance of hookers. We made small talk, exchanged names, aksed about where we were stationed and how much money we would be spending for their service.

We gave them a price of twenty dollars, which was acceptable for an hour. However, when my girl and I got to our room, she said that she was not a hooker and dated when she knew what she was getting into and that she trusted the cab driver. Besides soldiers had too much to lose to get into trouble. She said if I ordered something to eat and gave her another ten dollars, she would stay for the night. This was because I looked like a nice guy to her and that one day, I would make for a good man or husband to a nice girl. I thanked her and gave her twenty dollars to order some food even though I was not hungry yet, but I thought I might be before the night was over. The girl went out and returned with greens, rice and beef tips, candy yams and cornbread. She said there was a soul kitchen around the block from the hotel; we both disrobed with the light on and touched and admired each other's bodies. We talked; she asked me where my home was and I told her it was located in Clermont, Florida; it would take several days to get there from here. We talked some more and then we made love with the light on. Before the night was over, we made love several times and when the morning came she kissed me on the cheek and ask me to take care of the girl that I would find when I got home. She also told me not to forget her and that she would not forget me. I gave her another twenty dollars and she left.

Home

During my first week at home, I bought a 1960 maroon Thunderbird; my mother and father had to co-sign for me. I also started seeing a girl name Odessa Marie Brown whom I had known all my life, though she was a knockout. She was in college fifty-seven miles north of my hometown of Clermont, in Ocala. I also started to work for my brother, where the workday started at 6 am and ended at about 6 pm. After my shift, I would make the drive to Ocala to see Odessa. I am sure I was in love with her. However, we only had about three weeks together before I told Odessa I was going back into the army. She wanted a token, as she called it, an engagement ring; I was not ready for that because I had no idea where I would be assigned. On the 25th of February 1963, in Jacksonville, Florida, I was reenlisted in the United States Army and was assigned to the 6th Battalion 9th Artillery at Ft. Sill, Okla. It was a newly formed organization with 175mm Guns, the biggest in the Army inventory, and Eight Inch Howitzers, the second biggest gun in the army inventory.

When I arrived at the 9th Artillery at Ft. Sill, there were just a few men assigned to the unit. Once the organization was complete and tested, we would be assigned to a station in Germany. I had completed three years of active duty and was sure of my Sergeant E5 promotion within the next few months; the army regulation stated that unless you were in pay grade E5 or E4 with four years of service, you could not own ship a vehicle to an overseas command. I wanted to take my 1960 Thunderbird to Germany with me, as it would be the perfect car to run with the German Mercedes on the Autobahn. The Thunderbird had a hundred and sixty on the speedometer, and the autobahn had no speed limits. I requested an extended leave past the 14th of October 1963, that would give me four years of service. After working very hard to prove myself to the Battalion Commander, my leave was granted, and so I would have over four years of active duty. I would be able to ship my car, plus I would have more time to see Odessa – who still wanted a token. I wrote to her several times a week up until my leave that started on the 2nd of October 1963.

Upon leaving, I had enough money not to work. Odessa and I did a lot together, but there was no sex; she said that she was saving herself for marriage. We kissed every time our eyes met, and we touched every part of each other's bodies. One time, she let my hand inside of her pants, and I touched her most sensitive inner part; she had an orgasm right in my hand. Of course, she slapped me and never said anything about it. While I was home, she transferred from the junior college in Ocala to a four-year college near Jacksonville. This shift meant I had to drive a greater distance to see her. I visited Odessa at her dorm, and at night, we visited the local nightclubs and made long walks along the beach. For sure, I was in love for the first time in my life, but I could not commit to marriage.

Prior to coming home on leave from Ft. Sill, I had worked two jobs and never went into town, I was doing everything I had to for the next Sergeant ES promotion, and I wanted to make sure that I got it. The Battalion was filling up fast, and training had begun. I volunteered to work with Personnel (S1) and operation (S3) when I was not leading a wire team in the field. In garrison, S3 had the duty of establishing the manning chart or the required workforce for each section called TO&E for the Battalion, and SI had the duty of cutting the order to assign each man to a position within the TO&E. SI would cut the stencil, and I would run the hand-operated printing machine to manufacture the orders.

There were five hundred and forty-two members assigned to the Battalion: five hundred and eleven enlisted men, twenty-eight officers, and three warrant officers. Each member got three sets of orders, so I hand-printed 1,626 copies of orders and made the proper distribution through the message center that I worked at when I was not in the field. There were four Wire Teams: Jones, Weekly, Goldstein, and me. Each team had four men assigned, with ten miles of wire. Within this Battalion, a common wireline would run for about 20 miles.

This meant each team would do about 5 miles on a common line, and I think my team always did more than our share. One day, while rushing to complete a line while testing the line between two points about a two-mile distance, I was at one point, and my driver was at the other. I encouraged him to hurry and pick me up and, in the process, be turned over to the truck with three men aboard. This was in early September 1963. I was sure this would cancel the promotion I had worked so hard for.

The accident had been discussed, the men had minor injuries, the truck was a loss and had to be replaced, and no one said anymore to me about the accident. I continued to work at the messager when I was not in the field with my new truck and new crew. On the 12th of October 1963, I left Clermont with several men, going to upstate New York to a work camp around Peekskill to pick apples. Passing through Georgia, a man we called O.C. was driving the Thunderbird, speeding, doing about eighty in a sixty-mile an hour speed zone; the music in my 1960 vehicle was loud when the local police pulled us over. The officer addressed us as boys and asked for O.C.'s driver's license and the insurance for the car. O.C. showed his driver's license, and I got the insurance from the glove box. He reviewed the license and insurance. Keeping them, he asked us to follow him. When we got to the county courthouse, he asked who Julius P. Montgomery was – the individual whose name was on the insurance – and I told him it was me. He said the driver of the car had to go before the county judge and pay a fine or go to jail. The judge came in, took the insurance and license, and asked the officer what the charges were. The officer said that these boys were doing eighty miles an hour in a sixty-mile-an-hour speed zone. The judge said the fine would be $120 dollars or one week in jail; we pulled together and paid the fine.

The judge admonished us and said, "You boys try and obey the law, you hear?"

From Georgia on, we looked out for the law. We made no stops except for gas through South Carolina, North North Carolina, Virginia, DC, Maryland, and Pennsylvania, making the trip from Clermont to the work campin in record time to Peekskill, New York From there, I would have to travel down pass tthe Hudson, New York City, to Brooklyn Navy Yard, where I would load my car for shipment to Germany. At the work camp, I met a young man who said he was going to Harlem and that if I gave him a ride, he would help me get over to Brooklyn, Navy Yard. I agreed to give him a ride into Harlem. It was the 14th of October 1963, and I did not have to be at the Navy Yard until the 19th of October, and my flight to Germany would be on the 21st. I thought I would spend some time in Harlem, which I did. I even met an old neighbor from Clermont on 125th Street named Juanita Curry. Later, I ran into the young man who I picked up from camp family, and we both had a few beers together.

Then, we all loaded into the Thunderbird and drove over to the Navy Yard; I let the young man drive. He pulled me right up to the building where I had to check-in. I went in with a copy of my orders and logged in on the manifest. I parked my car inside the cantonment area as directed, with the keys still in the switch. The car had to be in place no later than 15:00 hours on the 19th of October.

My orders were stamped and given back to me, and I was told they would get me breakfast and a place to sleep until my flight left on the morning of the 21st of October 1963, for Frankfurt, Germany. When I returned to where I parked my vehicle, I found that there was no car! I went back inside and reported that it had been stolen. The Military Police was called, who put me in touch with a New York detective of the 25th Prescient as this was where the suspect was from. We looked for the car for two days, and the case was turned over to the FBI. They asked where I had been in Harlem, and I told them my whereabouts. The officers knocked on the door, announced that it was the FBI, and had four young men come out into the yard with their hands on top of their heads. They asked if the man that took my car was among the four people standing there. I pointed out the man that I recognized. It was about eleven o'clock in the morning; the car was very clean and had a new shine. I was told I had to go downtown to the judge's office where this man would be charged with grand theft auto, and I would have to press charges against him. As a result, he would be put away for several years if convicted.

I was told I did not have to be present for the trial. I was given my keys, the car's fuel tank was full of gas, and I followed the FBI downtown, feeling relieved but a little shaken; it was now the 16th of October, and I still had three days to get the car to the cantonment area and catch my flight. Since leaving Clermont, I have learned a lot; I thought I was smart, but I learned that I was lucky. In fact, very lucky to have found my car in the biggest city in the United States; I drove back to the naval shipyard. I parked my car on the afternoon of the 16th. My flight departed from New York at 09:00 hours on the 21st of October 1963. The pilot said it would be about a nine-hour flight to Frankfurt, Germany and that we would be landing at the Frankfurt Military Air Base at about 18:00 hours. Waiting for my arrival at the Military Air Force Base was an army van, and th driver identified me immediately. We went to baggage claim and picked up my duffel bag, and I had one other carry-on as I was the only passenger. We drove through the streets of Frankfurt to McNair Kaserne, Hoechst, Germany; it was a small base just big enough to hold the Battalion. It was freezing, and we witnessed the ground covered in snow; I was ready to get inside.

I was assigned quarters with one other sergeant: Sergeant Jones, which was good. I knew I would be making Sergeant soon. If not, I would be assigned to the squared bay. My knee was at nearly 100% with all the training at Ft. Sill; it had not given me any problems. Jones told me that my wire team was waiting for me, and we would be going to Graffingville, a training sight, in about a week. I did not have much time to get my team ready for the move. Graffmville was about a hundred kilometers away – close to the East Sector. I had never been there but had heard a lot of war stories about the place. It was talked about all over the army by careers that had experienced the cold, mud, and poor living conditions associated with the training area. Our section sergeant was Sergeant First Class White: an E6. Some SFCs were E7s, and some were E6s s; it had something to do with the changing rank structure in the army. SFC White was an old-timer who had been to Graff, as it was called, and had horrible stories to tell about the place. His instruction that was drilled into the wire section of the communication platoon was, "Make sure you had all of your equipment and all of your personal field gear. Overshoes, field trousers, Gloves, hats and scarf, et cetera, and make sure that the section equipment is survivable."

The field training test was for thirty days. We were required to stay awake for thirty-six hours at a time, and I was told the mud and Snow were knee-deep. Four-wheel drive vehicles often were not able to move in the mud and snow and required chains on the wheels. Guns and heavy equipment had to travel by rail to get to Graff because they were not allowed on the autobahn. The wheel section of the Battalion departed for Graff on the 27th of October 1963 and arrived at base camp late, even on the same day. Each section was assigned a hut to store our equipment and one for sleeping quarters. Our sleeping quarters had a single stove in the center of the floor that burned coal. Each man had an individual love cot to sleep in. A fire had to be started and maintained in the stove in the center of the hut, and there was no toilet or shower.

There were a community toilet and shower facility at the end of the row of huts with hot water heated by a coal furnace; this fire, too, had to be maintained. There was also a common mess facility with gas-burning cooking units. The mess facility was sufficient; this was our Base Camp. On the 29th of October 1963, we started field training (ORT), where we would train for thirty-six hours without sleep moving from one designated firing position to another, firing the big guns, and laying miles of field wire from the Fire Direction Center (FDC) to the Observatory Post (move, shoot) and radio communication also had to be maintained. Our mission was to communicate effectively as if we were in a combat environment. Wire lines had to be laid between each gun battery and the headquarters switchboard A, B, and C. Battery; each was responsible for their individual wire lines, and headquarters was responsible for the twenty-mile wireline to the OP.

This responsibility was divided between four-wire teams, Jones, Weekly, Goldstein, and me. I was back at base camp on the 31st of October 1963, and I was promoted to Sergeant E5 for four years and seventeen days in the army with sixteen years to go; I had decided to make the army a career. I wrote to Odessa and told her about my promotion and that I did not have a picture of her. Soon after, she sent me a picture of herself and congratulated me. She also asked if this exchange meant that I would be sending her an engagement ring. However, I knew that I would not. I thought I should tell Odessa that I did not want to marry until I was back in the states. The next letter I got from her, she told me she was going to get married to a guy that she had been seeing before she began to see me, Sam McGee. For some reason, I did not think she would be happy with him. However, she wanted to get married. I wrote her and told her I would always love her and hope she would be happy. A while later, someone told me she had moved to Detroit with Sam.

To drive in Germany, one needed an international driver's license; you also needed a US Forces license plate for your car. I took the test for the international license and passed, and I also got license plates for my car. Upon my return from Graff, I picked up my car from the port in early December 1963, driving back from which was a new experience.

The Thunderbird was able to hold its own on the Autobahn. One particular evening, I topped it out at one hundred and fifty-four miles an hour, passing everything on the autobahn. However, I was sure there would be other days when I would be left in the dust of a Mercedes or Porch or the hog of some other autobahn. In the Thunderbird, on my first visit to Frankfurt, Specialist 4th Class Brown from the wire section and I met two crazy Germany Girls who wanted to have a foursome. So, the first time I was in bed with a white woman, there were two of them. I did not know what to think when the girls said we would share a single room for the night. At first, I asked what we would do in just one room, to which they asked if we did not want to make love to them.

"I think so!" I replied to them.

"Will I make love to both of you?" I asked them. They ask

"Do you want to?" They replied.

So, Brown and I agreed to make love to these two not bad-looking girls; both of them had dark hair and were about the same size, 5'9". They looked like they weighed about one hundred and thirty pounds; they said they were nineteen and twenty, respectively. We all got into the Thunderbird, and they gave me the direction to the hotel, where we would all spend the night. It was Saturday night, and, luckily, there was no formation at camp on Sunday. The hotel was only several blocks away from the bar; I drove the distance and found a safe parking space.

They asked for money for the room, went to pay the clerk, and got the key. The room was sixty German Marks or about $20 USD and was on the second floor of the hotel: room 207. We took the elevator, and when we got to the room, I had another surprise, there was only one queen-sized bed. However, it was no surprise to the girls. They both undressed and got on the bed.

"Why are you waiting? Do you want us to undress you?" They asked me.

They were both having fun and laughing. So, I thought to join in the fun and requested that I be undressed. It was the nineteen-year-old that took me upon my request. And the twenty-year-old began to undress Brown. Once we were all undressed, we were all in the small space of the queen size bed together, touching one another and going through every stage of having sex and enjoying each other's bodies. I was surprised again when both girls did not agree to change partners. My girl and I stayed on our side of the bed, while Brown and his girl stayed on their side of the bed until morning. We all went and found the Thunderbird and found a McDonald's for breakfast.

The girls wanted to hang out with us for the rest of the day. However, Brown and I were not so sure; we wondered why the two girls were inseparable. Did they feel safe when they were together? I was not so sure that I enjoyed the night as much with two girls and a guy, or if I ever wanted to have a foursome or threesome, I think one girl at a time is the best way to go.

Germany

I was now in Germany, and from my first night in the town, three years would be a new experience for 'Mammy Black Baby.' I had been told by a soldier who had spent several years in Germany that my 6'2", 195-pound frame would not escape Germany without being married to a German woman (*Frauline*). I disagreed with him, of course. (I am sure I will marry someone someday), however, it will be to a black woman and have black children when I do. I learned early on in Germany that *Fraulines* were attracted to me, so I played my game. I had a beautiful American car, I dressed well, and a 22-year-old sergeant in the U.S. Army; I had almost everything going my way. In December 1963, in between one-night stands, I met a nineteen-year-old *Frauline* named Virginia – I liked her a lot. On weekends I would pick her up at the Frankfurt Train Station, and we would get a hotel room for the weekend. We would go out to the local clubs near and around Frankfurt. The only thing about Virginia that was good but not good for her was she was a freak for good sex, and she never got enough.

One night, we were at a nightclub when three African gentlemen approached me. One had a knife pulled and asked, "What have you been doing with my woman, man?"

Virginia jumped in front of me and said, "No!"

And out of nowhere, a friend of mine that I did not know was in the club pulled a pistol to the African gentleman's head and told him to get out of the club are he would drop him where he stood.

Afterward, I asked Virginia, "Who was the African?" She told me that he was her old boyfriend who won't leave her alone. I thanked my friend for coming to my rescue and took Virginia to the train station, after which I did not see her again for several months. In January 1964, I was assigned to the Seventh Army Non-commissioned Officers' Academy in Bad Toelz, Germany.

The Academy is the most prestigious NCO leadership school in the U.S. Army. The school taught Drill and Ceremonial, Ground Navigation, Public Speaking, Lesson Plans, Principle of Leadership, Leadership Traits, Physical Training and Combat Operation Orders. Many students failed to pass the course. In fact, only 132 students pulled through. Student number 45 Montgomery, Julius P. Headquarters Battery 6th Battalion 9th Artillery Graduation, standing at Number 85, graduated 47 from the bottom of the class, which was not outstanding, but as many as fifty students had failed – I was happy to graduate.

Graduation day was on the 28th of February 1964. Three days after the Battalion, moved from Frankfurt Hoechst, McNair Kaserne (APO 757, US Forces) to Rivers

Barracks, Giessen, Germany (APO 169, US Forces). Five hundred eleven enlisted men made this move with me, out of which twenty-eight were Officers, while three were Warrant Officers.

From the 24th of January, the same year, until the 28th of February, the Thunderbird was in a compound at Frankfurt Hoechst. I had to go to Frankfurt to pick up my car, so I thought I would look up Virginia for one last night with her. I found her at her favorite nightclub, The Sloes Bar. She wanted to know where I had moved to, so I came clean; we agreed to ride to Giessen in the Thunderbird and for her to take a train from Giessen back home.

We selected a nightclub in Giessen, had a few drinks, and got a hotel for the night, Virginia was her old self, and I thought that I was going to miss the great sex that we enjoyed together or would I look her up again in her favorite hangouts in Frankfurt. I knew she was not a one-man woman, but neither was a one-woman man. We were two of a kind made for each other in the early morning hours, lost in a sea of lust and pleasure. On the 1st of March, Virginia caught the train from Giessen back to her home near Frankfurt. I reported to my new duty station in Giessen. I was sure there would be many new Fraulines willing to be seen with the tall black solder in the maroon Thunderbird in and about Giessen, Germany. Rivers Barracks was a small compound compared to an Army Post. It had a Motor Pool for the large guns (each gun section had a small building to house equipment necessary to maintain a gun section). Another for wheel vehicles. Large hanger-like buildings to service the large guns and another for wheel vehicles, building to service wheel vehicles. There were smaller buildings for communication equipment, such as radio and wire sections.

In the compound's center was a parade field for the military, such as ceremonial events; the flagpole and a two-story large building housed Battalion Headquarters at the head of the parade field. Two-story large Barracks that housed personnel faced the parade field on two sides. And at the end of the parade field facing battalion headquarters was another large building that housed the NCO Club Snack Bar Reenlistment Office, the Chaplain Office, and a general meeting room. Other facilities included an EM Club (the Rendezvous) and. A chapel, a barbershop, the USO, and aparket lot the compound was enclosed, with a front and rear gate. Guards were posted at the front gate, and the back gate was only opened during training exercises. The barrack's capacity is approximately six hundred men. NCO rooms were separate from squared bays that were quarters for personnel in pay grade E4 and below. As a young Sergeant just out of the Seventh Army Noncommissioned Officers' Academy, SFC White, the Chief of the battalion wire section, wanted me to bunk with him. This was the last place I wanted to be. I knew it would not last long because I would have a busy schedule. 1) I needed a lot of room for my civilian clothes and shoes 2) I would be coming and going most of the time. And 3) I did not have the time to devout to talking army and about the troops, and I knew that was all he was about.

I tried for an after-duty job as a bouncer at the Rendezvous Club. The manager hired me and would work there for the next three years. I enjoyed the work of keeping the peace. Everyone soon learned that I was a no non-sense fair guy, So I had very few problems with the enlisted men that were about my age. There were always a few who wanted to test you, but after several out headfirst, they got the message. The Rendezvous closed at 2200 hours (10 pm); the time for bed check for soldiers in pay grade E4 and below was 2400 hours (12 midnight) for me. This was a good time to go downtown Giessen to check out the bars. Most of the soldiers have already returned to post, leaving their girlfriends free to do as they pleased. Early on, I met a young Frauline who was a bar girl (girls who got men to buy them drinks that were only colored water but very expensive). She had asked me to buy her a drink. I told her I did not buy drinks for girls that I did not know. She said that she would buy me a beer, and she did. I asked her what time did she get off? She said she got off when the bar closed and after she got paid for her night's work. I ask if I could drive her home. She asked what kind of car I had; she guessed Mercedes because I dressed so nice. Like someone that would drive a nice car. I told her I did drive a nice car, maybe nicer than a Mercedes. She said she would think about me driving her home.

I sat at my table along, and she sent over another beer. When the club was closing, she asked me to wait for her. I waited for her with the third beer that she had bought for me, and once she and the other girls and the manager got through talking in Germany over the night profit, she came to my table and said less go! Her Name was Renada, and if I could think of someone, she looked like it would be Elizabeth Taylor. Renada lived in a one-bedroom apartment on the second floor of an apartment house about half a mile from the 'Star Bar' where she worked. The apartment had very little furnishing and was heated by a steam heat radiator. After we were in bed and had made love, she asked if I would let her drive my car. I asked if she had a driver's license. She said no; I told her when she got a driver's license, she could drive my car. She said that eell, then I would be her gigolo. I asked her what a gigolo was. She said it was when someone was kept by a woman.

I asked her if she was saying she was willing to keep me. She said yes, as long as I was good to her and did not hit her or abuse her. I told her I would try to be her gigolo. She asked if I would pick her up from work every night from the 'Star Bar.' I told her I would pick her up when I could. This was in March 1964. What Renada wanted from me was to be there at the "Star Bar" to pick her up and to sleep with her. She did not keep me. I had a paycheck from the army and a paycheck from the Rendezvous each month. I had a car payment and a Taylor that kept up my wardrobe. I had to buy shoes and gas for my car. No, she did not keep me! But we had a good agreement I would be there for her, and the sex between us was good, and I did not have to give her any money. However, on weekends we did do things together that I paid for. We went to other nightclubs and did other things together. We had an agreement that I would not sleep with any of the other girls from the "Star Bar." But that did not work. On two occasions, I broke this agreement one was with a very young blond girl that always flirted with me even when Ranada was present. One night she played sick and asked if I would take her home, and as soon as we were in the Thunderbird, she kissed me on the lips and asked if I would make love to her.

I asked her where and she said she would show me. She stopped me on a dark street, and we made love in the back seat of the Thunderbird. Afterward, I dropped her off in front of her house and watched her go in. On another occasion, I was visiting the bartender's house from the 'Star Bar,' and a young girl that worked the bar on weekends was there, and somehow, she got me to make love to her on the couch in the living room with others in the dining room. Somehow Ranada learned of both occasions and told both girls to keep their hands off her man, or she would kick some ass! However, she said I was her man and "she knew what she had to do," whatever that meant. The relationship between Ranada lasted for the full time that I was in Germany, with me breaking the agreement with a one-night stand once in a while. The opportunity always presented itself at the Rendezvous; there was always Frauline willing even in the back of the Thunderbird. The soldiers called me 'Superman.' My duty at The Rendezvous and in Germany was not all bad. We at Rivers would go to designated firing positions, and about two load-out alerts a month, with the big guns, we kept the equipment ready for combat; we had other sections that would go to all of their assigned positions. These were mostly practice alerts. If it was the real thing, we would also go into combat from these positions. These guns had nuclear capabilities and were prepared to take on any Soviet threat.

Our other training was at Graff, once in the summer and once in winter to fire the big guns. After many years in the army, our old wire Chief SFC White was not allowed to reenlist. We had a new Wire Chief (SFC Duncan) who was more civilized and managed the section, with everyone pulling his weight. Under SCF Duncan (A Black Man), Graff was much easier; the impossible was not attempted. For example, SFC White would try to lay the wireline across the country without first reckonoton it. He would look on the map that may or may not be up to date and instruct the wire teams to take the close distance between two points, often running into impassable terrains such as swamps or ditches. We would waste hours winching our way out or calling for assistance. Our Platoon Sergeant Master Sergeant Rominger would reprimand SFC White for taking shortcuts, and he would try taking shortcuts repeatedly and again. He was rarely successful, making the entire wire section look inefficient. Under our new Wire Chief (SFC Duncan), the wire teams followed known routes, sometimes laying two to five miles or more wire but getting the job done. In garrison under SFC Duncan, we had a more constructed training program such as Standard Operation Instruction (SOI) and Standard Signal Instruction (SSI); this gave the communication persons the ability to receive and send coded messages. Training is a must a when a unit goes to combat. The new leadership in the wire section gave the communication platoon a new direction. And duty at Rivers Barracks Giessen Germany was good. With alerts only about two times a month and training at Graff only two months out of the year gave the small concern a lot of time for parades and ceremonies; the small parade field got lots of use, making the concern more patriotic with two units in one morning. On the small concern, there was a parade every Saturday with my 6'2", 195 pound frame. I was one of the Honor Guards (Color Guard) that led the parade for almost three years that I was at Rivers Barracks Giessen, Germany; another Honor Guard was Sergeant Gross, also about 6'2" and 200 pounds (Black Soldier).

Being an honor guard called for standing for thirty minutes at a time, then the marching caused my knee injury problems, but I liked the spotlight, so I did not complain. Working at the Rendezvous Club, Honor Guard, having a steady girl to pick up every night, and being a wire team chief made the time pass fast; however, I did find time with Renada when she took off from the "Star Bar" to go to other nightclubs and restaurants. Renada never stops bugging me about driving the Thunderbird. One night we were out on a deserted road, and I gave in to her request. She took the wheel, hit the gas, and ran directly into the guard-rail on the side of the road, causing several hundred dollars in damage to my car. All she could say when I said, "See, you have destroyed my car, new I should have never let you drive!"

"Yes, but we will make great love tonight!" at that point, I was not sure if I wanted to make love to her, or even put up with her anymore? But I took the wheel, and we went on to the next town, to a small bar, and ordered a bottle of wine. She tried to talk about all of the other girls that she knew I was sleeping with, I told her that was talk, and I told her I was going to make her pay for the repairs on the car, and she said that she would, but she insisted that I was sleeping with other Fraulines.

I asked her why she ran my car into the rail, and she smiled. I told her if I thought that she could drive and run my car into the rail on purpose, I would beat her ass. She wanted to dance, but I did not feel like dancing; I knew I would get the car fix as soon as I could. I looked in the German telephone directory and found a body and paint shop that would repair the car and paint it for seven hundred dollars. The following week I put the car in the repair shop for repairs and changed the color to a metallic blue. I did not like the blue as much as the maroon, but it was OK, and everyone did not recognize the car so easily. I did smack Renada once; she was again bugging me about sleeping around and said she could do the same if she wanted to, and there was several Sergeant that knew me and had asked her to be their woman because I was not good for her. I smacked her and told her not to discuss me with other men, but I think she did sleep with a couple of guys in the Giessen area. We never had a real fight about it because I think we had a good sleeping arrangement. She worked the club for drinks, and I picked her up once I got off from the Rendezvous Club. The sex was good, and we enjoyed being together around and about Giessen in the Thunderbird.

On the 26th of April 1966, I was called to Battalion Headquarters and told that my duty tour in Germany had been curtailed. I served in Germany from October 1963-April 1966 for two and a half years. SFC Turner was detailed to drive my car to port for shipment to NJ. I was told that I would depart Germany for Fort Dix, NJ, from Rhain Main Air Force Base on the 30th of April 1966. I was authorized thirty days leave and will report to USA AMC (OCS) NLT on the 26th of May 1966. Upon arrival at Fort Dix, NJ, I traded the 1960 Thunderbird for a 1966 Chevy (Super Sport) with the paperwork for my Thunderbird and my orders. I drove non-stop (except for gas) to my hometown of Clermont, Florida. I felt bad that I did not tell Renada goodbye. I wonder how often a GI had left Germany without telling his Frauline a goodbye?

Renada had asked me to marry her on several occasions. I had told her my mother would not approve of me marrying a white woman. She had asked if I would give her my mother's address so she could write to her. I never did. I never thought I was too good to marry a 'Bar Girl'; I just thought maybe I loved her or maybe not. I also believed that a mixed marriage in Florida would not work in 1966. However, some black GIs from the south did marry their Fraulines. Odessa was now married, so there was no one girl in Clermont for me.

Home again

So, I made myself available to the field. Within the three weeks that I was in Clermont, I slept with four or more women there for the taking, and the black community of Clermont is tiny. I remember when Eddie and I first left Clermont in 1959; I had been reluctant to approach a woman for sex. Now, after Fort Jackson, Thailand, and Germany, it is not a second thought and is a part of every thought of mine. I guess it has always been so, but I had been taught to respect women, and I still do. But I have also learned that women are a little different from men when it comes to sex. In Fort Jackson, it was sex for money; this was quite simple and uncomplicated. In Thailand, it was also sex for a very low price. In Germany, I never met a prostitute; however, I know that in Germany, some towns are famous for prostitution, the same as strip clubs in Las Vegas, and I am also sure some 'Bar Girls' in Germany did have sex for money, but I have never approached them that way, nor was I ever approached in Clermont to pay for sex.

The times that I paid for sex were because it was convenient for me to do so. Like in Oakland, on my return from Hawaii, I thought the woman was going out of her way to render a service. We had no other connection, nor did we wish to have it that way – once again, it was just convenient! I had feelings for maybe only one girl in high school – Vivianloria Thompson. I was only sixteen, and then there was Odessa. Ranada, too, was an arrangement, but maybe I did love her.

But now, I was on my way to Fort Sill for the second time in my short career of four years. During my previous tour at Fort Sill, I was too busy trying to get promoted for girls. This time, I was sure, would be different; I was now a sergeant with a new sports car, and I was sure I would have more time. My drive was a long one in 1966. The Equal Accommodation law of 1965 had just been passed, and motels in the south were still not accepting colored folks.

Clermont to Fort Sill was about sixteen hundred miles, so I would drive straight through, stopping only for gas and at rest stops during daylight for an hour or so at a time. For safety reasons, I was afraid to stop at night; the drive took twenty-four hours. Upon arrival at Fort Sill, I was assigned quarters at Staff and Faculty Battery with others that taught at the Officer Candidate School (OCS). My 1966 Chevy still had temporary license plates, and I had an international driver's license. I visited the Department of Public Safety and got a driver's handbook and Oklahoma plates for my car. A week later, I took the driver's test and failed the driving part of the test. The instructor said I drove with only one hand on the steering wheel and the other on the gearshift. It would be two weeks before I could take the driving part of the test again. As an instructor, I taught Officer Candidate Student, Radio Procedure, Standard Signal Instruction (SSI), and Standard Operational Instruction (SOI). For instructors that had quarters at Staff and Faculty Battery, there were no formations.

There was a bulletin board where information was posted. I had a friend who was also my driver the last time I was at Fort Sill. He had wrecked my truck with two others aboard, and I had to sweat getting my promotion. Major Boardingham lived in a small town (Anadarko), North of Fort Sill. He also had a sister that I had seen only once, and I thought she was really cute. I wanted to get to to know her then, and now maybe I could. On my first weekend at Fort Sill, I drove to Anadarko and looked up Major. He introduced me to his sister, Alfreader, the beginning of a six-month relationship. The following week I re-took the driving part of the driver's license test, and this time, I kept both hands on the steering wheel; I passed the test and finally got my Oklahoma driver's license. During the next six months, I only talked to two other women (who were friends), and the third was Alfreader. The drive from Anadarko to Fort Sill was less than an hour-long, and I could easily make it every day. The town was small, and there was no motel available to colored people, so most of my sex encounter with Alfreader was on a country road in the back seat of the Chevy, except when we were in Lawton or Oklahoma City, where I could gain access to a motel.

I made friends with several other Fort Sill Soldiers who had girl's friends in Anadarko or Chickasha, a town just west of Anadarko. Sergeant Jackson, Sergeant Watson, and I would meet at a small restaurant, Sarge Place, in Anadarko with our girls for hot links and beer. Across the street was a barbecue restaurant with the best barbecue in Oklahoma where Barbara, Major's wife, worked that catered to mostly white people. We would often do take-outs (of pork ribs and beef brisket). Anadarko was almost like home, the comradeship between us was good, and we knew almost every colored family within the small colored community. Major had a good job (working at the local carpet factor as a carpet dyeing expert) according to colored standards, and with his wife, Barbara, he had a nice home for themselves and their two children. He was someone that was looked up to within the community.

There was also a great deal of respect for young army sergeants such as Watson, Jackson, and me. All of us were concerned about being shipped out to Vietnam; we all knew we would be shipped sooner or later. However, in the meantime, being an instructor at the Artillery and Missile School for Officer Candidate Students at Fort Sill was a really important and prestigious job. Each block of instruction was subject to inspection by a superior officer that would often critique and, if found not to be up to par, could reflect on the instructor's annual evaluation report. Getting ready for a block of instruction required research and practice. Annual evaluation reports were the means by which a soldier's career was dictated. Among the lot, SSG Jackson was the most respected because 1) he was one grade higher than the rest of us and 2) because of his job (an Artillery Fire Direction expert), which was rare for a colored soldier in the sixties. The job required one to be good at math, slide rules, and algorithm, and he worked in an Artillery Fire Direction Center, the heart of an Artillery unit.

Often colleges and universities Reserve Officers Training Candidates who would become Artillery Officers would Train with the school during the summer. I was assigned to teach a Standard Signal Instruction (SSI) and Standard Operation Instruction (SOI) class for College and University students. And in one of my classes was a university student from Clermont, Florida, by the name of Mack Fogle. Mack was from a single-parent family, and his mother was Ms. Rose. All of his brothers were outstanding; Albert, who was my age, was a community organizer. George was an outstanding football player who, unfortunately, was killed in a car accident before he could play at the next level, and Geane was an apartment and property manager.

Mack, after completing his military obligation, owned property in several cities, including Clermont, Florida, that his brother Geane managed. On the 7th of October 1966, I received orders for Vietnam with a departure date of the 15th of November, 1966. The orders read that the individual will arrive in Vietnam wearing khaki trousers and short sleeve shirt. And will have in their possession basic required summer uniforms, work uniforms, and combat boots. On the 15th of October, I visited Anadarko for the last time and told everyone I was en route to Vietnam after a thirty-day leave that I would spend with my family in Florida.

I headed the Chevy toward Chickasha on highway 62, from where I would take highway 81 to 35 to 10 to 75 and finally into the Central Florida turnpike into Clermont. The trip would take about twenty-four hours, and I would have traveled across Oklahoma, Texas, Louisiana, Mississippi, and Alabama. I would leave my car with my sister Gloria and her husband Speedy and fly out to Fort Lewis, Washington. My thirty days at home would be in the same small town of Clermont.

With the old Jim Crow Southing laws, there was little for a colored person to do for entertainment in 1966. But for the most part, girls were willing, and again, for the most part, entertainment was in the back seat of the Chevy on a country road. There was no golf at the country club or drinks at the local bar with the guys, nor were there motels that were available for a guy and his girl. But there was war, and soon, I would be in the heart of it. On the 12th of November 1966, Speedy, my brother-in-law, took me to the Orlando airport, where I bought a ticket for Tacoma, Washington, to be processed for air departure to Vietnam from Fort Lewis.

Vietnam

O n the morning of the 15th, troops, including myself, were bused to the McChord Air Force Base for departure to Camp Alfa, South Vietnam, with a layover in Japan, for refueling. At the layover, we were not permitted to leave the aircraft. For twenty-three hours, we were on one aircraft. Upon landing in South Vietnam, we departed the aircraft in single file through a single gate; the compound was encircled with razor wire with guards in elevated sandbagged bunkers with machine guns every fifty feet or so. It looked like a war zone! We were housed in large tents with sandbags about knee-high around each tent; I did not feel safe. We were briefed and were told through a loudspeaker announcement that we were to get on the floor until an *all-clear* was given; there would be three formations a day, and at each formation, we would be given an assignment to a unit somewhere in South Vietnam.

I still felt unsafe. I was in a war zone without a gun! After two days, on the morning of the 17th of November 1966, I was given an assignment: Battalion 69th Armor in Pleiku, the Central Highlands of South Vietnam. At about 10:00 hours, I was on a Caribou Army Cargo aircraft headed for the central highlands of South Vietnam. It was about an hour-and-a-half long flight. Upon landing in Pleiku, we witnessed a tall, 6'3" white soldier with starched jungle fatigues, a 45-pistol strapped to his side, and an M16 rifle; with his hand in the air, said anyone for the 69th Armor.

I held up my hand, and he walked over to me with his hand extended and said, "I am Sergeant Summerville, better known as 81 Charley Fox Trot. I am the company supply clerk and your transportation to Company A. The company is presently on-road security with forwarding base camp about 15 miles south of Pleiku. I'll take you out tomorrow after we get you your basic combat gear and a m16.

"There's one issue," I told him. "Are you a Communication Sergeant replacing Sergeant Jackson?"

"Oh! You will be his replacement for some time. He is our Commo/Operation Sergeant, mostly operation," he said. Sergeant Summerville was a very friendly, likable, and talkative individual.

He gave me a quick history of the unit. The unit is really the Third Brigade of the 25th Infantry from down south around Hobo Woods that escorted the Fourth Infantry Division to the Central High Lands. They are like on loan to the Fourth Infantry Division. The Fourth Infantry Division Third Brigade is still down South with the 25th Infantry. We still wear the 25th patch. We call our base camp Third Brigade Hill. The ride from Pleiku Airstrip to Third Brigade Hill, was a short one, upon arriving, Summerville told me where I would sleep; less get you your issue. I was given a cot, sleeping bag, a shelter, half tent pegs, rope, tent poles, three sets of jungle fatigues, three OD T-shirts, shorts, jungle boots and an M14 rifle, a bandoleer of ammunition, a steel helmet, and a bullet proof vest. He told me to pack my khaki and other gear in a bag that he gave to me with a tag to put my name on and gave me a place to store it in the supply room. You will need them a year from now.

The following morning, we headed for the forward base camp. Once outside of base camp, he told me to put a clip in my rifle and put on my bulletproof vest; we were about forty miles per hour on the dirt road with jungle on each side, and he said this was combat. He said our tanks were positioned at each checkpoint along the jungle road with Infantry in between. It was time for him to check in with forwarding base camp by radio to tell them he had departed base camp with the new "81Zero" (Communication / Operation Sergeant) "81Zero This is 81 Charley Fox Trot Over."

"81Charley FoxTrotThisIs810, Over"

"810 This Is 81 Charley Fox Trot Departing Base CampWith The New810 Will Contact You When Reached Check Poin Alfa, Over." Check Point Alfa is now a hard-top road, and we could see the M48A3 Main Battle Tank with its crew on-road security duty. Sergeant Summerville pulled into the checkpoint and introduced me to Pappy, Platoon Sergeant of the third platoon, and three of his men, who put in an order for beer and sodas on his next trip out.

Summerville contacted forward base camp and reported that we were departing checkpoint Alfa for checkpoint Bravo. As we passed checkpoint Bravo, we waved and radioed to forward base camp that we had passed checkpoint Bravo and would report in at checkpoint Charley, the last checkpoint before reaching forward base camp. Beer, sodas, and cigarettes were combat issues for combat troops and could be picked up at the G4 lot at base camp; ice was another story. That had to be bought off the local market. We reported passing checkpoint Charley and would be at the forward base camp in fifteen minutes. Upon reaching forward base camp, I was introduced to the company 1" Sergeant, a man of Asian descent from Hawaii, who introduced me to the company Commo/Operation Sergeant. Sergeant Jackson (A Colored Sergeant) is a laid-back kind of guy that plays the Guitar. His assistant, Specialist 4th Class Cathguarth (Also Colored), was the company radio repairman. Road Security was laid back kind of duty for a tank company.

It was the same old thing every day, so there was not much for a Commo/Operation Sergeant to do but take sit-reps (Situation Reports) from the checkpoints; most reports were negative reports. Infantry was also on duty with each tank both the tankers and Infantry made their report to the tank platoon leader, who was a Lieutenant. The Lieutenant made his report to the Operation Sergeant every hour, who made a record for the company commander. However, without this security, supplies and resupplies could not reach a division-size unit, thereby cutting off operation within an area or theater. Road security in combat operations is a must, if not by tanks, then by escorts, heavy-armed wheel vehicles that lead supplies through a suspected enemy area. My armor tank company during the Vietnam war was made up as follows. Five tanks per tank platoon and two tanks assigned to the headquarters platoon. The Company Commander had his own tank. He also had a jeep with a driver. The 1" Sergeant supervised the dozer tank. He had his own jeep and driver. The Supply Sergeant had a 1/4 ton truck and a jeep driven by the supply clerk. The Mess section had a 24-ton vehicle and a driver, and five cooks. Motor Sergeant had a 1/4-ton truck, Vehicle/Tank Retriever, and five mechanics. Ammunition Sergeant had 2½ ton vehicles with two helpers. Any changes) Communication/Operation Sergeant had an M113 Armored Personnel Carrier Modified to Carry Radios Used as the Combat Mobile Headquarters for The Company. Everything that happened within Company A, 1st Battalion 69th Armor came through the Mobile Headquarters. The mission was received by code and had to be decoded by hand; this sometimes took hours using Standard Signal Instruction (SSI) (Road Security Was the Exception Because There Were Few If Tank Platoon Organization: Each tank's personnel number consists of the platoon number, followed by the vehicle number. There is no number one; instead, the number six is used as the universal command number.

Company Commander 6

Platoon Leader 1 Platoon 1-6 (1" Lieutenant)

Line Tank 1-2(Staff Sergeant)

Line Tank 1-3(Staff Sergeant)

Platoon Sergeant and Second in Command 1-4(Sergeant 1st Class)

Line Tank 1-5(Staff Sergeant)

Platoon Leader 2nd Platoon 2-6(1" Lieutenant).

Line Tank 2-2Staff Sergeant)

Line Tank 2-3(Staff Sergeant)

Platoon Sergeant and Second in Command 2-4(Sergeant 1st Class)

Line Tank 2-5(Staff Sergeant)

Platoon Leader 3-6 3rd Platoon (1" Lieutenant)

Line Tank 3-2(Staff Sergeant)

Line Tank 3-3(Staff Sergeant)

Platoon Sergeant and Second in Command 3-4(Sergeant 1st Class)

Line Tank 3-5(Staff Sergeant)

Tankers Responsibilities

Tank Commander: He is responsible for the vehicle, its maintenance, and performance in battle and is also the most likely to be killed in battle.

Gunner: Normally in control of the main gun and the second in command of the tank.

Loader: Responsible for feeding all weapons and keeping supplies stocked

Driver: Drives tank and maintains engine, tracks, and electrical system

As Commo/Operation Sergeant for Company A, 1" Battalion 69th Armor from December 1966 to November 1967, working as the extension of the company commander, I received operation orders sometimes in code with groups that exceeded one hundred. (While on-road security, the operation order was within a known area and would probably read no change from one day to the next.) However, in every enemy contact or during normal operation, as operation sergeant, I was available to assist. Suppose the tank commander needed ammunition, fuel, air support, medical extraction of the wounded (Medevac), food, vehicle extraction or repair, radio repair, Infantry and engineer support, maps, and direction to known enemy contact where a tank could assist. In Vietnam, my call sign was 81-0, which was available to company A, 1" Battalion 69th Armor 24/7.

On one occasion in February 1967, while on-road security, with the forward base camp stationed at the Oases, a platoon of Company A tanks was moving on a road south of Pleiku near the rock quarry when command-detonated mines exploded, disabling all five tanks. The Platoon Leader called 81-0 for assistance. I called Captain DeMount, who was the company commander during that time. His instruction to the Platoon Leader was to buckle up and load canister rounds, and if the enemy mounted any tank, for each tank to fire canisters on each other. In the meantime, I called the Air Force to deliver NAPALM on each side of the road where the tanks were downed; I gave the Air Force the location on the map. Upon identifying the target, the pilot radioed, the target was identified, and two low-flying aircraft dropped their load of NAPALM on each side of the road of the downed tanks; I called for Infantry to search the area for bodies or enemy activity. We received a negative report. The Infantry maintained security for the tanks until they were repaired. Engineers were called to sweep the road for mines and both the Infantry and engineers with the tanks until they reached their new position.

This was the most activity I experienced during road security during my short time as operation sergeant for A. The following week, while still at the Oases, I received a one hundred and six-word group for tanks platoon with assigned Infantry to search suspected areas for rice in 50 100 pound containers and retrieve upon receiving the day's mission that took me most of the night to decode using a gas lantern and the assigned Standard Signal Instruction(SSI) Captain DeMount who doubted the mission until he had confirmed it with the assigned Infantry company commander that was given a rendezvous point to meet with the tank platoon. The day's mission was an active one, with tanks calling in each time they discovered a stash of rice. Several hundred pounds of rice were found. It was retrieved and given to the Montagnard Chiefs of the Central Highlands, who had first discovered the rice and reported it to higher headquarters. This was a major accomplishment. It had shortened the Vietcong food supply for several weeks or even months.

In March of 1967, Company A, 1 Battalion 69th Armor, was given a new mission. The company will be assigned to support the 1" Cavalry Forward Division at LZ. English (Bong Son). The order was for Company A to road march to Qui Nhon and board a Navy Ship (LST) on the South China Sea north and make a beach landing on the Bong Son Beach, about a twelve-hour voyage. The plan did not work. The Navy Ship was not able to make a beach land because the ship bottomed out, and the tanks would sink if they tried to go inland. The plan was revised. The ship returned to Qui Nhon, and each vehicle of company A was assigned to a single landing craft and made a twelve-hour vehicle landing craft. A Vehicle Tank Retriever, also weighing 52 tons assigned to a single back north on the South China Sea. Seventeen Tanks, every 52 tons, were assigned to a single landing craft. Two 2 1/2 Tons trucks each assigned to a landing craft. Two Jeeps trucks assigned to a landing craft. A ¼ ton truck assigned to a single landing craft. The M113 Communication/ vehicle sassigned to a landing craft. Each unit had a radio was communicate with the other.

I was assigned to a tugboat with radio and maintained the status of each unit. The idea was if any landing craft got into trouble, the tugboat would come to its rescue. The combat voyage beaching at Bong Son Beach was reminiscent of the Normandy invasion. We took the beach without any causalities and road marched into Bong Son city and on to Landing Zone (LZ) English without any major incident. The outstanding memories of Bong Song are the day-to-day enemy contact at the forwarded location of the company and the impact awards of The Purple Heart, Bronze Star, Silver Star, Soldier's Medal, and Medal of Honor also:

General Orders Number 878: the 16th of April 1970

AWARD OF THE VALOROUS UNIT AWARD TC 439 The following AWARD is announced.

By direction of the Secretary of the Army, under the provisions of paragraph 202. 1g (2) AR 672 5-1, the Valorous Unit Award is awarded to the following named unit of the United States Army for extraordinary heroism while engaged in military operations during the period indicated:

The citation reads as follows:

COMPANY A, 1ST BATTALION, 69TH ARMOR, 4TH INFANTRY DIVISION distinguished itself by extraordinary heroism while engaged in military operation during the period the 30th of May by 1967 to the 3rd of July 1967, in Binh Dinh Province, Republic of Vietnam. While in support of the 1 Cavalry Division (Airmobile), unit personnel participated in numerous tank-infantry assaults on well-entrenched and heavily armed North Vietnamese Army and Viet Cong forces. Using the shock effect of Armor to the fullest, they aggressively engaged the enemy with 90mm guns, coaxial machine guns, and often times due to the close-quarter fighting, utilized hand grenades to dislodges to dislodge the enemy from his well-fortified position. Demonstrating great determination and a remarkable grasp of the tactical situation, the men of COMPANY A, 1st Battalion 69TH ARMOR, 4TH INFANTRY DIVISION skillfully located hostile emplacements and ably supported ground assault troops by delivering the heat of battle. Tank crewmen employed their vehicles as shields, and despite the intense enemy fire, they venit dismounted their vehicles suspiciously, and A, 1ST courageously assisted wounded comrades and evacuated them from the battle zone. Their brave and selfless action saved many lives and won respect and admiration of those with whom they served. The men of COMPANY A, 1ST BATTALION, 69TH ARMOR 4TH INFANTRY DIVISION, displayed extraordinary heroism and devotion to duty which are in keeping with the highest traditions of the military service and reflect distinct credit upon themselves and the Armed Forces of the United States.

The impact award of The Medal of Honor was awarded to SFC Hazelip (which was downgraded), The Silver Star was awarded to SFC Baggy, The Bronze Star Medal was awarded to SSG Trump and to several other members of Company A. The Purple Heart Medal was awarded

to Sgt Bell, SSG Watanabe and many others of Company
A, (The Medal of Honor was also awarded to Dwight H.
Johnson, a friend, of Company B, 1" Battalion 69th Armor.
Johnson's citation states that the Medal was awarded on the
15th of January 1968. This is a misprint. I was in the country
when the award was made, and I departed Vietnam in
November 1967.)

In November 1967, upon arriving at Pleiku, from the
Bong Son Plains by way of Qui Nhon and Mang Yang Pass,
Company A set up base camp south of Pleiku with on-road
security. Captain Allen was Company A's new commander.
All of the men of Company A were restless, road security
was boring, and now Company A was in a no-fire zone.
After being in a free-fire zone for the past eight months. The
local villages had been all searched by Infantry and Military
Intelligence. Dogs had been used to detect anything out of
the norm. Intelligence had left with me a Frequency to call in
case of suspected enemy activity. However, SFC Baggy, the
First Platoon Sergeant, reported receiving fire from a nearby
village and requested permission to take the village out! I
told him we were in a no-fire zone. He requested to speak
with the Company Command Captain Allen.

I called Captain Allen and First Sergent Quinton
to the operation bunker and told them the First Platoon
Sergeant, SFC Baggy, called and reported receiving fire from
the local village. I gave Captain Allen the information from
the intelligence report. Captain Allen requested that I get

SFC Baggy on the radio, and I did. He asked First Sergeant Quinton what his evaluation of SFC evaluati Baggly was? First Sergeant Quinton told Captain Allen that SFC Baggy was a Non-commission Officer of the highest caliber and recipient of the Silver Star Medal. After a few words between Captain Allen and SFC Baggy, Captain Allen gave Sergeant Baggy permission to fire on the village. On the command radio net, the command was given to Cease Fire! Cease Fire! Those in the village that was still alive were immediately evacuated by helicopter (Medevac). However, I saw many that were not alive and others that were dieing. There were broken limbs and mangled bodies. All were women and children. It was a massacre. The following day SFC Baggy was relieved of his duties. I was picked up by the Military Police and charged with another infraction (Fraud?) My records were flagged (no action could be processed on me).

Fort Meade, MD

My file was assigned to the 6th Armor Calvary. Regiment. Fort Meade, MD. After leave I reported to Fort Meade in December 1967. For several months while under flag, I had no assignment to a TO&E slot. After my record had been reviewed and after several interviews with the local commander at Fort Meade, the flag was lifted in March 1968, and I was assigned to A, Battery 2d Sqd 6th Armor Cavalry Regiment. On April 4, 1968, Reverend Martin Luther King was felled by an assassin's bullet. The violent death of Dr. King brought an immediate reaction to rioting in black ghettos around the country. The 6th Armor Calvary was only twelve miles from the Washington, DC area. The unit was quickly assigned to the DC area to assist local law. Enforcement. It was rumored that the rioting in the DC area was controlled by the likes of the Black Panther Party, Stockley Carmichael, and H. Rap Brown. I was attached as a radio operator with the DC Police Department, which assigned me to a patrol car that reacted to hot spots, and/or sightings of Carmichael, members of the Black Panther Party, or H. Rap Brown. Fires were everywhere; in fact, it seemed that the entire city was on fire. My job was to inform the commander where the Army troops were needed for riot control or where the heavy consecration of would-be rioters was.

During the rioting, everyone was a looter. Police car trunks were filled with everything thinkable from Stereo Equipment and jewelry to cases of the best whiskey that they off-loaded from time to time in key locations within the city. During the rioting, "The God Father of Soul," James Brown agreed to put on a special concert to calm the riot. He was pumped through all the television channels, and he requested that everyone go home and stop the burning. The 6 Armor Calvary Regiment boasts about six hundred members, and the Battery made up about one hundred and twenty members, the number that was under my control. The riot lasted about a week. We slept in gymnasiums at high schools in our sleeping bags within the city communities. Each soldier was armed with an M16 rifle, and ammunition could be issued upon the request of the commander. These were serious times within this country. Once the cities throughout the country came to calm, military unity was reassigned to normal duty at their respective military installation.

At Fort Meade, I was assigned as Communication Chief for How Battery and was promoted to SSG E6 on 27 August 1968. During those months that I was under flag, I supported myself by playing poker with a partner (1sgt Joseph Barker) who was a card shark; he taught me the way around a poker game. In fact, during that time, I bought a new car 1969(442) Oldsmobile. After the flag was lifted and after the DC riots, I stopped playing poker for a living because I had an army paycheck. Playing poker for a living is not easy as one may think. In fact, it was an odd way to try and make a living. The Washington, DC, and Baltimore area was full of action. There was everything you could think of, from orgies to opium and pot-smoking parties. However, I did continue to see several of the girls that I met during these times. One was Gladys, from Lumberton, North Carolina, who was living with her sister Betty in Baltimore. Betty was one of Sergeant Barker's girls. Both sisters loved to party, and Gladys, only eighteen, had no sexual hang-ups. She lived for sex.

Another girl I met during my flagged period was Eleanor, from Annapolis, Maryland, who was a divorcee and wanted to get married. She always talked about building Hope's chest. She introduced me to everyone she knew as her future husband. When I told her I was not in love with her, I had to call one of her friends to stop her from crying. She said she would sue me for breach of promise. When I told her I never promised her I would marry her, she said she had a witness that I did. There were many other women whose names I can't remember. However, I remember their personalities, sex drive, and how much they liked the nightlife of D.C. and Baltimore. I was so ready to leave Fort Meade

Korea

Upon reenlisting on the 24th of February 1969, I requested an assignment to Korea. My port call date from Fort Lewis, Washington, was the 29th of April 1969, and I would arrive at my new duty station on 1 May 1969. I would do two additional months at Fort Meade in March and April, and I would have one month in Clermont. During this time, I tried to stop seeing Eleanor. However, she called my Bachelor Enlistment Quarters(BEQ) non-stop. I saw Gladys, who wanted to set up camp at my BEQ and did a pretty good job of it. I saw her even when I did not want to see her. It was always about sex. In early April, I told Gladys I was going home; she said she would meet me in Clermont after she went home to North Carolina if I would send her air fair. At first, I told her I would; however, after being home, I called and told her I did not have the money because I had to travel to Fort Lewis at the end of the month, and she was upset. Clermont was always the same, and the same old girls were always available and willing. However, this time it was a little different. I had to make a decision on who I would leave my new 1969(442) Oldsmobile with. For whatever reason, I decided to leave the car with my young brother Wilbert. Who did not have a car. The reporting time to Fort Lewis was No Later Than (NLT) 1200HR 29 April

1969. Enlisted members will arrive wearing Khaki trousers and short sleeve Khaki shirts and have in possession basic allowance of uniforms. The flight departed Fort Lewis at 1600HR and arrived in Seoul, Korea, mid-day on May 1st, 1969.

Korea was a cross between the training areas of Germany in Graf. And Vietnam, the living arrangement t was like Graf; in Germany and the working condition was more like Vietnam. The troops were housed in Quonset huts, heated with radiators. There were common toilet and shower facilities at the end of each row of Quonset huts, except for senior noncommissioned officers or those that were in senior noncommissioned officers' positions who had private facilities. Officer's quarters also had private toilets and shower facilities. In a Battalion size organization of M110 and M107 Artillery, guns capability of delivering a nuclear warhead into North Korea. It was made up of three Gun Batteries, a Service Battery, and a Headquarters Battery. The Battalion were surrounded by villages of mostly women and some men that worked at the military concern as houseboys who shined shoes and cleaned quarters for officers and senior noncommissioned officers for a price. Women offered the America GI anything, from home-cooked meals Korean style to sex. This was a contractual agreement between the GI and the Korean kept women called "YOBO" These small villages were set up outside of each Battery area to better serve the Gis. Many Gls married their "YOBO" and brought them home to the states.

I was a Staff Sergeant E6 who worked in a senior position from the time that I reported for duty in Korea until I left a year later after being given an assignment. My first order of business was to find a good houseboy, I found one in Mr. Kim, and then I visited the Village to find a "YOBO" I was introduced to a cute young thing with a quarter's American name of Debby, Debby had a young daughter about two years old. I agreed to try Debby as a "YOBO" for one month, and if it worked out, we would think of longer terms; the cost for rent for the first month was forty dollars. It was understood that other costs, such as food, would be as needed during the month; I paid Debby the forty dollars upfront. I was set.

My First senior position was as communication chief, an E8 position assigned to Headquarters & Headquarters Battery. The communication chief was in charge of a platoon of about forty men. The sections that made up this platoon was as follow: A field wire section that was normally headed by a Sergeant First Class E7, but under my command was headed by a fellow Staff Sergeant E6 with about twenty men. Men and equipment common to a field wire section were as follows Five three quarter ton trucks each with a Sergeant ES team chief, an E4 assistance team chief, an E4 and two E3s with ten miles of field wire, an A-frame for laying field wire and two field telephone for testing wire lines. A switchboard section with a three-quarter ton truck with trailer, two switchboards with necessary terminals, and four men; one E4 and three E3s. A radio section headed by a fellow Staff Sergeant E6, two radio operators E5 per radio truck, and four AM single sideband AM106es with radio teletype capability of communicate with the United States. A radio repair section with an E5 and an E4. The Communication headquarters section was made up of one Captain, the communication officer, an E4, and me, who was responsible for Standard Signal Instruction and Standard Operation Instruction, and in general, the operation of the communication platoon. The mission of the Battalion was to 1) Move, 2) Shoot, and 3) communicate. Communication was key in every facet of delivering a warhead to a designated target. Upon the arrival of an E8 Master Sergeant Berry, I was assigned to another Senior Position within the Battalion. This time it was the Intelligent (S2) section, also a section within the Headquarters Battery of the Battalion.

Early on in my assignment to Korea, I received two alarming letters from home from two different sources. A letter from Gladys is telling me that she had missed her period and could be pregnant. A few days later, I got a letter from her that she had caught her period. I was relieved. The other news from home was that my brother Wilbert had wrecked my new 442 Olds, and State Farm Insurance company had said it was beyond repair and had paid off the finance company of $2626.40. The insurance company also sent me a small check that made up the difference in the appraised value of the car. I visited the Post Exchange and applied the check toward the down payment on a 1970 Corvette. The Intelligent (S2) section of the battalion was almost like the communication headquarters of the communication platoon, but with a wider scope. Specialist 4th Class (Churchill) was the intelligent clerk, and a Captain, (Waltman), me. Made-up the S2 section. The files of the Battalion Intelligent Section covered every facet of the operation of the battalion. The S2 files are classified from unclassified to Top Secret. Storage of a nuclear warhead, moving of a nuclear warhead, security, Inspection of nuclear facilities, always under constant inspection and no room for error in preparation to fire a nuclear warhead.

Errors in an inspection based on the error could mean the removal of the structure of the unit. In this job, there was little time to s spend with your "YOBO" in the village. Files were always being taken from the S2 section, and it was my job to make sure the file was in the right place when it was returned. A file out of order could cause the breakdown of continuity for the battalion. I was on top of my game, and during the time that I was the Intelligent Sergeant, the battalion had no problems within the S2 section. Another job of the S2, was to process all security clearances within the battalion. This required direct communication with the FBI and NSA for background investigation to obtain security Clearance. Everyone within a nuclear battalion required a security clearance. Processing clearances within its itself was a full-time job. After several months I was relieved from the position and was assigned to another E8 position of Operation Sergeant (S3). This also was a demanding job responsible for training within the battalion. My replacement was Master Sergeant E8 (Stanley). Shortly after Stanley took over the S2 section, the battalion failed an inspection due to filing errors within the S2 section. This caused alarm throughout the Battalion.

The Battalion Sergeant Major had a nervous breakdown and was sent back to the states. For several weeks the Battalion received assistance from higher headquarters. It was on equal footing again. For whatever reason, no one was relieved of their command; however, several repairmen were given, which could cause serious problems in future assignments and promotions for a person of the command structure, including the Battalion Commander. As a S3 Sergeant, my third E8 position within the battalion since my assignment to the battalion was another high profile and heavy workload position. I was responsible for all the training within the battalion on a daily bases and special training, including familiarization and zeroing of personally assigned weapons. I was also responsible for field training and firing of the M110 Eight-Inch Howitzer and M107 175MM Guns that could deliver a nuclear warhead into North Korea.

These training exercises sometimes took place in the heart of winter, in 20 below zero weather along the demilitarized zone of South Korea; however, the most demanding exercise within the battalion involved almost all members. And maybe called at any time: When a nuclear alert is called, this requires members of the battalion to man their assigned post. Three authentication cards from three separate safes located in the S2 section require three key personnel to open an assigned safe and pull their assigned card, call cookie from each safe. When the card is open, if they all match, this could mean all systems go for the firing of nuclear warheads on their designated target unless there is a follow-up call to stand down. Nuclear alerts were called several times a month, both day and night. And key personnel had to be ready to react. Reaction time was within the hour, so persons in senior positions had to stay close to their posts. This meant that often time senior personnel "YOBO" visited them within their quarters, which required an escort for security.

Between assignments from Battalion Intelligent Sergeant to Battalion Operation Sergeant, I was assigned as Chief of Firing Battery within A, Battery of the Battalion. This was another key position responsible for four Eight Inch Gun sections, which were the nuts and bolts of an Artillery Battalion. I was assigned as Chief for only a brief period long enough to learn and experience the real hardship of a Field Artillerymen; a projectile or (warhead) weighed several hundred pounds with a fuse fitted to the projectile is required to be loaded into the breech of the gun by two men and rammed into place by an automatic rammer. Black gunpowder called charges is measured and put into place; behind the projectile and the breach is closed. A detonator is placed into the breach, the data from the fire direction center is relayed to the chief, and feed the gun instruments. Data, including deflection, elevation, etc., is given to the

Chief of the Section before the chief of the section gives the order to fire the gun. When the order to fire is given by the Chief of Section, a rope attached to the trigger mechanism on the breach is pulled, firing the gun. This is basically what a member of a gun section experiences when firing an M110 Eight Inch Gun or an M107 175MM Gun. However, much more than that is required. First, an orienting angle is Established, and the battery is laid at the battery level. At the headquarters level, surveying teams spend many hours surveying targets.

Also, at the headquarters level, Fire Direction uses instruments, maps, and computers to give effective data to the guns. And without good radio, AM & FM together with wire communication none of the above is possible. As the S3 Sergeant, I was also the Platoon Sergeant for S2, S3, forward observer (FO) who directed Artillery Fire from an Observation Post many miles from the gun in placement and the Fire Direction Section. During my assignment of one year in Korea, I served in every key NCO position accept survey, another E8 position within the headquarters battery. I was only an E6 with nine years of service. From my own observation over the years, if I were white, I would have been promoted to E7 during this period. On several occasions, the subject was brought up promoting me, but it was turned down because of time in grade and time in service, so they say. I also had one account on my records of disrespect of an officer at Fort Mead. I think if the black mark was not on my record, they would have had to promote me based on my track record during my year in Korea. But this was the sixties.

There was one other thing during my assignment. A black E6 who was about seven feet tall and about three hundred pounds from the medical section said I was an uppity nigger, and he wanted to kick my ass. He gave me a hard time every time he got the chance, especially during meals around other blacks. He was three hundred pounds or over, and I was 6'2" and about one hundred and ninety pounds. I agreed to fight him in a boxing match with an official referee. I explained that I had no reason to fight him other than to get him off my back: I had nothing against the big guy. The fight was set up as a battalion event and would be held at the concern gem. SSG E6 Gray of headquarters battery would be the referee. I was much faster than the big bully and got in some good punches during the first round. I think everyone in the gym was pulling for me. However, in the early minutes of the second round, the big guy caught me with a haymaker and knocked me out. I am sure I had a concussion because a month later, I was still having headaches from the devastating blow to the head. I served in Korea from April 1969 through March 1970. I should have served through April of 1970. However, ISG Colon of Headquarters Battery worked a deal with personnel to cut my tour short because it was rumored that a Private from the communication platoon, together with a 2nd LT, would bring charges against me for hitting the said Private.

I don't remember hitting anyone, but I do remember giving orders to several enlisted men in a restricted area (S2) who had to much drink and/or was high by other means, and one had said he would tell his Lieutenant that I had physically assaulted him and would bring charges against my black ass.. I suspect the Lieutenant himself was buddies with the said Private and may have also been a bigot. ISG Colon said the Private had several witnesses, and the Lieutenant had agreed to press charges against me. I agreed with the ISG and agreed to leave Koren a month early. A lot had to be done to get me out of the country. 1) I had to pack; I had a lot to pack Because I had so much time in my quarters spent due on my duties and had a lot of stuff. I had stereo equipment: A reel to reel Sony Tape Recorder, A record changer, Two Large Speakers, A Kenwood Amplifier, and stacks of records and tapes. I also had my basic military issue. 2) I had to have an assignment. The ISG said the assignment could be got by telephone, and I could be out of the country within days or as soon as I was packed. He said this could not be done for anybody, but I had served the battalion well and should not have to go through Something like this; he also said this would probably mean I would not be receiving any medals that I deserved, but I had a long career ahead of me, time for medals and accommodations. I had saved the boxes that my stereo equipment came in, so I was packed within several hours after getting the word from the ISG. My stuff with my military issue was taken to I Corps Headquarters and would be processed out upon getting an assignment.

Fort Hood, Texas

The following day I got my assignment. To Fort Hood, Texas, Headquarters 7th of 6 Infantry of the 2d Armor Division, I was assigned as Headquarters Company Communication Chief. I was again in an E6 position after serving in several E8 positions in Korea. My record showed that I had served in several E8 positions; however, I don't think anyone gave a dam. In 1970 division was authorized to promote to E7; however, the Department of the Army would take over this responsibility in the next physical year. Everyone on a Division list for promotion to E7 would be promoted prior to the Department of the Army taking this responsibility. I was not on a Division list for promotion. This meant several years could pass before I could be promoted. I knew of many undeserving E6s who were white that got their name on the Divisions list through favors or just because they had the time in the Army. I am sure if I were white with my record, I would have got on the Division list.

Several weeks after being at Fort Hood, my stuff from Korea arrived, my stereo equipment with my whole baggage, and my new corvette was also ready for pick-up in St. Louis, Mo. I took a two-week leave, picked up my stereo equipment and whole baggage, and locked it in my assigned quarters. I bought my car through the Post Exchange, so I needed Post Exchange paperwork to get the car financed. I got the car financed through the credit union on the post and flew to St. Louis. To pick up my car. I drove to Clermont, Florida, stayed for a couple of days, and went back to Fort Hood. I had almost everything. I had a suit for every day of the week, over twenty dress shirts, and a new corvette. But I should have been promoted to E7. I had worked for a promotion, and now it looks like it would be several years before I get the promotion. In May of 1970, I met Sergeant First Class Portwood. SFC Portwood was my platoon sergeant in Hawaii in 1960, more than ten years past. I told him that I did not make the Division E7 list after being in an E8 position for the past year in Korea. He told me that he had more than twenty-four years of service and was only an E7 but was happy with his career. He said rank was not everything. He said the position was more important than rank. I told him I was not happy with my current position and had requested a position as an Intelligent Analyst. He said that an Intelligent Analyst spent most of his time in the field grading division units, and I would not be happy in that position. He told me he was the assistant to III Corps and Fort Hood Career Counselor and could help me become a Career Counselor.

In this position, there would be little or no field duty, and you will have an office to yourself, with no requirement to make formations, and would come under the supervision of the Adjutant or the Battalion Commander. The Career Counselor Office had Special furnishing air-condition, a wooden desk, a leather high back chair, and leather office furnishing. You also would have clerical support at III Corps and Fort Hood level. About this time at Fort Hood, I saw several girls. Francis from Waco, Beth in Killeen, and Robbie in Austin; of the three, I was serious about Robbie, who was separated from her husband and had a two-year-old son (Joe). On the 28th of January 1971, my request to become an Intelligent Analyst was granted, and on 1 February 1971, I was assigned to the 163" Military Intelligence Battalion (Combat). The Battalion Mission was to test combat units and combat surveillance equipment. This was during the heart of the Vietnam War, and the unit was under extreme pressure and in the Field 100% of the time; in fact, the unit set up teams to rotate in and out of the field, testing units for combat readiness and combat surveillance to be used in Vietnam. SFC Portwood had advised me correctly about field duty as an Intelligent Analyst. Not only that, when I was assigned, there was only one black, an E4, assigned to my Intelligence Platoon; I was assigned as an assistance platoon sergeant. Most of the members of the platoon were draftees with four years of college, including the one black E4.

As an assistant platoon sergeant, I had a hard time getting anything accomplished, which was a first for me. During my first month after being assigned to the 163rd MI Battalion in late February, I made a request to attend the career counseling and recruiters course at the USA Adjutant

General School at Fort Benjamin Harrison, IN. I requested
SFC Portwood's assistance. For one to be selected to attend
the career counseling and recruiters' For one course, a packet
had to be submitted with a handwritten assay as Incl.#1
subject "My qualification for assignment as an assignment
as an Army Career Counselor/Recruiter."

My essay reads as follows: "I believe in loyalty
to any unit or organization that one might be a part of. I
entered the United States Army on October 12, 1959, with a
tenth-grade education; my first TOE unit was Headquarters
and Headquarters Battery Second Battalion Ninth Artillery,
and station at Schofield Barracks, Hawaii. There I took and
successfully completed the High School General Education
Development Test (GED). I have a GT score of 115 in area
aptitude; I have served in four overseas commands Hawaii
from May 1960-May 1963, Germany from October 1963 to
May 1966, Vietnam from November 1966-November 1967,
and Korea from May 1969 to April 1970. I have a total of
seven years and six months overseas service. I have no bad
time or Court-Martial; I have a conduct and efficiency rating
of excellent in every command that I have Court served.

I began the essay with the statement, " I believe in
loyalty" during my early years of army life, I felt that most
of the enlisted ranks were loyal to their fellow soldiers and
leaders, and during those enjoyable army days, the thought
of becoming a career counselor or recruiter never entered
my mind, however, the past four or five years most men in

uniform only know loyalty as a word from the dictionary, understand me now; I say most men in uniform. There are still some soldiers that are loyal, and these are the ones that I would like to see stay in t the army. From reading different articles on the all-volunteer army, I feel that all the things that it takes to build and maintain a good fighting team can be put back into the army. In January Army Magazine I read Yesterday, while reading Gen. Howze article who had been a commander for a great part of his life, Gen. Hamilton H. Howze (Retired) has commanded Tens of Thousands of men at one time, wrote in part, I have taught leadership to 10,000 extensively and written many pamphlets. But I do not believe that I could (even were 1 35 years younger and stronger) successfully command a company in the circumstances prevailing today, not if one defines successful command as including the capacity to take that company successfully into battle against a powerful and determined enemy" The General was speaking of todays army and the poor discipline that exists.

I believe if I am assigned as a career counselor or recruiter, I will be able to help retain or recruit the young men that have self-discipline, and any commander could command effectively. I will be willing to go anyplace in the United States or abroad, if so assigned, to content with all the Anti-war demonstrations and all the work and hours that might be involved in any type of whether to seek and find the young men that have the qualification the wiliness and loyalty to become a soldier. I want to become a recruiter for the long hair hippy that does not yet know where he is going in life but has all the potential to become a leader anywhere, including in the army. I am sure there are men in the army as well as future soldiers who need and want good career counseling; the army has an excellent record of informing these men of the possibilities of a successful army career. I know I could contribute a great deal to the already outstanding record. If selected for a position as a recruiter or career counselor, I will always consider the need of the army as well as the individuals I recruit or council. Once again, I am grateful to the United States Army for giving me the opportunity to request the type of duty I want to perform while serving the United States of America. On the 21 of June 1971, I was accepted into the recruiter/career counselor program with a reporting date of 13 July 1971 to attend class number 6 of the Recruiting and Career Counseling Course at Fort Benjamin Harrison, Indiana.

On the 11th of July, I departed Fort Hood in my new Corvette. I stopped in St. Louis and arrived at Fort Ben. On the morning of the 13th of July 1971 and signed in and was assigned quarters; two other black students were assigned to my quarters. There were three sleeping areas with a common kitchen living area, and a dining area. While at Fort. Ben. I drove to Columbus in my Corvette and visited ISG Barker. 18G Barker was a poker partner back in Fort Meade when I was under flag from Vietnam. He was also the partner responsible for my promotion to SSG E6. On another weekend, while at Fort Ben, I attended a Jazz Concert in Cleveland, Ohio.

On August 17, 1971, I graduated from the recruiter/ career counselor course. My Military Intelligence MOS was withdrawn as a primary MOS and was awarded a primary MOS of OOE40 (Recruiter/Career Counselor). After the recruiter/career counselor course, I took a month's leave to Florida. I drove myself. I drove my corvette from Fort Ben to Florida and asked Robbie and Joe to join. Robbie had filed for divorce, and I had thought of asking her to marry me. Robbie and Joe flew to Florida and met my family, and the three of us drove back to Texas in the too setter corvette. On our way back to Texas, we stopped in New Orleans to try and buy a six-pack of beer, and we were told niggers were not served there. I was assigned as a Battalion career counselor for, the 163 Military Intelligence Battalion (Combat), effective 14 Sep 1971.

As a Career counselor, I was co-located with another Career counselor. We had separate and private offices. I had my own parking space where I parked my 1970 Corvette Stingray. It was quite impressive for the men of the battalion, and I built a very good rapport that was good for 1" term enlistment. More than ninety-nine percent of the enlisted men of the battalion were white. I made no formation and prescribed my own uniform; mostly, I wore a class B uniform with short sleeves during the summer months and a class a, army green uniform during the winter months. I was scheduled to talk with an enlisted member about every six months about his career within the army and try to get a commitment for him to reenlist. I had a good record for first-term reenlistment. By this time, I saw very little of Beth and Francis. However, I did run into them at the NCO club, where I met both of them while working as a bouncer. I told both of them I was getting married, but Francis would not let go, and I had several subsequent One Night stands with her. Beth was a slim Good Looking white girl who played the field, so we just became friends. On the 28th of April 1972, Robbie and I were married, and the Corvette was traded for a mobile home, and we were located in Stagecoach Mobile Home Park in Killeen, Texas, close to Fort Hood. I stopped working at the NCO club and did not see Francis or Beth again.

During my assignment as the Battalion Career counselor for 163d MI, I received many letters of appreciation, recognition, and/or commendation. However, I also received some misleading "Enlisted Efficiency Reports," the most important entry to an enlisted member's military record. From May through October 1973, I received three "Enlisted Efficiency Reports." One 3 May 1973, that was a regular that recommended that I be promoted ahead of my contemporaries. Report On August 1973, I received an all-around perfect report that recommended that I be promoted immediate, and on 30 October 1973, upon being drafted for duty with the U.S. Army Recruiting Command, I received a third report that recommended that I be promoted immediate but gave me an excellent in attitude as appose to an outstanding. I was drafted for the Fourth Recruiting District Fort Sam Houston, Texas, with a duty station in

Del Rio, Texas. After several hours on the phone, I was successful in being relieved from an assignment in Del Rio, Texas, to Dallas, Texas, with duty at Killeen, Texas, of the Waco Recruiting Zone. I had a reporting date of 19 November 1973.assigned to the Waco recruiting zone, there was only one black recruiter. (SFC Grubbs) assigned to the Temple recruiting station, and it was clear that no other black recruiters were welcome. In the 1970s, there were few black recruiters assigned to the U.S. Army Recruiting Command. SFC Campbell was the commander of the Temple Recruiting Station and had accepted me at the Temple Station and said that I would be assigned to the Temple Sub-Station (Killeen).

At Killeen Sub-Station, there were two recruiters, one white (SSG Corley) and one Mexican (SFC Garcia). The first Saturday after I was assigned, SFC Campbell picked me up at the Killeen station for a trip to the Dallas Recruiting Main Station to meet the Commander and the Recruiting Main Station Sergeant Major. The Sergeant Major said to me, "I see you were assigned to Del Rio how did you end up in Dallas" I told the SGM that the Del Rio area was mostly Spanish speaking, and I do not speak Spanish. His reply was you are the first soldier I ever known assigned because of race. I told him I thought race had anything to do with the assignment. It was because I did not speak Spanish. He told me to wait outside, and the commander would see me. I waited for more than an hour and was told the commander would see me some other time. By this time, SFC Campbell had already left for Temple, and I asked Master Sergeant

Butts, the Waco zone commander, if I could catch a ride with him? He said that he was going back to Waco, and I could ride that far, which was about fifty miles from Killeen.

I understood that I was not welcome. I only had about five dollars and could not catch a bus to Killeen, so I accepted MSG Butts' offer, hoping that he would change his mind and have someone drive me to Killeen; there were two other recruiters of which one was the driver. But they did not change their mind and dropped me off on 1-35 in Waco. I was in Army uniform and was left to hitchhike home. A Mexican Family picked me up. That had just enough room for me in their small car. They had their children and live chickens in a cage in the back seat. I road with them for about thirty miles and again was dropped off along 1-35 and the cut-off to Killeen. My thought was what a way to start an assignment. But I knew that it would not get any better, and unless I made this assignment work, I would never make E7, and this could very well be the end of a good career.

Recruiting Duties

I would apply everything I learned at the Recruiting and Career Counseling Course at Fort Ben. 1) Know your area of assignment. 2) Develop centers of influence 3) Look professionally. I had several things going for me. I was 6'2" tall, about 200lbs, and made a military uniform look good. I knew many key personnel in the Fort Hood area who would help me. I was willing to work hard developing high school counselors, and I would put the time in to be successful. MSG Butts assigned me to an area that had no support, not even a telephone (Gatesville). The area was twenty miles away from Killeen, and I was not assigned a car as recruiters usually are. I asked what was I to do about transportation? He said I had to use my own car, and the Army would reimburse me for mileage. My wife and I had only one car now that I had traded my corvette for a Mobil Home. My wife was a nurse and worked in Temple, more than twenty miles from Stagecoach Mobil Home Park in Killeen. Somehow, we worked it out; my wife caught a ride with a friend, and I used the family car as my recruiting car. Our car was a 1970 Plymouth Duster without air condition. This was ok during the winter months; however, during the summer, I remember the Texas temperature being as high as 107 degrees.

Also, upon my assignment to recruiting duty, I had a low "Enlisted Evaluation Data Report Score" (83); recruiters that were already assigned had scores of 120 or higher. What I was not told was that they had study material. And studied as a group for the test. The owner of the Mobile Home Park where my mobile home was parked was born and raised in Gatesville, Texas, so I asked him to take me around the small town just north of Fort Hood and introduce me to the Townspeople. He was glad to help. First, he introduced me to the City Manager and asked if there was free office space for an Army Recruiting Station. The city manager had a storage space up stare, cleared out, and set up a desk, and I told the substation commander in Killeen that I had set up a recruiting station in Gatesville and needed a telephone put in. By this time, I had already enlisted two for the Army since my assignment to recruiting duty on 19 November 1973. Somehow a work order for a telephone was approved, and I was set up to canvass the areas around and about Four Hood. Some days I would work from 2 AM to 10 PM, wake up at 2 AM, pick up an Army applicant, drive him to Dallas for enlistment and get back home as late as 10 PM. A normal day often would be from 6 AM to 6 PM; the applicant had to be tested to qualify for enlistment. The nearest test site was Waco, fifty miles from the sub-station in Killeen.

An applicant is picked up at 6 AM paperwork for testing must be completed sometime. There would be as many as ten applicants that would be transported in a van assigned to the sub-station. Normally start at 9 AM and over at 12noon. Applicants that pass the test would be scheduled for physicals and given a dated to be processed at Dallas and then driven home. In early February 1974, I drafted a six-page letter to the commanding generals at the U. S. Army Recruiting Command Fort Sheridan, Illinois. The letter explained how Master Sagearnt Butts, and the incoming Sergeant Major of the Dallas District Recruiting Command had received me when I had first requested an assignment with Dallas. The letter also explained my re-assignment from duty as an army recruiter from Del Rio to the Dallas District Recruiting Command with duty at the Temple Recruiting Station. The reason for re-assignment was Del Rio was a Spanish-speaking area, and I did not speak Spanish. I also informed the commander how I Had been deposited along 1-35 fifty miles from Killeen when I had first requested an assignment to Dallas. However, this letter was not about my early experience with the Dallas Command. It was about signing an "Enlisted Efficiency Report" after successfully being assigned to the command. I reported for duty with the Dallas district on the 19th of November 1973. It was now the 11th of February 1974, time for my efficiency report. For more than three months. I had made and exceeded my assigned recruiting objective, with little or no support from the command,

The last straw was Master Sergeant Butts made a request of me to sign a blank efficiency report. I told him I would not sign the report and would write the Army Recruiting Command at Fort Sheridan, Illinois explaining how I was received in this district and how I was asked to sign a blank efficiency report. I explained to MSG Butts that I personally would like to stay at my assigned station because I had established a good rapport with the people and the schools and knew that I was the school that assigned the area to a high-producing area. He only said he could not further develop the understanding while I did not trust him to give me a fair report, and he would see me later. I let SFC Campbell see the draft of my letter to the Commanding General at Fort Sheridan, Illinois, a copy of my knowledge that the contents of the letter would be leaked to MSG Butts. On the 28th of February 1974, I was called to the Temple Recruiting Station to meet with MSG Butts. He gave me a completed copy of my enlisted efficiency report to read and sign. The report was perfect except for "Comment of Rater."

He said, "At this time, I do not consider SSG Montgomery as having 1SG potential." I did not agree with that comment; however, with the report being perfect in every other area, I did not see how the report could hurt my chance of being promoted to E7.

I was also given to study my "Enlisted Evaluation Data Report." In 1973 my score was (83) and in material for 1974, the score was (139) I was also given a 1972 six-passenger ford without air-conditioning as a car. In July of 1974, I was awarded the "Army Commendation Medal. And finally, I. Made the list for promotion to E7, which would take some months before I could pin on the strips and get paid for the promotion. I feel the promotion is about five years late, thinking back to Korea, such as when I worked hard worked in several E8 positions, a position equal to MSG Butts, who gave me time early on in my assignment to the Dallas district. I think back to MSG Jones and Prior, who were black men and E8 working as intelligent and early as 1960, respectfully, as an operation sergeant Korea as only an E6. But as SFC Portwood (a white man) said, rank isn't the only thing position count for something, as I learned as a Career Counselor with the 163 Military Intelligence Battalion. The best position I ever had as a soldier.

During the month of June of 1974 1 had an assigned enlistment objective of four. I enlisted 28, or 700% of the assigned objective, and a Dallas record. When one thinks of this, it will seem impossible, but the record speaks for itself. To do this, it takes almost an around-the-clock effort to get maybe two hours of sleep a night when one considers the District Recruiting Command being 150 miles from the recruiting station. That was in June of 1974. Today was November 19, 2009, 35 years ago and I would bet the record still stand if one would take the time to research it. During my assignment with the Dallas Recruiting Command from November 19, 1973, through October 1978, during these five years, I was always in the top 1% for production. In June of 1975, I was awarded the "Meritorious Service Medal." The highest medal for administrated type duty within the enlisted ranks. In November 1976, I was assigned as "Station Commander" for the Killeen Recruiting Station with two assigned recruiters. SFC Corley and SFC Bacon, a "Medal of Honor" recipient. It was through SFC Bacon that I learned that Dwight Johnson, also a "Medal of Honor" recipient and a friend from my unit in Vietnam, had been shot and killed in his hometown of Detroit. Dwight was the third African American recipient to be awarded the "Medal of Honor."

I remember the day that the news was received over my unit radio. It was in late October 1967. However, the citation on file states that it was 15 January 1968. I don't know how the dates got mixed up, but I remember what I was doing when the news came over my radio: I was preparing my track to leave LZ English, a 1st CAV area in the Bong-Son Plains, and a free-fire zone to Pleiku the Fourth Infantry Division area. The news that Johnson was shot and killed brought back every action and interaction of the Vietnam experience. The one experience that was at the forefront of my mind was the massacre in Pleiku after leaving a free-fire zone in the Bong Son Plains. There were many times that I did not agree with the body count being combat kills. But thought them to be collateral kills that I had to record as combat kills and report them to higher headquarters. Company A, 1 Battalion 69th Armor, had a combat kill ratio of three hundred to one. I knew Johnson and have a copy of his citation for the "Medal of Honor," and now that he had been shot and killed in his hometown, along with the way I was received into the recruiting command, makes me think the second time on how loyal I could continue to be to the U.S. Army.

On 3 November 1978, I made an inclined a local church because I felt I had a to-be station. I am also Commander of the Killen Recruiting Station. Reassigned I from my position as "Station calling on my life and could only obey this calling through the divine inspiration of the Holy Spirit. Earlier on 26 July 1978, I wrote the Department of The Army to review my official personnel file and received an answer on 16 August 1978. I agree with the review; however, I cannot agree why conditions at the unit level put me in those positions to have a lesser evaluation than my white peers when I was out producing them. Sometimes when thinking about how the "Pleiku Massacre" came about first, I think it was a reaction to an African American being awarded the "Medal of Honor." As the unit operation sergeant of Company, A, I Battalion 69 Armor 1 received a letter of Appreciation for being the most outstanding operation sergeant for an Armor unit within the Republic of Vietnam. From Captain William, the commander of Company A, who was the commander at the time of the award of the "President Unit Citation"? I remember how out of control some of the company A tank crews were after we departed a free-fire zone to a control fire zone.

And with me being an African American, I was sometimes rendered incompetent to be an operation sergeant by white tank crews after being in the position for almost a year and during the time of heavy contact when we were in a free-fire zone. I finally made E7 after receiving poor or lesser evaluations from my white peers over most of a Five year period until awards, medals, and/or accommodations were based on production. When recruiting became a numbers game, my evaluation could only go one way, and that was up. However, I feel my promotion was about five years late in coming. After resigning my position as the Killeen Station Commander, I was ordered by my LTC Fenn, Jr. Dallas District Recruiting Command to undergo a psychological evaluation. Diagnostic Impression: No mental disorder. Summary And Recommendations: SFC Montgomery scored within normal limits on all psychological tests. His current adjustment difficulties at work seem to have been brought about by a combination of factors, primarily his non-selection for promotion to E8. He feels that he has been highly productive and should be elevated to positions of increased responsibility. In summary, this case can best be resolved through the opening line of communication between SFC Montgomery's quality and his command. In 1978 I had the highest rating within the command I when was the factor.

However, I was not "Recruiter of the Year"; it was the decision of points was the District Recruiter Commander LTC Fenn, Jr. To give the award to a white recruiter with the highest number of enlistments when the award was based on quality enlistment. Later during the year, I understood LTC Fenn, Jr. Was relieved of his duties as the Dallas District Recruiting Command for not supporting the "Equal Opportunity Program" On 15 December 1978, I laterally Transferred from Dallas District Recruiting Command to Oklahoma after 15 days leave. Prior to departing the Dallas

Recruiting Command, I was told I would be a Station Commander (in a supervisory) position, not on production, and I would have Army leased housing. However, upon being on hold and being reviewed by the Oklahoma Commander, I was told there was no leased housing and that as an E7 I was responsible for my own housing. However, I would be given time to locate housing for my family. I asked the commander if he had received an Enlisted Efficiency Report on me, and he checked with his SGM and said they had not. I asked the commander if I could call the United States Army Recruiting Command because an Enlisted member does not supposed to be transferred from one command to another without an EER. And I He said I could use the phone and gave me the General of the Recruiting Command.

I called and was put on, hold, until the Commanding General picked up the phone. I told him who I was, and that I was without an EER prior to being assigned to the Oklahoma recruiting command and was also told I would have army housing by the Dallas District Recruiting Command, but upon arriving at my new duty station, I did not have an EER, nor was there army housing for me. He said he would get my record and have his SGM call me back within 24 hours The Oklahoma commander ask that I visit my assigned recruiting station recruiting station upon arrival at the station founded four white recruiters, all were Staff sergeants E6s waiting for me.

The husband-and-wife team was the top producer. I did not like the idea of a wife team working out of the same station because I felt this was a disadvantage to the other recruiters assigned to the station. I spent the day at the recruiting station to see how the recruiters would receive me. My money was running low. However, after leaving the recruiting station, I checked into a motel and made a call to my sister Gloria and asked that the company "Johnson & Montgomery" extend me alone of $1500.00 to move my family to Oklahoma City. I gave her my telephone number at the motel and asked her to call me back between 8:00 p.m. and 10:00 p.m. I waited in my room for the call but did not receive one at about 10:30 p.m. I called her back, and she said that they had not had the time to talk and asked if I could call her back the next day. I told her I would. I could not sleep thinking about what the recruiting SGM would tell me the following day. I hope that he would say I could not be Reassigned without receiving an EER. The following morning, I reported in at the Oklahoma Recruiting Command and had a cup of coffee outside of the SGM office. I waited for about two hours.

It was a little after 10:00 a.m. when the SGM called me into his office to accept the call from the USAREC SGM. The SGM first congratulated me for sustaining such an outstanding recruiting record over the past five years. And that he was sorry for what I have been put through during the past few months. He said it was the commanding general decision that I return to the Dallas Recruiting Command until I receive an EER, and since the last EER I received was a special EER, the command could not give an adverse EER within a six-month period. I return to Dallas. I had to put up in a motel with no pro-dim from the army; I waited all day the second day without seeing the commander. On 9 February, I was called a side by A GS4, MS. Lorrayne Hoover; she asked whether I had received my orders. I told her I had not. She gave me a copy and told me to report to anyone within III Corps and Fort Hood because I was being set up by the commander LTC Fenn. If I had not witnessed the action of the commander, there was no way that I could believe that an active duty LTC could stoop so low or prove to be an outright bigot.

However, during the FY of 1978, I received many letters of appreciation from general officers without his endorsements. Based on my accomplishment during FY 78, I should have been named the recruiter of of the year" however, it was given to a white recruiter with a lesser accomplishment. (The psychological evaluation during December 1978! Why?) On the third day, I was told by the DRC SGM to go home until I received my orders that would be mailed to me. Upon returning to Ft Hood I reported to DONALD W. JAUCH, III Corps & Ft Hood, who told me to contact ISG Marsh. I contacted ISG Marsh and was told he did not have any orders on me, assigning me to his organization. During the first week of March, I reported back to SFC JAUCH and he again directed me to 1SG Marsh, who said he had no orders for a SFC Julius P. Montgomery. I

Called ISG Marsh from MSG Graves offices in early March about my orders and again was told he had no such orders. Finally ask SFC Jauch to put in writing that I had reported to him about my assignment I also got a written statement from SGM Graves that I had signed in to his office,

Several days after calling ISG Marsh office from MSG Graves' office, I was called at my home and ordered a report to ISG March's office in uniform. When I reported, there were several officers awaiting me, a Major, Captain, and an SGM the Major was from the III Corps JAG office. He was the first to ask me where I had been for the past 32 days? I told him I had been at home when I was not trying to find out what unit I was assigned to within III Corps & Fort Hood. I told him that I had visited ISG Marsh offices and was told they did not have orders assigning me to his unit. I told him I also visited SFC JAUCH at III Corps & Fort Hood, and had him sign a copy of orders that were given to me by Ms. Hoover. Ms. Hoover told me to get a witness that I made an attempt to sign in at III Corps & Fort Hood in writing. I told the Major that I had my orders signed by SFC JAUCH and by MSG Graves of the 1" CAV. That I made an attempt at III Corps and Fort Hood several times and was told there were no orders assigning me to Fort Hood. Sign in at III; I told the Major that during the past few months, LTC FENN, the Dallas Recruiting Command Commander, has had me undergo a psychological evaluation, tried to process me out of his command without an EER, and now tried to set me up to be AWOL or in this case a deserter Because it has been over 32 days since I was assigned to a unit.

I told the Major I wanted to see the III Corps Inspecting General (IG). I gave the major a copy of my orders witnessed by MSG Graves and SFC Jauch. And he said I had his permission to see the III Corps IG. Everyone in the room except ISG Marsh and the JAG officer left the room without a word. The JAG officer called the III Corps IG's office and told him that he had a hot case that needed immediate attention. When I got to the III IG's office, he said he thought this was a case for the Department of the Army IG and said that he would get the Army IG on the line and let me talk to him directly Once on the line with the Army IG, I gave him a history of my assignment under LTC Fenn. He said he would pull my record and advise me once all the details were worked out. The III Corps IG told me to go home and wait for his call, that I would have a temporary duty at Fort Hood until I could be re-assigned to another duty station. I was home two days when I got the call from the III Corps IG's office. I would have a temporary duty as the NCO in charge of the Fort Hood Army Community Center. The center was a central location where soldiers processed in and out of Fort Hoods, had ID cards and passports made, shipped hold baggage, and was received by a welcome committee to the post. I was to handle all perceived problems within the center and find a solution. I was not at the center long before I got my permanent change of station orders.

Germany Again

On the 27 March, I got my orders assigning me to Germany. On 2 May, I received an amendment to the orders assigning me to the 2nd Battalion 92nd Field Artillery. I got a nice letter from Command Sergeant Major Floyd English welcoming me to the unit. My port call was from Charleston, SC. I would take my 1965 Chevy El Cameo; I would drive to Charleston, process my vehicle, and catch my flight out of Charleston to Frankfurt, Germany. I was impressed I have never been received into a unit so nicely. In fact, the word from the Sergeant Major was: with your cooperation, we will be able to apply a little more of the personnel into personnel" I would be in the country on 10 May 1979.

Upon My arrival, SFC Rudy Garcia received me at the Frankfurt airport in an army sedan. I was taken to the NCO bachelor quarters in Giessen, Germany. I only had my army issue of clothing in my duffel bag and carry-on baggage containing two changes of civilian clothing. The NCO bachelor quarters were located about four miles from the unit, which was a good morning run. I would have to run the four miles to my office co-located with 2nd Battalion, 92nd Field Artillery, my parent unit, on Rivers Barracks at Giessen, Germany, until I picked up my 1965 Cameo, my car, which would not be in port for another month. The El Cameo was some car; I had redone the body and painted it with several coats of white licker. It had a 350cubit inch engine with a full race cam. And could outrun almost anything on the road. I used it to pull my 16 "bass boat" I had driven it to Clermont, FL, and got more looks than my 1970 corvette that I traded on a mobile home.

I enjoyed the El Cameo more than I had enjoyed any of my prior cars, it was a good hook for first-term enlistment. I had a private parking area in front of my office. With the 163 Intelligent Battalion, I also had a private parking area in front of my office with the 92d Field Artillery. Where I would park my El Cameo. The assignment to Germany with the 92d was ideal. With one exception, I was away from my family. My office was co-located with two other career counselors and the concerned chaplain. I was also an ordained lay minister, so it was ideal to be co-located with the concerned chaplain. Germany had a lay pastoral program, so I was allowed to pastor a congregation at the concern chapel. Being a career counselor and a pastor went hand and hand. I was able to counsel the soldier and invite him to church at the same time. Being a pastor also gave me other advantages: I could use army transportation, i.e., buses and vans, also buildings.

I had pastoral clerical assistance for typing and reproducing Sunday programs and making public announcements within the Giessen army community. Moneys took up during Sunday morning services were ours to use for whatever program I selected to sponsor within the Giessen army community. Over and above all, lay pastors in Germany was able to communicate with churches within the United States and program guest speakers from churches, seminary, and other religious organization. When I got the notification that my car was in port, army transportation was provided to pick up my car. I was so excited that I failed to check the water in my radiator. There is no speed limit on the autobahn, so when I hit the autobahn, I open the Chevy up to about 90 miles an hour. About fifty miles from the port, the engine ran hot and locked up on me. I Found some water along the autobahn and filled the radiator, but the car did not cool down for an hour or more. I finally got it started and made my way to the nearest town along the autobahn and found a farmer who gave me enough water to fill the engine block. I made it into Giessen. However, I knew the Chevy would never be the same. I was really hurt. The car ran, but it leaked oil and did not have the power it had prior to breaking down on the autobahn. From the outside, it was still impressive, but driving it was a letdown. The reenlistment program within the 92nd was on fire, and monthly, I got some means of appreciation from the commander LTC Whitmore. However, I was still had problems Johnson, the Vietnam War, and ELComeo coping at night. I could not put LTC Fenn, out of mind

On Sunday mornings was my finest hour. The congregation at the river's concern was about 150 members strong. There were three other ministers. Grant, Watson, and

Wilson, after service normal, we would be invited to Sunday dinner by members of the congregation. Once or twice a month, we would dispatch a bus from the Giessen Army Depot and visit other congregations within Germany. There. Be food served, and things conducive to good fellowship would be promoted: Guest speakers and group discussions were common. In August 1979, I was the guest speaker when the area conference was held at the Rivers Chapel in Giessen, Germany. My topic was "and they spoke with other tongues" Acts 2:4. The message was well received, and people were overjoyed; they were dancing and praising the Lord in the Holy Spirit.

After service, we had dinner in the basement near my office. We had a wonderful time. Another advantage of being a lay pastor was we made all f the classes of the full-time chaplains. However, I had not decided if I wanted to stay in the army past twenty years, and I had not received an EER after leaving the Dallas Recruiting Command, and if I was going to be promoted to E8, I needed an EER for that period. On 4 August 1979, I wrote The Secretary of the Army and told him I had not received an EER since leaving the Dallas Recruiting Command. On the 21 of August 1979, I got a letter stating that my request would receive a complete and impartial review, and I would be advised of the final decision as expeditiously as possible. In October 1979, I took leave from Germany for several reasons. 1) I had not received my EER from LTC Fenn, and without an EER for that period, I could not make the 1980 E8 list, and if I did not make a list for sure, I would retire; and I thought I stood a better chance of retiring by making my case at Fort Hood. 2) All my monthly pay went to my wife in Texas, and I had asked her to mail me a money order for $125.00 to arrive in Germany on the 1st of the month, and I was not receiving the money order on time. 3) I wanted. To make sure that all my bills were up to date prior to retiring from the army, it was reason to doubt if I was not receiving the $125.00 a month. 4) With all I had gone through prior to going to Germany, I had a good case to ask the army for a reprieve in the form of a job subsequent to retirement or disability if a job was not forthcoming.

Prior to departing Germany, I requested retirement after 20 years of service and asked Chaplain Ackley and Chaplain Batluck to write a supporting letter. In October 1979, I reported on a sick call at Darnall Army Hospital, Fort Hood, Texas, and was treated as an outpatient for depression and was assigned to Operational Support Battalion 13th COSCOM Fort Hood, Texas. As I suspected, my personal finance at home was in disarray. I considered divorce but decided against it because I already had enough on my plate. The doctor advised me for several months during my assignment to Fort Hood that I had an outstanding record, and the army felt that I should return to Germany to work in my primary MOS. However, the doctor told the army that I would be admitted as an inpatient if I received orders to return to Germany. On 10 March 1980, I was admitted to Darnell Army Community Hospital as an inpatient for depression. The Honorable Marvin Leath House of Representative 1331

Longworth Building Washington D.C. intervened on my behalf to have all personal belongings return from Germany to Sergeant First Class Julius Montgomery.

Retirement

I was retired on 1 September 1980. After twenty years of service with the U.S. Army, I did not attend my retirement ceremony. I had lost all respect for what I would have given my life to defend just a few years prior. However, I did feel bad not returning to Germany because it was a good assignment. The commander LTC Whitmore was fair and allowed me to run my reenlist program. I had a good rapport with the Chaplains and the other lay ministers. I had been offered a larger congregation at a division-size unit just several miles from Giessen.

I turned it down 1) because my car was not running very well, 2) I did not think I could devote the time to a larger congregation and have a good reenlistment program and 3) I needed to come home to see what problems my wife was having. Another lay minister from the Church of God and Christ took the congregation and, I understand, had great success. I chose to come home and was now circa. My first job after retirement was with Central Texas College as a Learning Center Instructor, and I was assigned to Headquarters 1 Battalion, 8th Cavalry 1st Cavalry Division. December 1980, I was contacted by the Department of The Army Inspecting General office. I was offered a job as a department of the army "Recruiting Specialist" he stated that this was the reprieve I had asked for before my retirement. I told the IG that I had not been retired for six months, as was the requirement to be employed by the government following active duty. The IG office told me that that requirement would be waver, and if I wanted, the job paperwork would be forwarded to me to get a physical at Fort Hood, and I would subsequently report to

Civilian Recruiter

Fort Jackson, South Carolina, to be sworn in as a department of the army GS7; my assignment will be with the Columbia SC District Recruiting Command. I accepted the job. 1st December 1980 was my last day as the learning center instructor for the 1" Battalion 8th Cavalry. I got an outstanding letter of appreciation from the commander LTC Kendall; that said in part that my learning center was the standard against which other learning centers at Fort Hood were measured. Upon reporting to the Fort Jackson Civil Service Office, I was told that I could not be sworn in as a GS7 because I had only been out of the army for three months.

I told the officer in charge that I was told that I would get a waiver for the other three months. He told me there was no waiver on file, and I would have to come back the following day after he had looked into the matter. I asked the officer if I could leave my phone number, and he would call me once the problem was resolved. He said okay. I was staying with a friend that I knew in Columbia. I gave him the phone number and returned to my friend's house about five miles from the civil service Office. The next day about 2:00 p.m., the civil service office called me and told me that the waiver was approved and to report to the civil service office to be sworn in. I was driving our new car a 1980 Mazda that my wife had talked me into buying after I started working at Fort Hood as a learning center employee.

After being sworn into the Recruiting Command, again I was to report to Captain Hooper. Upon reporting to the Captain of the Columbia District, I was told by captain Hooper I would be working out of the Greenville area and possibly assigned to Easley. I drove 125 miles to Greenville and was told they did not have orders assigning me to their command, and until they did find someplace to stay and get in contact, within a couple of days I drove to Clemson, said to myself. This is "Dallas" all over again. So I got into my car and met a find gentleman eager to talk with me, and we found that we had something in common... We both had a background in military intelligence. He was in charge of Clemson University and agreed to put me up free of charge in one of the apartments on the fourth floor of the university. I would check with Greenville and ask if they knew concerning my assignment to the Greenville area. They told me they had not. Finally, I told them I was going to Florida for the weekend and would check with them once I was back in the area. On my return, they accuse me of levying without permission. My response was permission from According to Greenville. I had not been assigned to Greenville upon my departure to Florida for the weekend. Even though I accepted the job as a recruiting specialist on 5 January 1981, I had not yet been given a responsibility, on

12 January 1981. Another recruiting specialist and I were given orders to attend a recruiting course at Fort Benjamin Harrison, IN.

Upon returning, I was told I would be assigned to Easley Recruiting Station, Easley, S.C. where SSG Hyche was the station commander and would be my immediate supervisor. I wouldn't say I liked the idea of being supervised by an E6, someone I outranked and had many more years of experience, but this was something I could live with. I met SGT Brown, who was a clerk at the Greenville headquarters, who told me that it was out that it was the objective of the Columbia Recruiting Command to "kick me out of recruiting and to destroy my reputation as a department of the army civilian" because I had caused many problems For the Army Recruiting Command during my years of active duty. My wife called me and asked if she could fly to Indianapolis and meet me after I graduated from recruiting school. She wanted to ride back to Greenville with me and look for a house. I told her she could fly to Indianapolis, and we would take it easy riding back to the Greenville area.

After graduation, I picked my wife up at the Indianapolis airport and took a slow ride to Greenville. We made several stops at motels and ate at good restaurants; it was a good winter trip in our new Mazda. It was like a second honeymoon, something we needed after the almost break-up after Germany. Upon arriving at the Greenville area headquarters, I asked for some time off to find a place to stay.

However, after meeting several real estate agencies, I never knew it would be such a problem. I realized that the piedmont of South Carolina was a very prejudiced area; for a black man would be very hard to establish the necessary rapport to be an effective recruiter. And if what Sergeant Brown said about the recruiting command would make it hard for me because of the problems I had caused during active duty, I was becoming somewhat worried and wondered if I had made the right decision in accepting this job. My wife and I spent three days looking for a house we could buy. However, it was almost impossible to find a reasonable deal for two reasons. 1) Interest rate was at 20%, and 2) the houses the agencies wanted to sell to blacks were not acceptable.

Finally, we gave up and one of the real estate agents found me a place to stay, with her single son who had a spear bedroom. My wife caught a flight out of Greenville back to Texas. We had three cars a 1978 Ford double cab F-150 pick up, a 1980 Mazda, and a 1970 VW. I continued to look in the paper for a house that we could lease with an option to buy and found a house advertised as an "executive special" I called and made an appointment to see the house. The agent was on Bob Jones University Board of Directive, and I think had something to prove. The house was located in an upper middleclass neighborhood and had 3600 square feet of living area. I was impressed if only I could afford the house. The agent said he wanted my family to have the house; and would give me the bargain of my life. He would lease the house for just $500.00 per month. I accepted his offer. I called my wife and told her I had found a house and she should make an attempt to rent our mobile home. She said she already had someone who wanted to rent our mobile home. So, the only thing left to do was make an arrangement to move from Texas to South Carolina.

The army was obligated to one move after retirement so our move would be free. I would have to fly to Texas and drive one of the two cars that were still in Texas and sell the stuff that we could or did not want to ship. We had a John Deer tractor with trailer that we would sell there were other stuff that we could leave with our neighbors that could be picked up at a later time. We made the trip from Texas my way of Florida, for the most part the children traveled in back of the improved camper on back of our F-150, I drove the pick-up and my wife drove the VW. The trip took three days with a one-day layover in Florida. Two days after we arrived the moving van with our household goods arrived I house was located in Taylors. SC a Suburb of Greenville SC and about eighteen miles from Easley SC, my assigned duty station. My job was to recruit for local Reserve Units and for the ROTC collage program, at Clemson University. Within the Greenville area, there is about six active Reserve Units and about the same number of recruiters recruiting for those unites. Making the assigned objective should not be a problem if the recruiter is given the cooperation necessary to do the job. Leads of Persons being discharged from active duty come down through the area headquarters. If these leads are described to each assigned recruiters this will account for about half of the recruiter's objective.

However, if the leads are given to a selective recruiter, it gives an advantage to the recruiter that gets the lead. It is easy to overlook one recruiter in favor of another recruiter. In the up Piedmonts of South Carolina where an African American have a hard time establishing rapport to begin with it is almost impossible to make an assigned objective without leads from area headquarters. During the three years that I was assigned to the Greenville area I got no leads from area headquarters. And personnel assigned to the six-reserve unit gave me negative cooperation. I think from the commanding general who lived in my neighborhood to the lowest technician assigned to the six reserve units new me and worked to see me fail, something I have never did during 21 years of active duty. Sergeant Brown of the Greenville Headquarters told me that it was the objective of the command to see me fail and he even put that in writing. During the next few captures of this book, you would think I should have given up the fight however, I will never give up. I have lost many hours of sleep and even had nightmares because of the obstacles placed in my path but I hope that this book can be an example to someone else who Was pressed to fight the good fight, and never gave up. From the outside looking in one would think I had an idea job.

I had an assigned automobile I could wear suite and tie if I so choice and for all practical purposes I worked from 9-5 an averaged eight hour day. However, within the reserve units and the ROTC program I was a good assigned to recruit for almost no one would talk to

Me "I was the transparent nigger" in the government car that was seen in the hill country of South Carolina wearing a tie. These towns included Walhalla, Seneca, Clemson, Pendleton, Westminster, Easley and Pickens. The few African-American I saw in these areas was most subservience, and "knew their place" The employment in the area was logging, sawmills and textile mills. I was employed and assigned to work this area on 1 December 1980 and was assigned my first recruiting objective in February 1981.

Resignation as Civilian Recruiter

I resigned from my position as a recruiting specialist on 3 September 1983; of the two years ten months as a recruiting specialist in the piedmont of South Carolina, I never made my assigned recruiting objective. I first graduated from the Recruiting and Career Counseling Course on 17 August 1971. I was assigned my first objective on 3 December 1971 and my last objective on active duty on December 1979 (eight years). I never missed an assigned objective while on active duty. I had an average of 167% lifetime while on active duty. At this point, the question is, why? On 15 June 1983, I saw Doctor Joseph J. Nannarell at the Department of the Army Federal Building in Greenville.

DIAGNOSIS: 1) Depressive disorder 2) Paranoia. The recommendation was I be given a two-month leave of absence from my job. On June 23, 1983, I was requested again to undergo a psychiatric evaluation by the Greenville area commander Captain Harold E. Neal, Jr. This time; the doctor was Dr. Perry Irvine Lupo: Mr. Montgomery is a 42-year-old married black male seen for evaluation on 7-21-83 and a follow-up visit on 8-05-83. The patient began by stating that his problems began in 1978. When he was on active duty as a recruiter in the service when he started "having problems with recruiting command," he reported at that time that the commander had him undergo psychiatric evaluation and that it "found no psychiatric illness." Apparently, from that time, he was later assigned to Germany and returned to the States. He was on active duty until September 1, 1980. Since then, there have been numerous problems which Mr. Montgomery went into great detail about and brought a volume of information in letters that he had compiled.

I reviewed these and the material sent to me by the civilian personnel office. Dr. Nannarello at the Veteran's Administration Outpatient Clinic in Greenville has also seen Mr. Montgomery, and I believe you have copies of these records, which I have also reviewed. He began going to the VA early in the early in. Dr. Nannarello diagnosed him as having Depression and Paranoia to the point that he was given a 2-month leave of absence from work. When I saw Mr. Montgomery, he had not returned to work. He reported that he had learned that the office and personnel had already been prejudiced against him before he even came to this area. He has found this area to be very prejudiced. He cannot work with the personnel here and therefore has not been able to meet his requirements. I believe you already know his claims about the situation here, as described in Dr. Nannerello's evaluation and letters he has written to your various offices. Mental status at the time of assessment shows the patient to be a well-developed, well-nourished black male who appeared his stated age. He was appropriately groomed on both occasions. He is very verbal and cooperative. The effect was not inappropriate. However, processes were logical and goal-directed. There did seem to be the evidence of paranoia, which was only in relation to the job situation, the personnel there, and this part of the country. Other than in that realm, testing appeared to be intact. Due to the paranoia, judgment and insight could be said to be impaired. Briefly, the patient is from Florida. He grew up in a fairly large family. According to him, there was a good deal of racial prejudice in the area he grew up in. His mother, on several occasions, warned him to stay out of trouble with white people. There is a lot of competition between him and his brothers. He joined the service and, for several years, did well and became one of the top recruiters. His problems began as he stated in 1978 1) A friend from Vietnam who was the 3rd Black to win the Medal of Honor was shot and killed in Detroit. And 2) the prejudice of LTC Fenn of the Dallas Recruiting Command. And I would judge from the volume of information from your office and these letters that he has compiled that this has been an ongoing problem since that time. He draws a small amount of disability from the service and his retirement pay.

From these two interviews with Mr. Montgomery, I agree with Dr. Nannarello on the diagnosis of Depression, Depressive Neurosis, and Paranoia. The paranoia seems fairlywell encapsulated and not generalized to all situations. Most of these seem related to the service, the civilian recruiting jobs, and this part of the country. Regarding defense mechanisms, he appears to use denial, projection, and a good deal of intellectualization and rationalizing. In my opinion, as the situation stands and has been over the

4-5 years, I do not feel that Mr. Montgomery can work in his present capacity; or other words, he is disabled to work in his current capacity. On September 3, 1983, 1 resigned from my position as a "recruiting specialist" I founded a non-profit COTA, or Churches Organized to Assist; I also signed up as a full-time student at the university of south Carolina (Spartanburg) COTA held a news conference in Greenville and were on the evening news. Our objective was to assist young people by having them discover the successful person within the community (we will call the discovered person community heroes). The student will write about that person's success and post the composition in a special place in the public library. Subsequently, the student will find venues where the Community Hero will speak; these events will be used as community fundraisers. These funds will be used as scholarships for participating students. We would recruit churches as venues for the organization's fundraising. The program would also act as a writing program for the participating student.

While working on a COTA program and cooking dinner for the kids, I left a burner in the kitchen with a pot of fatback that I would add some green beans, too, for dinner. I forgot about the pool and left for the printing shop printing booklets for the COTA program, and when I returned, the house was in flames. More than 150.000 dollars in damages were done to the house. I was not employed. The COTA program was just getting started, and there was no one to take over the COTA program for me, even with a six-member board of directors. My wife was still working, but we had no clothes on our backs and only a small amount of money from the bank. Our neighbors raised about a thousand dollars for us, and we moved in with friends to find a place we could afford. Our friends, where we found temporary housing, lived in government-assisted housing, and the neighbors reported us to the housing authority. So, we moved before we could find a good place to live. The apartments that we moved to were called "Ducketts Apartments" from the outside looked well, and even inside, the apartment looked OK. There were only two bedrooms, and we had six in our family. At night the apartment came alive with roaches and rats. My depression was fully blown. I saw a doctor twice a week and was on medication, but I still had crying spells, and it Was hard to get started in the morning.

However, I knew that I had to get started. I was still in school and had to maintain a grade of C to get the VA check. We still had two cars; we had sold the VW to one of our real estate agencies, so we had the 1978 super cab pickup and the 1980 Mazda. The age of our children was 4-17. Our renters in Texas had moved on, so I had to go to Texas and try and sell the property or fix it up for rent? I took the pick-up with my foster daughter's husband to help me move some of the things I had around the place to a friend's house. Upon arriving in Texas, I had serious problems with headaches and numbness on one side of my body. And crying spells. It was bad that I checked in at the Army hospital. The doctor at the hospital checked my vital signs, gave me some pills, and told me to check in with my doctor when I got back to Greenville. My son-in-law and I moved all the stuff out of our outhouse and around the mobile home, i.e., cement mixer, mortar box, shovels, hoes, etc. All over to my friend's house, who ran a large home for boys.

I also talked to several pastors about COTA and suggested using my mobile home as headquarters, but there were no takers. The problem was I was not well enough to sell the program and needed some moral support until I was well again. I was still a student at the university, and it had been two weeks since I last attended class. However, I had good grades and should be able to pull out of f the semester with an overall grade of C to maintain my VA check. I did not have the time or support for the COTA program in Greenville. So I thought after finishing the semester at the university selling my property, and finding somewhere for my family to stay, I would move COTA to Clermont, FL, find a fundraiser, and give 100% 10 COTA. I put the property on the market for $40,000, hoping I would get at least $25,000 and I would buy or lease a place in Greenville.

COTA or Churches Organized to Assist

Ifounded a non-profit COTA, or Churches Organized to Assist; I also signed up as a full-time student at the university of south Carolina (Spartanburg) COTA held a news conference in Greenville and was on the evening news. Our objective was to assist young people by having them discover the successful person within the community (we will call the discovered person community heroes). The student will write about that person's success and post the composition in a special place in the public library. Subsequently, the student will find venues where the "Community Hero" will speak; these events will be used as a community fundraiser. These funds will be used as scholarships for participating students. We would recruit churches as venues for the organization's fundraising. The program would also act as a writing program for the participating student.

While working on a COTA program and cooking dinner for the kids, I left a burner on in the kitchen with a pot of fatback that I would add some green beans, too, for dinner. I forgot about the pot and left for the printing shop printing booklets for the COTA program, and when I returned, the house was in flames. More than 150.000 dollars in damages were done to the house. I was not employed. The COTA program was just getting started, and there was no one to take over the COTA program for me, even with a six-member board of directors. My wife was still working, but we had no clothes except those on our backs, and we only had a small amount of money in the bank. Our neighbors raised about a thousand dollars for us, and we moved in with friends until we could find a place we could afford. Our friends, with whom we found temporary housing, lived in government-assisted housing, and the neighbors reported us to the housing authority. So, we moved before we could find a good place to live.

The apartments that we ents" from the outside look good, and even on moved to was called "Ducketts Apartments" the inside the condo looked OK. There were only two bedrooms, and we had six in our family. At night the apartment came alive with roaches and rats. My depression was fully blown. I saw a doctor twice a week and was on medication but still had crying spells, and it was hard to get started in the morning. However, I knew that I had to get started. I was still in school and had to maintain a grade of C to get the VA check. We still had two cars; we had sold the VW to one of our real estate agencies, so we had the 1978 super cab pick and the 1980 Mazda. The age of our children was 4-17. Our renters in Texas had moved on, so I had to go to Texas and try and sell the property or fix it up for rent? I took the pick-up with my foster daughter's husband to help me move some of the things I had around the place to a friend's house.

Upon arriving in Texas, I had serious problems with headaches, numbness on one side of my body, and crying spells. It was so bad that I checked in at the Army hospital. The doctor at the hospital checked my vital signs, gave me some pills, and told me to check in with my doctor when I got back to Greenville. My son-in-law and I moved all the stuff out of our outhouse and around the mobile home, i.e., cement mixer, mortar box, shovels, hoes, etc. All over to my friend's house, who ran a large home for boys. I also talked to several pastors about COTA and suggested using my mobile home as a headquarters, but there were no takers. The problem was I was not well enough to sell the program and needed some moral support until I was well again. But I needed money to support my family. I applied at the Lincoln-Mercury Honda dealership and was hired as a car salesman, I was successful, and the pressure I was under seemed to dissipate. It was like a new beginning. My average income as a car salesman was about $1500 a week plus my army retirement. I was still a student at the university, and I was not attending class. However, I had good grades and should be able to pull out of the semester with an overall grade of C to maintain my VA check if I made all the finals.

My income was good. However, I did not have the time or support for the COTA program in Greenville. So I thought we would find time for COTA after finishing the semester at the university, selling my property and buying a house. I got an offer for the property shortly after putting it on the market for $40,000. However, after the buyer looked at the property and did some investigating, the offer was they would pay off the property and give me $5,000; I agreed. I was still selling cars two years after we bought a house in Greenville. All the old problems had also returned. I was seeing a doctor at the VA two times a week for what he said was depression. He said I had symptoms of "post-traumatic stress disorder" (P.T.S.D.), I had controllable crying spells, and I had talked to most of the leading pastors in Greenville, Columbia. A great part of South Carolina, but none wanted to sponsor a program outside their church's norms. I thought other churches would follow if I could get one church to support the program. But the answer I got was that the church membership did community. By giving the only,

The student had to put forth an effort.

COTA would help answer this is that the student community. I see leaders not wanting to take on the responsibility of sponsoring students that they had to teach to read and write. In other words, the church did not feel the students could write about the community patriarchs and matriarchs in their workbooks with very little unity. I help the student and guidelines to write about the community patriarch and matriarch. As a child, I had to write! For my community, as an adult, when that same greeted during the 20th Century. After the close of the semester at the COTA program, Our youth need to know what our parents, grandparents, and community! At the university, I quit my job as a car salesman in Greenville, packed my car, and moved to Florida with less than a hundred dollars to my name. I had faith. My greatest accomplishment is accepting Christ as the leader in my life. This did not happen until I was past thirty until I was past thirty years old. As a young man, I saw women as sex objects and nothing more. Programs such as COTA can change the way young men and women think of their community and themselves.

When I think of my life, I see many personalities that most were no good and self-fulfilling; as a black man, I think I have led a life that could be beneficial, especially for the young I also feel that my life has seen great hardship that could have been avoided. The first step to avoiding pitfalls in life is to seek out good leadership. I don't think I did that in my early years. I was so afraid to trust anyone because of the options given to young black men. But now, I can identify with those who made better decisions than I and those who made worse. My effort in writing this program is to offer an option to those Who would accept it. By reading this book, you know a lot about me. By this time, you should see if you would consider accepting a program I have written to better one's station in life. I am 68 years old and have done most of the things that one would think a 68-year-old black American could have done with his life in America, especially in the America South. I am married with four children and fourteen grandchildren by now; you know I served in the U.S. Army and as a department of the army civilian, accounting for about twenty-four years. I am offering a family program, "PG" The book (autobiography) is about my life, and the program is about what you could do to better your station in life. COTA was founded in Greenville, South Carolina, in 1986.

Patriarchies/Matriarchies Children Fund was founded in Austin, Texas, in 1995 COTA (Churches Organized To Assist) was our hope that churches would support youth programs where the youth of our community could write about the success of seniors and successful members of the community.

This was a hard sell to most communities; however, we did have some success in Florida and Texas; but not enough success, and we thought the name change would enhance the success of the program, so we changed the name to "Patriarchies/Matriarchies Children Fund" aka "Hero's." The objective of the program was the same. At this point, I think your question should be why a total autobiography asks one to participate in a community program. I thought you should know that I am no angle. I have had some successes and some failures. However, I am still standing; I want to point out some contacts the program has had starting from as early as 1988. The program made headlines in the Orlando Sentinel Sunday, March 20, 1988, after establishing a learning center in Clermont, Florida; the objective of the center was to research the Lack County black community and record their contribution to the learning center upon arriving in Florida it took me only a few weeks to get a building and organize a support unit to build the program.

The program was also on the Greenville evening news. However, after fourteen months in Florida, my health was not improving, and fundraising was slow, but there was hope. Several ministers from the Greenville, SC, area were willing to offer their time, but my health was not improving.

Hospitalization

In July 1988, after discussing it with the board in Florida and South Carolina, I agreed to be hospitalized at the VA Medical Center in Augusta, GA; I was hospitalized from July 1988-2 December 1988. On August 19, 1988, I wrote to vice president George Bush after he accepted the nomination of the republican party for the office of president of the United States. The letter to the Vice President explained in detail the problems I had from 1979-1988. I wrote to the Vice President again on November 5, 1988. However, he had already addressed my August 19 letter through Dr. Mark W. Wolcott. His letter reads: Your letter of August 19, 1988, addressed to Vice President George Bush, has been referred to our office for reply. Your letter clearly describes your hazardous military service and the psychological and personal difficulties you have experienced since that time.

We know that you are currently in treatment at the Augusta Veterans Administration Medical Center and have spoken with your staff physician, Dr. Amarasinghe. We are encouraged by the progress you are making and urge you to continue to work with your therapists during this hospitalization and, after you are discharged, in outpatient care. I was discharged in December 1988 and medically retired in January 1989 with 100% disability.

Hoping to keep the program vibrant, on March 5, 1991, the program was introduced to the president of Prairie View A&M University as a tool for students to interact and identify patriarch and matriarch who had made local and national contributions. The university suggested that I invite other colleges into the program and write a grant to impairment the program. During the 1994 & 1995 school years, we established a club on the campus of "Gordon A. Bailey Middle School with more than 25 members. The club members interacted with local military organizations, including members of the National Medal of Honor Society, Lyndon B. Johnson Library, Congressman Lloyd Doggett, and Col. Carmine A. Vito, USAF Ret. And the first to fly a U2 spy plane over the Soviet Union. On February 7, 1998, the Hero's TM Club unveiled "The Lyndon B. Johnson Patriarch Poster" at Givens Recreation Center. Subsequently, on October 30, 1999, those on the poster as community "heroes" was honored at Mt. Olive Baptist Church as an "Affirmation of 20th Century Heroes" the guess speaker was Mr. Harry J. Middleton. Mr. Middleton is the author of "The White House Years." He is the former speechwriter for President Lyndon B. Johnson and director of the LBJ Library and Museum.

Memorial of Dwight H. Johnson

The first public program Hero's TM did in Texas was Memorial Day May 29th 1995 "A Memorial Service" for Sp5 Dwight H. Johnson. A Black Medal of Honor recipient. First we called Dwight hometown: Detroit MI and asked that the Mayor do a Proclamation the answer was they would do a proclamation, and we offered to present a plaque to the Mayor honoring Dwight. The answer was they was not really into Medals of honors and did not know if the mayor would have the time to accept the plaque on the city's behalf. I flew to Detroit and was not able to get an appointment with the mayor and the proclamation was given to me in the hallway of city hall. I still have the plaque in the hope of some future date; the sitting mayor will be honored to accept the "Dwight H. Johnson" Memorial Plaque." The Dwight H. Johnson Memorial Service:

Silent Prayer…………………….Congregation

Prelude………………………..Organist

Posting of the colors…………..Maj. Alex Morales (Army Ret.)

Reading of the Scriptures………Maj. Gary Offineer (Army Ret.)

Invocation...............Rev. Sterline Lands II, D.D.

Musical Selections...........................Choirs

Eulogy......................…...A Time to Mend
- Rev. J. Paul Montgomery Member of the Deceased
Combat Unit

A Hero's Reflection. Msg. Roy Benavidez (Army
Ret.) Medal of Honor Recipient Presentation of the Memorial
Plaque...Msg. Roy Benavidez (Army Ret.) and Rev. Raphael
Smith, D.D.

Recessional..........................."Battle Hymn of
the Republic"....Congregation

Postlude, Organist

The Eulogy: "A Time to Mend" Rev. J. Paul
Montgomery (Member of the deceased combat Unit)

To mend: To set something right which has been
wrong. Text: Ecclesiastes 3, Romans 12. Eccl. 4-9:

A time to weep, and a time to laugh;

A time to grieve and a time to dance;

A time for scattering stones, and a time for

gathering stones together;

A time to embrace and a time to refrain from embracing

A time to find; and a time to lose;

A time for keeping, and a time for throwing away;

A time to tear, and a time to repair;

A time to be quiet, and a time to speak up;

A time for loving, and a time for hating;

A time for war, and a time for peace;

What does one get by doing the right thing at the right time?

Romans 12:1 say that we should present our bodies as a living sacrifice, to be used by God, and we should not look for a great return. (To present our body as a living sacrifice is the right thing to do.)

Does not a soldier do just that? He presents his body as a living sacrifice, for the betterment of His country, and for the most part, he asks little in return. The Book of Ecclesiastes tells us our Greatest return from God is through our works, our works and abilities are God's gifts to us.

Today we are here to honor our fallen heroes-those who in fact presented themselves as living sacrifices those who did great works, and for most part, did so because they too felt it was the right thing to do. In particular today, we want to honor heroes who have gone above and beyond the call of duty Medal of Honor recipients. The Medal of Honor was first presented in 1863, during the Civil War. Sixteen free blacks were recipients of the highest honor during that war. After the Civil War (during the 20th Century) only four blacks to my knowledge received this highest honor. We will honor one of these four here today. We have tried to have representation here today across the racial spectrum of America, for all Races of Americans fought together, and many died together.

I am reminded today of a warm August morning in Fort Sill Oklahoma. I was a 21-year old soldier my battalion was in training for an overseas assignment to Germany. Preparation included our becoming re-familiarized with our personal weapons. After a march of about ten miles to the rifle range, we found the range in a bad state of repair. After removing the covers from the prefabricated foxholes, we found webs! Within these webs were deadly Black Widows, hundreds of them, as if they had taken over the range due to its poor state of repair, or because the range had not been used for such a long time. In these webs we saw the skeletons of various insects. The black widows had sucked the life out of the insects and left only skeletons hanging in their places. On that warm summer morning at Fort Sill, Oklahoma, we had to call off target practice and call on the post engineers to come out and exterminate the black widows within those deadly webs.

In many cases when soldiers have returned from war, they come from having presented their body as living sacrifices. They come home and find that they, too, are caught up in deadly webs. While in this deadly entanglement the innermost parts of their beings are sucked until only a skeleton remains in place. They become numb with little or no felling. They come to have little or no concern for self or family. They become drug or alcohol dependent. They become a nuisance to our fast-paced American Society. And too often those who have offered their bodies as living sacrifices are pushed to the Point of taking their own lives. This seems like a better reward, after having offered themselves so completely as living sacrificed. America, we can do better, and must do better. For America, if you look around, you can see the Fruit of their work and their sacrifice. It is called freedom. It is schools and universities. It is the Home in the suburbs. It is called, "The American Dream."

Verse 16 of Ecclesiastes 3 reads, "And moreover, I saw under the sun that in the place of justice, that wickedness was there; and in the place of righteousness, that iniquity was there." I submit that the government and the churches have shown little compassion for soldiers who have gone to distant lands to sacrifice themselves with the best of interest of the church and government in mind. Today we can also say that the compassion which has been shown has come too late for many, for those who have been left as skeletons hanging in the black widow's webs, or those who have been pushed to the point of suicide.

Ecclesiastes 3:22 reads "Wherefore, I perceive that there is nothing better, than that a man should rejoice in his own works; for that is his portion." If you find it possible to consider the soldier today, I pray that you would understand the work these soldiers wrought through blood, sweat, and tears and that you would allow the soldiers or their loved ones to have their portion. They have earned it, and it is their gift from God.

The scripture says, "for who shall bring them to see what shell be after them? We, as men and as women, should enjoy whatever gift God has given us. This is all that we have. The Bible tells us that God give us ability, in other words, our works, and that is no greater enjoyment. In Romans 12:6 we read, "Having then gifts differing according to the grace that is given to us, prophecy according to the proportion of faith". In other words let each of us be compassionate toward the rest, based on whatever gift God has to us. Consider what part your works play in our communities, and consider also how another helps you. It is time for mending in every facet of our society. We can only mend by working together, and helping one another.

Sp5 Dwight H. Johnson had many talents. He was an outstanding soldier. He was agile. He used his agility to defend and rescue fellow soldiers. He was a quick thinker. He used this skill to overcome almost insurmountable odds and bring a dire situation under control. He was caring. He used this gift to carry others to safety in the most dangerous conditions. Now, we remember and honor him. He is an example to all. With this example before us, we should start a new day. We should give freely of ourselves as God has given to us freely our different gifts. With our gifts we should mend those things that we Find broken within our society, and through this giving of ourselves we will enjoy the gifts from God, who made the heavens and earth.

Hero's in Schools (patriarchs/ matriarchs)(aka Hero's)

During the 2001-2002 School Year, the program was offered to the Austin Independent School District as an After-School program. The program was short of personnel and could only be placed in one school. (Kealing Middle School) Quick Facts about the program: 1) Confidence builder 2) Provides Instructor 3) Serves grades 6-12th 4) 10 students per class 5) 30-60 minute sessions 6) Suited for 4, 6, or week Sessions 7) Ideal for a classroom 8) $7.50 per session per student.9) Description: This program is about finding heroes within your community and ways to interact with each hero in a positive environment. 10) Objectives/ Academic Area Emphasized: Building confidence. 11) References Available Upon Request, 12) Previous School District Experiences: Gordon A. Bailey Middle School during the 1994-1995 school year. The students interacted with the following community heroes: Harry J. Middleton (Director LBJ Library), Mrs. Robbie Alexander (Matriarch of Mt. Olive Baptist Church), Mr. Chester Watson (Patriarch of Mt Olive Baptist Church); finding and recognizing our patriarchs and matriarchs is the first step in building a support system between our communities, i.e., colleges universities, government, non-profit organizations, and the corporate community in establishing a strong support system for our community youths, grades 1-12.

Another recognition program to follow this recognition will be a program to recognize siblings of our patriarchs and matriarchs. These siblings may be recruited from corporate, labor, government, entertainment sports, and other communities who agree to support our patriarchs and matriarchs programs. The youth of our communities in grades 1-12 will now come together using the patriarch, Matriarch, and siblings to construct an adopted community family tree. This family tree, made up of a wide spectrum of our demographics, including our government, sports, corporate, labor, and other communities, will work together to ensure our children have the best possible chance of being all they can be. Be a part of this initiative by signing up and supporting Patriarchies/Matriarchies Children Fun, Inc., AKA Hero.

The following list of names is some of the early community personnel I have asked to sign up to be community heroes. Most have biographies filed in the local library

1. The Honorable Wilhelmina Ruth Fitzgerald Delco-Former State Rep.
2. Former Attorney General Dan Morales-Former State Attorney General
3. Former Councilman Willie Lewis-Former City Councilman

4. Former Chief Michael C. McDonald-Former Asst. Chief of Police

5. Former Mayor Gustavo L. Garcia-Former Mayor

6. Mr. Charles W. Gates-Director of Aviation

7. Former Sheriff Margo L. Frasier-Former County Sheriff

8. Judge Brenda Kennedy-Judge

9. Representative Dawnna Dukes-State Rep.

10. Senator Rodney Ellis-State Senate

11. Lt. Gen John Q. Taylor King, Sr., Ph.D.-Chancellor and President Emeritus of Huston Tillotson University

12. The late Rev. Raphael C. Smith, DD-Former Pastor Mt. Olive Baptist Church

13. Elder Sylvester Copeland-Former Pastor P.E.H.C. Copperas Cove, TX.

14. Pastor Kennedy Young-Pastor Olivet Baptist Church

15. Dr. Grant Coffman-Founder Olivet Bible institute

16. Mrs. Fairy Chism Barlow-Olivet Baptist Church

17. Mrs. Betty Meshack Mann-Olivet Baptist Church

18. Pastor J. Townsend-Peaceful St. James Baptist Church

19. Mrs. J. Townsend-Peaceful St. James Baptist Church

20. Mrs. Brenda Johnson-Olivet Baptist Church

21. Mr. Chester Watson-Mt. Olive Baptist Church

22. Mrs. Robbie Alexander-Mt. Olive Baptist Church

23. Mr. Harry J. Middleton-Former Director L.B.J. Library

When a person agrees to be a "hero" of "Patriarchies/ Matriarchies," a book, preferable a biography or autobiography of the twentieth century, will be placed in a special place in the library in the name of the "community hero/ matriarch or patriarch." Theses books will become the topic of discussion in the "heroes book club" on Saturday mornings. Our kids need help to be all they can be. This especially holds for black kids. I hope this program attracts the attention of all of our community. I have needed help throughout my life, and for the most part, I received that help in one form or another. Being a black kid, things did not come easy. Being a black man, at times, life seemed impossible, but I kept asking for help several times. I asked the President of the United States for help and then the Vice President. After 26 years of federal service, my help came from 100% medical retirement.

Made in United States
North Haven, CT
08 April 2023

35215550R00183